"...Not bad for a South Texas boy"

A Story of Perseverance

Federico Peña

Cover Design: Linda Gallegos
Cover Photo: Reese & Co Portraits
Editorial Assistance: Susan Brooks

Library of Congress Control Number: 2021910959

ISBN Print: 978-0-578-92582-0
ISBN eBook: 978-0-578-92583-7

About The Author

Describing a challenging life journey from the small border town of Brownsville, Peña details his transformation from his original dream of practicing conventional law, to a passion for fighting for the underserved. He discovers a rekindled hope in America by lobbying for education reforms in Colorado and then serendipitously becomes a state legislator. Surprising political pundits, he is elected as Mayor of Denver where he blazes through a calamitous recession, builds a new international airport and modern convention center. He invests in neighborhoods, preserves historic buildings, and brings major league baseball to Colorado.

As Transportation Secretary, he helps restore Los Angeles from its 1994 devastating earthquake, introduces new transportation safety standards and technological advances, and supports significant infrastructure investments. As Energy Secretary, he fashions a national energy policy, invests in clean energy technologies, and travels the world fighting for America's interests. He becomes the first Latino to lead two federal departments in our nation's capital.

Today Peña, a successful businessman, remains engaged in local, national and civlc affairs and is highly sought for advice and leadership.

Peña aims to inspire Americans who have lost faith in our country through his life's challenges and his regained optimism for America. He provides guidance for our nation's leaders with long-term strategies for the 21st Century.

Ultimately, he believes that if a boy from South Texas can make a difference... so can you.

Contents

Introduction

I've had an incredible journey. From the South Texas border town of Brownsville, where I was raised, to City Hall in Denver and the revered institutions of our nation's capital, my eventual story would likely surprise the University of Texas English professor who expected so little from this "South Texas boy." The comment was inscribed on a college essay. It took years to understand the nuances of the message as one of UT's few students of color.

Ironically, my ancestors founded Laredo, Texas, fought in the Civil War and, like other Latino families, have contributed to building this nation since long before its founding in 1776. Yet, the low expectations I encountered at UT are still all too common for Latinos in the U.S. We have been part of the fabric of this great land for centuries, and yet must still fight for recognition and representation.

As a young man, I dreamed of becoming a lawyer, inspired by the television show *Perry Mason*. I was intrigued by the fundamental principles of our political and judicial systems. Civic engagement was not new to my family. My Grandfather,

Eduardo Peña, served on the Laredo City Council for nearly a quarter of a century. My Father, Gustavo Peña, set an example for civic engagement as a mayoral appointee to the Brownsville Public Utilities Commission. Who could have imagined that one day his third son would serve the country as its Secretary of Energy?

I persevered and earned my law degree, even though I was initially denied entry into UT's School of Law because, I was told, it was unlikely that I could complete the coursework or pass the bar exam. Perseverance was not something I was conscious of...I just kept going. I've always had hope and I've always believed in future promise. And although I've lost my footing from time to time, becoming disillusioned by social injustice, discrimination, and wrongly initiated wars, I've never abandoned my work for change and reform.

Leaving Texas, on my way to the west coast, I planned a short stop in Denver. Weeks became years, and my unlikely political career took shape. As a Colorado legislator, I fought for equal funding for rural schools and bilingual education. As Denver's Mayor, I asked citizens to *Imagine a Great City*, and together we found the courage to build it.

I expected obstacles along the way, but at times they felt more like landmines. I became Denver's first (and only) Hispanic Mayor, with nearly half of voters opposing me. Like our country today, Denver was a divided city, and even so, we brought people together to build the *Great City* we imagined. Although at times the opposition had familiar racial undertones, I kept working, believing we could come together to build something with promise for everyone.

In Washington, I served as Secretary of Transportation and Secretary of Energy, the first Latino to head two federal departments. I found myself in the company of kings and strongmen around the world. But I also had the joy of working side by side with thousands of talented people who dedicate their lives to government work. It was a great experience. I encourage everyone, Latinos in particular, to embrace public service.

I believe Latinos are integral in addressing 21st Century challenges as we work to grow our economy, build a critical work force, and defend our nation. Today's President, Joe Biden, has challenged us to "restore the soul of America." Americans from every ethnic, racial, and religious background will be needed in this effort. Diversity of talent is our unique asset.

I encourage you not to lose hope during these challenging times but to look for the opportunity to use your talents in service to your community, your city, your state, and your country. If a kid from South Texas can make a difference...so can you.

Preface

Imagine a Great City

It was a beautiful spring day in 1982 as I drove across town from my office in Colorado's ornate capitol building in Denver. The Rocky Mountains looked splendid—their snow-capped peaks glowing brilliantly against an amazing blue sky. It is a sky that exists only in Colorado as far as I can tell, a major contrast to the humid and heat-laden sky of Brownsville, Texas, my hometown on the border of Mexico. I was in my fourth and—I hoped—last year in the state legislature. Having announced that I would not seek a third term, I was looking forward to returning to practice law with my brother Alfredo. Politics, I had decided, was no longer for me.

From the start I had considered my service in the legislature a temporary commitment. In addition to representing the unique interests of my constituents in District 5, I focused on education reform. In my four years, I'd seen a number of legislators who had overstayed their welcome. They had served for ten, twenty, or even more years, and I wondered why they were still in office. Some remained effective; others had lost their drive or were no longer attentive to their constituents. I did not want to become one of them. Four years was enough to accomplish something of importance. It was time for me to pass the torch. My decision had a practical side. I was a member of the minority party, and it was unlikely that Democrats would take control of the legislature anytime soon. Although the incumbent Governor was a Democrat, Dick Lamm was undergoing a political transformation that often collided with some of my own Democratic principles and values.

As I drove into west Denver, I noticed that the leaves on the trees were green and full. I parked my banged-up blue Volvo in the crowded lot at the Don Quijote restaurant and crawled over the gearshift to exit from the passenger door. A few weeks earlier, someone had slammed into my driver's side, disabling the door and its lock. Since the door would no longer close, I tied it shut with a rope. Though I could afford to fix my car, I was simply too busy. Plus, putting work ahead of such a mundane but necessary task was a deeply ingrained habit.

I loved the Don Quijote restaurant. It was an unassuming place tucked into a cramped parcel of land that often required jumping the curb in order to park. Its owner, Señor Calvo, was from Spain. He served both Mexican and Spanish delights like *torta de huevo*, ham hocks, and a wonderful *paella* that rivaled my Mother's. His restaurant drew a diverse crowd that relished his unique dishes.

"*Como estas, Señor Calvo?*" I asked, as I always did when I walked in the door.

"*Bienvenido, Peña, que dicen los politicos?*" he always replied, with a sly smile.

Señor Calvo's restaurant had only a handful of tables. The dining room was plastered with huge posters of bullfights and exotic paintings of Spanish landscapes. So much art adorned the walls and ceilings that I'm sure it was something of a fire hazard. A small television tucked in the corner usually showed soccer games from somewhere in the world, while Señor Calvo's grandson often scampered beneath the tables.

The owner's two sons, Davíd and Alejo, worked at the restaurant. Davíd was the waiter and Alejo was the cook. I knew them well, as my brother and I sometimes played basketball with them at a nearby school on the weekends. As expected, I found Alejo in the kitchen and asked, "*Que hay de comida?*"

"*Todo es especial,*" he shouted back, laughing.

The jovial atmosphere at Don Quijote always invigorated me, as did the conversations I'd have with Señor Calvo. Often, he would reminisce about his native country and grumble about the former Spanish dictator, Francisco Franco, while worrying aloud that the fire department would someday force him to take down his imposing and probably flammable posters. "*No puedes hablar con ellos, Peña?*" he would anxiously ask.

On that day in May 1982, I was looking forward to a hearty lunch and the company of my friends John Parr, Tom Nussbaum, and Bill Rosser. I assumed we were going to celebrate my four years in the statehouse and my impending retirement. They were there waiting for me, and I greeted them warmly––completely unaware that they had been plotting behind my back.

John and Tom served in Governor Lamm's administration, and I had worked closely with them on a slew of issues during my two terms in the legislature. Bill was co-director of the Chicano Education Project, a Colorado civil rights organization. In the early 1970s I was hired as the organization's attorney. All three men were passionate about their work and politically sophisticated.

Over a round of beer, we bantered about the latest political intrigue at the capitol and speculated about who was going to run for my soon-to-be vacant legislative seat. Halfway through the second round, however, the co-conspirators began to reveal their true intentions. They had no interest in toasting my imminent retirement from politics. Quite the opposite: they wanted me to run for Mayor of Denver—against a powerful incumbent candidate from a prominent family that had been active in Colorado for generations.

When I realized I had not misheard them, I almost fell out of my chair. "Are you guys nuts?" I asked.

My friends had definitely let their imaginations get the best of them. I did not see myself continuing in politics—and I certainly had no intention of ever running for Mayor.

The idea of running against the indomitable Mayor Bill McNichols was as incredible as the idea of visiting Pluto. I thought the whole notion was crazy. For starters, I was not prepared to run for such a high-profile office. I was young, only thirty-five years old, and still mostly unknown in Denver. Without broad-based support throughout the city, I would be tilting at windmills like Quijote himself. And yet my friends dismissed my arguments as frivolous. From under the table, they pulled out stacks of documents that contained graphs and tables of demographic, political, and electoral data. As they wove a narrative of how I could win the election, an astounding realization overcame me: *they were dead serious.*

"Look, Federico," John Parr said, "Denver is ready for a new kind of leader. We all know the city is adrift."

Tom Nussbaum chimed in, "And you're articulate, smart, and have a solid reputation in the statehouse."

While I sat, almost too stunned to react, they seized the moment to present their calculations about Denver's electorate and its potential. My crafty friends knew that facts and figures and a sound argument could influence me. And so, on they went about voter registration and voter turnout numbers. My body buzzing warmly from my second beer, I listened, mostly bemused. But my friends, each taking a turn, continued to explain the reasons I could win. As they did, I could not resist doing my own calculations. I was not a Denver native and not well known in the city, despite being a legislator. I had been a controversial civil rights attorney, and I'd protested against the Vietnam War in college. My mind drifted to my teenage days when my Father had taken me along to *cafecitos* in Brownsville where his friends drank coffee and discussed what mattered to them politically, with special regard to what was going on at City Hall. Those sessions were held in the back room of Mayor Tony Gonzales's pharmacy, where I would sit a short distance from the conversations as I watched Mr. Gonzales occasionally leave the meeting to fill prescriptions for his customers. There were times I was asked my opinion, and my heart would race as I offered a brief response. Maybe my heart raced a little that day at Don Quijote too.

But I was not at a *cafecito* back home. I was having a serious conversation with serious men about running for Mayor of Denver.

The incumbent, Mayor Bill McNichols, came from a powerful and prominent political family. His brother, Steve McNichols, had been elected Lieutenant Governor and then Governor of Colorado. Their Father had been City Auditor of Denver for more than thirty years. The Mayor had been elected three times and was in his fourteenth year. He enjoyed name recognition above 90 percent. Mayor Bill seemed solidly entrenched in his position. He had more than $200,000 in his political war chest—serious money even now, but an unimaginable sum back then. Trying to raise money for a political novice like me against a rival like that would be a fool's errand.

And there was the question of my birthplace. The people of Denver and Colorado are not known to be fond of Texans. My Mother, years later, would put a fine point on it: "If someone from Denver came to Brownsville to run for Mayor," she said, "I wouldn't vote for him."

It seemed to me this story would have an end before it mustered a beginning.

Or was the idea that crazy?

The crux of my friend's strategic argument was voter turnout. Their data documented voting results of mayoral elections during odd-numbered or "off years." Voter turnout in off-year elections was usually low, around 51 percent. In even-numbered years, like the year Pat Schroeder ran for her Denver-based congressional seat, voters turned out at a rate of 70 percent. *Voilà!*

"All we have to do is secure that kind of turnout," Bill said with a smile.

"Something that's never been done in an off year," I pointed out.

To my starry-eyed friends, it still did not matter that I had 3 percent name recognition, no money, and no prospects of matching what the Mayor could spend. They seemed impervious to the fact that I was young and single. Nor did they care that I was Latino in a city with a small Hispanic population—about 18 percent then—in a state and region with a checkered racial history. Were they forgetting the *eñe* over Peña, which would immediately give some voters a reason for concern?

My canny *compadres* knew how much I enjoyed Mexican food and beer and that the combination would have a favorable effect on me. The combination reminded me of being back home in South Texas with my Tejano buddies. When we gathered for barbecues, there was always Mexican beer, *cabrito* (baby goat roasted in an open fire pit), tamales, and, if we were lucky, my Mother's exceptional paella.

As I savored the delectable food from Señor Calvo's kitchen, I had a more relaxed state of mind and found myself intrigued. After more talk over the longer-than-expected lunch, I told my friends what they at the minimum wanted to hear: "I'll think about it."

Leaving the restaurant, I felt a kind of odd excitement. I was more surprised—struck, even—that my friends had such faith in me, and was equally flattered that these otherwise sober *politicos* believed I could win a Denver mayoral race. They were not political neophytes. John Parr and Tom Nussbaum had helped mastermind the statewide initiative that had convinced Colorado voters to reject the Winter Olympics in 1972 after the games were awarded by the International Committee. They argued that the games would be costly to taxpayers and damage the environment. They were master strategists who were adept at detecting political and social undercurrents. The voters' rejection of the Olympics propelled them to the gold medal podium of political thinkers, landing them key positions in Governor Lamm's administration. Bill Rosser had been a community organizer long before he co-founded the Chicano Education Project. He had keen political judgment honed while working with everyday people. It was hard to imagine these brilliant tactical thinkers wanted me to run for Mayor of Denver.

I lived a few blocks from my brother Alfredo, so I stopped by on my way home to tell him about the fantastic encounter I'd just experienced. He was equally puzzled. Alfredo had come to Denver to attend the University of Denver Law School. He had established the private practice that I joined before I ran for the legislature in 1978. Alfredo had observed city politics close up while practicing law before the Denver county courts, located near the Mayor's office. He often came into contact with numerous McNichols appointees and had a taste for municipal politics. He was very much aware of the McNichols political machine. While he'd been supportive of my two previous legislative campaigns, his intuition and experience made him sensibly skeptical about my running for Mayor. "Not only is McNichols known everywhere," he noted, "he's got a reputation for being a strong-willed politician."

I knew my brother was trying to break it to me gently that my chances of winning an election against Mayor Bill were slim, but the thought of running had already begun to turn in my mind. I continued to think about the possibility over the next few days and became intrigued enough to seek out the opinions of fellow legislators, a few community and neighborhood activists, and others who had contemplated a mayoral run.

While some scoffed at the idea, others were fascinated. Listening to them, I concluded that I should take my time to determine if I genuinely wanted to run and if I truly believed I could win. I was not interested in running, losing, and then preparing for a later election as other politicians do. I had never conducted my life by testing the waters.

Although I had been a State Legislator from Denver for four years, I had not fully appreciated the power and influence of the office of Mayor. McNichols ran the city through his cabinet. With no City Manager, he appointed the powerful water board, and oversaw the nation's sixth-busiest airport. A strong Mayor with a much broader vision of the city than the one McNichols held could bring great change to Denver, unite its citizens in a new undertaking, and perhaps improve the quality of life of almost half a million people.

I approached some State Legislators as well as members of City Council. Councilman Sal Carpio from North Denver had established himself as an up-and-coming leader, and it was generally accepted that he would run for Mayor. When I approached him, he said he was in fact thinking about taking the plunge. I told him I would not run if he decided to. He had a larger following and had been involved in city politics for many years, and I respected him as an astute and knowledgeable individual.

I received mixed responses from people whom I respected, and it caused me to do a deep soul search of my own desires and abilities. I knew I was smart, hard-working, and thoughtful enough about the issues facing the city to run for Mayor. I had sufficient political experience to give me the confidence I would need to contend with other candidates.

I knew much of Denver. I had spent hundreds of hours in the community, walking door-to-door in my legislative campaigns, addressing neighborhood organizations, and meeting with many diverse citizens. I could relate to individuals from almost every walk of life and every ethnic and racial group, yet I had doubts about being able to attract support from a broad cross-section of Denver. At the same time, I sensed there was an undercurrent in the city that other, long-standing elected officials did not appreciate. Many people believed the city was adrift and felt excluded from participating in municipal policies. Thinking about the electoral data, I wondered if we really could increase voter turnout. I had been elected to the state house in a district about one-tenth the size of Denver but with only a 30 percent Latino population. Could I present myself in a similarly positive fashion to the broader community? I believed I had the raw ability to win and to transcend whatever biases people might have about someone they did not know well. Even someone with an *eñe* in his last name.

Thanks to the talented friends and associates who were encouraging me, I became confident we could put together the political organization needed to run an effective campaign. There were, however, the questions of money and low name recognition. But first things first: I had to make a decision.

As time passed, Councilman Carpio was having difficulty deciding whether to run. Other Council Members who were thinking of joining the race concluded they could not prevail against the powerful incumbent Mayor or District Attorney Dale Tooley, who was likely to run.

Meanwhile, I sketched out my platform, thinking more expansively about what I could do as Mayor and shared my ideas with others. Community leaders began offering me ideas. Environmentalist Tony Massaro had specific thoughts on how to clean Denver's dirty air. Attorney Steve Kaplan suggested how the City Attorney's office could be reformed. Others suggested how the City could partner with neighborhood leaders to clean up dirty alleys and remove unsightly graffiti. Urban policy expert Tom Gougeon deluged me with strategies for improving city planning and moving aggressively on a new airport. The University of Denver Law School's Dean and former Manager of Public Safety, Daniel Hoffman, shared his ideas about improving the police and fire departments. Businessman Bruce Rockwell emphasized the need for a new convention center. Educator Katherine Archuleta had ideas for improving our public schools.

The more excited people became about the possibility of me as Mayor, the more they inundated me with their innovative ideas to propel Denver forward. Armed with proposals for almost every aspect of city life, they poured out their frustrations about the incumbent city administration and offered their dreams and hopes for a greater city.

These discussions, loaded with so much optimism and enthusiasm, were all incredibly encouraging. I believed that Denver had great potential and, with bold leadership, could be catapulted into a much brighter future. I came to appreciate that I was not alone in my thinking and that thousands of like-minded citizens could be mobilized in a new political movement. The notion that we could generate a 70 percent voter turnout in an odd-numbered year started to take hold in my mind.

More importantly, I knew I had to put my beliefs to the test. I had been deeply moved by President John F. Kennedy's call twenty years earlier asking Americans what we could do for our country. I had come to love Denver, and I cared deeply about its future. I knew I was going to raise a family here. I truly believed we could do better, and I trusted that thousands of citizens shared my passion. I believed that I needed to accept the challenge and run.

As word leaked out that I might run, hundreds of citizens began to express interest in volunteering to help. Even before we could get organized, people were moving swiftly ahead of us with support. I was getting calls from people I admired, people I wanted to hear from, and people I had never met.

Tom Nussbaum and his wife, Sherry Seiber, a criminal defense lawyer, offered their home to strategize. Sandy Widener, John Parr's wife and co-founder of the popular weekly magazine *Westword*, joined these sessions, bringing her wit and energy to our discussions. For hours, our core team talked and debated––always with the idea that we had to propel the city forward.

One night, after several glasses of wine, we were imagining

thousands of volunteers, imagining the excitement of a fresh new face in mayoral politics, imagining the great changes we could bring to our city with an invigorated and talented team, when Sandy blurted out: "Imagine a great city!" Suddenly, it all made sense. All my conversations with friends, all the ideas of elevating our city to new heights, all the dreams so many had of invigorating Denver were capsulized in a collective imagination of a great city. And thus emerged a slogan that would remain in the hearts and minds of Denver citizens for decades—"Imagine a Great City."

I decided I would run.

Part One: Texas (1947–1973)

1. Family, Faith, and Fortitude

How could I run for Mayor of Denver if I was not a Colorado native? I was born in Laredo, Texas, on March 15, 1947, at the old Mercy Hospital. My parents, Gustavo José Peña and Ana Lucila Farías, named me Federico Fabián. I was baptized later that year in the Cathedral of San Agustín, the same church where my parents were married. Our ancestors have been baptized, married, and buried there for more than 200 years. Though we moved from Laredo before my first birthday, the town remains an essential part of my life. We were raised in Brownsville, and my siblings and I spent a lot of time in Laredo visiting our grandparents and cousins. My experiences as a young man in both of these south Texas cities would carve troubling and long-lasting impressions. Most Americans would not understand how the subtle and not-so-subtle indignations Latinos experience impact our lives.

Brownsville was in some ways very much like Laredo: overwhelmingly Hispanic, poor, and hot. Oddly, Brownsville felt more isolated than Laredo, even with its seaport. For my family, the blockbuster news in 1948 was not our move to Brownsville.

Fifteen months after my birth, my Mother gave birth to triplets. In the 1940s, doctors did not have today's technology to identify multiple birth pregnancies. My Father loved telling the story of that memorable day in June of 1948.

Gustavo and Lucila already had three sons under the age of five: me and my older brothers Oscar and Gustavo Jr. So, when the doctor entered the waiting room to announce the arrival of a baby girl, my Father was elated. Just as he was beginning to process being the father of four, the doctor returned. "Congratulations, Mr. Peña, you have another baby, a boy!" Dad's eyes always twinkled telling the story. After just a few minutes of sitting with the amazing news, the doctor reappeared.

"Congratulations...you have another baby boy!"

As Dad would tell it, he thanked the doctor and asked him not to return.

October 2003, Peña family in front of San Agustín Church in Laredo, Texas. Left to right: Alfredo, Alberto, Ana, Gustavo, Mom, Oscar, Dad, and Federico. Photo courtesy of the Peña Family Archives.

The change in my Father's demeanor, as he realized his family had grown from three to six children within a span of minutes, must have been pronounced. The doctor later explained he'd only ever heard one heartbeat, but my five-foot-tall Mother would later confide she'd known something was different with that pregnancy all along.

The birth of Ana, Alfredo, and Alberto, my triplet siblings, was unique. Their arrival represented the first successful birth of triplets in South Texas, and they quickly became the talk of Brownsville. When my parents' friends came to visit, they would brush past me in their rush to get to the triplets. I became almost irrelevant. My two older brothers, Gustavo and Oscar, had already established their own identities. I, at fifteen months, fell immediately into the middle of the pack.

The Brownsville of my youth was ragged, its flatness even more pronounced than Laredo's. Its old wooden homes looked wind swept, and its palm trees leaned from the constant pressure of Gulf winds. Sometimes they would topple from the force of the pounding hurricanes that stormed in from the Gulf of Mexico. We were always afraid of hurricanes. When we learned one was coming, we would quickly board up the windows, secure the outdoor tables and chairs, and bring in the dogs. When the winds howled and the electricity went out, we lit flashlights and candles and prayed the roof wouldn't be blown off. After the storms passed, we drove around Brownsville to survey the damage. This life experience affected me deeply. Decades later as Secretary of Transportation, I would find myself assisting Gulf Coast communities in recovering from their own storms. I understood their fear and suffering.

The city's tired and aged streets, lined with palm trees that never looked like the postcard versions peddled by the Chamber of Commerce, squared a small business district downtown. This area contained a few historic homes owned by the town's founding families and was surrounded by modest neighborhoods. In the small-town center, the Majestic Theatre served as a favorite escape. I remember seeing Roy Rogers and Dale Evans movies there as well as my first 3-D movie. The old federal courthouse and post office sat across from the theater. Shortly after I was

born, my Father opened a cotton brokerage office in Brownsville for the Longoria family of Nuevo Laredo, Mexico. The Gulf
Pacific Cotton Agency was housed in Brownsville's historic train
station, a place I came to love. The agency was the U.S. subsid-
iary of Empresas Longoria, a successful Mexican company. My
Father was responsible for marketing Mexican cotton. We grew
up watching ships sail from the port of Brownsville loaded with
cotton, destined for mills around the world.

I attended Sacred Heart Elementary under the reign—and
in the rein—of no-nonsense nuns clad in imposing black habits.
From day one in kindergarten, they called me Fred. Back then
the name was unimportant; I was a five-year-old boy. When I
look back now, I know I was hurt by the change. They took away
the most personal and important part of my Latino identity, and
it took me years to have the confidence to reclaim my christened
name, Federico.

I remember hearing a visiting priest describe Brownsville
as "missionary territory" during Sunday mass while home from
college. It angered me. Even though our priests were from the
OMI, the *Missionary* Oblates of Mary Immaculate, I was startled to hear how we were still perceived. The word "missionary"
confirmed an attitude that we were poor, uneducated, lacked
sophistication, and needed to be "saved" by the all-white order
of priests. My Father was an educated, successful businessman
who traveled the world. We enjoyed a nice life. Why did they
view us this way?

I was immersed in the ultraconservative teachings of the
church, which no doubt instilled in me an unwavering respect
for authority, institutions, and prayer. The nuns and priests
said prayer would help us throughout our lives. Thus, I prayed
every day; I prayed before taking a test, before taking the field,
before eating, before going to sleep, and when I awoke each
morning. I believed that if I prayed and did not commit a mortal
sin, only good things would come my way. If my prayers were
not answered, I would wonder what I had done wrong. So, I

prayed longer and harder and more often. To this day, prayer remains a force in my life. I now sense that God listens when I pray, regardless of the outcome. It gives me balance and peace and grounds me with meditation.

The Catholic Church was an amalgam of beliefs revolving around the promise of eternal salvation. There was one promise to which I paid particular attention. It involved taking Holy Communion the first Friday of every month for an entire year. I was taught by fulfilling the "First Friday" requirement, a priest was guaranteed to be at my deathbed to grant absolution of my sins, assuring speedy entry into the celestial kingdom after my last breath. Having complied with this earthly requirement a number of years in a row, I wondered if I could then sin all I wanted since I certainly must have already secured this sacred guarantee.

These were the dimensions of my spiritual development, complemented by my Mother's involvement in parish life and the Peña boys' service as altar boys. Whenever Fr. Sexton needed to fill in servers on Sunday, he only had to call our home and a full complement of us would hustle to the church. Thanks to my strict Catholic upbringing, I was raised to be "a straight kid." I performed well academically and was never disruptive in class. My parents made it clear that being irresponsible was not an option.

My Mother spoke English and Spanish flawlessly. She was warm and loved all six Peña children with passion. She helped us with our homework, took us to baseball practice, the library (it was air-conditioned), swimming, and shopping. She was the den mother for our Scout troop and hosted activities in our home. Mom had the grace of a princess, and I never heard anyone speak ill of her. How could they? She was kind and considerate to everyone. She was secure in her roots and could confidently interact with people from all walks of life. She learned to swim at age fifty and later took French classes. She loved our local community playhouse and was active in our church and school. Incredibly, she was willing to move her historic family rooted in Laredo to the largely unknown town of Brownsville because she loved our Father and joined his adventure willingly.

1959, Peña Alter boys at Sacred Heart Church in Brownsville, Texas.
Left to right are Gustavo, Oscar, Federico, Alfredo, and Alberto.
Photo courtesy of the Peña Family Archives.

When we misbehaved, we heard the common response of Mothers back then, *"Just wait till your Father gets home."* Ours was a strictly disciplined home. Dad imposed his military training from Texas A&M and World War II. We were expected to be well-behaved. If we veered too far, my Father used a belt to get our attention. Being belted on the rump was not that unusual in those days. For lesser offenses, he made us kneel on the wooden floor until our knees went numb. We were six children born within seven years, three the same age. It was a lot to manage, and we accepted that corporal punishment was just a part of life. We had an early bedtime and we were expected to be at the breakfast table promptly every morning. Gustavo and Lucila parented with pride and had high expectations for each of us. I was so focused on getting good grades, I was often awake earlier than the others to study in the bathroom, next to a small gas furnace that warmed me during cold winter mornings.

Every morning, my Father would bang on our bedroom doors. The ruckus of his knuckles, bulging with his proudly worn but weathered Aggie ring, sounded as if he were going to pound right through the door. "Up and at 'em!" he would yell. I can hear his morning shout to this day. Not wanting to risk his wrath, my two younger brothers and I would scurry into action in the bedroom we shared.

In the warmth of my memories now, the echo of my Father's door-banging is a nostalgic refrain, and those mornings seem magical. Not so much back then. We were a highly regimented family. No one dared talk back to our parents—*Yes, sir* or *No, sir* and *No, ma'am* or *Yes, ma'am* were the only acceptable responses. Learning respect for elders shaped my values and has served me well in life. As a young legislator, and later as a Mayor, I listened carefully to older advisors from whom I learned a great deal.

As a small child, I followed my Father almost everywhere. For years, I would drive with him to the post office on Sundays after Mass to get his mail. The first time we did this, I wondered who besides my work-crazed Father would be at the post office on a Sunday. To my surprise, he was not alone. Others were there performing the same ritualistic opening of their mail. I stood next to my dad, letter opener in hand, as he dutifully opened each envelope. He read every letter and, if one was of no importance, would hand it to me to discard in the trash can.

This experience taught me that Sunday could be a day of work, notwithstanding my Catholic instruction. I gleaned from my Father that work was paramount—more important, it seemed, than keeping Sunday sacrosanct. By my Father's standards, each minute of every waking hour, one should apply oneself in some constructive fashion. Relaxing on Sunday was not a good use of one's time. Even to this day, I feel compelled to be doing something productive every minute, and I find it difficult to simply relax.

It was my Grandfather Eduardo Peña who shaped the character of my Father and his two brothers. He owned a grocery store and served as a Laredo city alderman for almost a quarter of a century. My Grandfather had no time for foolishness from his boys; he needed their help to run the store. My Father was exposed to the business world and learned the importance of public service from his Father. He understood the importance of hard work and witnessed firsthand his Father's grocery store struggle to survive the Great Depression. He was formed by the times, and his circumstances made him into a man of strong character and intellect with a conservative nature.

Dad's solemn demeanor didn't keep him from relaxing and having light and casual conversations with others, including his children. Though not particularly athletic, he was adventuresome and loved to try new things. He built his own sailboat, fished, hunted, and learned to play golf. He read anything he could get his hands on, loved learning, and enjoyed exposing us to new ideas and experiences. But most of the time he was very strict. We had no comic books, no television viewing without permission, and no dogs inside the house.

And we also worked. From early teenage days, we swept cotton at Dad's offices, did construction work, and repaired and painted our home. I worked in a grain elevator where sorghum husks would imbed in my skin for days, not coming off with a bath. All the Peña children worked summers. Mom drove us to the Brownsville Savings and Loan on Saturday mornings to deposit our payroll checks. We weren't allowed to spend our hard-earned money...it was saved for college.

Public service and religion were of equal importance to Dad, who was as committed to the Rotary Cub as he was to the Catholic Church. He was very proud of his perfect attendance pin. When he traveled on business, including his trips to Europe, he made extra effort to not miss Rotary meetings. In much the same way, our family always sought out other churches while on vacation so we would not miss Sunday Mass.

Although my Father was a conservative businessman, both of my parents were Democrats. They believed in Franklin Delano Roosevelt. They had faith in America, and they sympathized greatly with people who were poor, making clear it was our responsibility to help those in need.

Gustavo and Lucila lived with open hearts and they accepted everyone. The handful of Jewish families in Brownsville who worshipped at a small synagogue were my parents' friends. Dad seemed to know them all, and they were always welcomed in our home.

My Father and his two brothers attended college in the 1930s, when it was largely unheard-of for Latinos from the small town of Laredo to go to Texas A&M, a testament to their personal determination and sturdy upbringing.

At A&M, my Father joined the school's renowned military Corps of Cadets and worked his way through the university as a janitor. Majoring in agriculture, he won a contest by correctly identifying, classifying, and grading cotton—a major staple of the Texas economy back then. The prize was a tour of Europe!

Dad graduated as a Second Lieutenant in 1938, two months after Hitler's troops marched into Czechoslovakia. In 1941, he and most of the Aggie student body went to war. Dad served as Captain in the 45th Coast Artillery in the Pacific Theater until 1945.

Like other members of "the Greatest Generation" who survived the Great Depression and fought in World War II, my Father rarely talked of the war. The only detail he shared was that his ship hit a mine in the waters near the island of Espiritu Santo in the Pacific Ocean. The island was a supply base, naval harbor, and airbase used by the Allied Forces. Dad was forever upset that when the mine exploded his commanders, graduates of West Point, were the first to abandon ship. He never revealed how many were injured or how he managed to leave with his troops, but he maintained that officers should be the last ones to leave a sinking ship. As a military school graduate, he understood the responsibilities of officers and was angry that those from our nation's preeminent military academy violated basic leadership tenets. His only mementos from the war were two spent artillery shells that he kept in our hall closet.

Dad's youngest brother, Augusto, also went to war almost immediately after graduation. Tío Augusto served in Europe from September 1943 to April 1946—almost the entirety of the war—with the 542nd Field Artillery Battalion of the famous Rainbow 42 Division. He received two bronze stars and the American Campaign Theater ribbon.

Dad's younger brother, Willie, enrolled in Texas A&M with the dream of becoming an architect. The attack on Pearl Harbor temporarily and dramatically altered his plans. Although he graduated in May 1942 with a degree in architecture, he was "shipped out" the next day, commissioned as a Second Lieutenant in the infantry. Willie's military service during World War II is chronicled in his book *As Far as Schleiden*, published sixteen years after the war ended. An intriguing book, it is filled with intricate details about the ugliness, irony, and sometimes humor of war. Schleiden is the place in Germany where Tío Willie stepped on a mine nearly three years into his deployment. He was seriously injured and lost his left leg. He described this life- transforming event: "An ear-splitting explosion numbed me as I felt myself rising, head bowed, in the air," and, "The thought flashed in my mind...I must not cry out like some men I'd seen hit and go into hysteria." He gritted his teeth to withstand the pain. His injuries were so severe that he spent two years recuperating in various hospitals. Tío Willie was honored with a Bronze Heart, a Purple Heart, and the French Croix de Guerre. At a Veterans Day ceremony in Houston in 2013, he was awarded the Legion of Honour Chevalier (Knight) medal, France's most prestigious decoration. In December 2014, he and four fellow Aggies were the subject of a Battle of the Bulge war exhibit in Belgium. My siblings and I were honored to represent him in Bastogne, where the Queen, our Ambassador, and other dignitaries also attended.

Tío Willie was undeterred by his injuries and long recovery. He returned to Texas A&M for a fifth year, hampered by a wooden leg that rubbed his stump so badly it gave him blisters. Not long after, he joined the architectural firm Caudill Rowlet and Scott, became its fourth partner, and pioneered the practice and theory of architectural programming. He co-authored the seminal book *Problem Seeking*, which is still used in architecture schools across the country. The William M. Peña Chair at Texas A&M University was established in my Uncle's honor, and he was inducted as a Distinguished Alumnus in 2016. I have always had a deep admiration for my Uncle.

My patriotic and proud grandparents had their three sons fighting in the war at the same time. Their service in the military and their professional successes were a positive influence on the Peña children. Our upbringing in south Texas, which imbued us with notions of hard work, sacrifice, patriotism, and belief in our democracy, was not unique. Millions of other Hispanic families across the country were and are similarly raised. Like many other Hispanics of my generation, we were taught that we had to be better and work harder than similarly situated Anglos. My parents taught us to be respectful of others, not to hold grudges, and to conduct ourselves with dignity and integrity. I hope that I have lived up to their expectations.

My family's history of military service, business success, and civic contributions is shared by millions of Latino families across the country. And yet, our Hispanic history is generally unknown. It is not taught in classrooms nor sought out by historians, yet it is vast and remarkable. We are a mixed heritage with roots in both indigenous and Spanish cultures. Our ancestors lived on this land literally centuries before European settlers dreamed of a new nation. We are misunderstood and disrespected and told to "go back to Mexico" by enraged individuals who are sadly uninformed. The ignorant statements routinely made by President Trump about a Hispanic judge, immigrants, and workers promoted false and long-held negative stereotypes. In "Forget the Alamo", the authors document the disgraceful attempts by the Texas State Board of Education to dismiss the historical contributions of Mexicans, Tejanos and Mexican Americans in public school history books. It is almost unfathomable that we must still fight to be recognized and respected. I am grateful for my upbringing and the role models in my family who have given me the strength and confidence needed to move past these indignations, even in today's anti-Latino immigrant climate.

2. Life Lessons and Legacies

"Are you an American citizen?" was a question often asked of us in South Texas. There were times I wanted to yell back, "Yeah...and I have been a lot longer than you!"

In the 1960s, crossing the border *into* the Mexican town of Matamoros was simple. Buying a twenty-five-cent bottle of Carta Blanca or Corona was easy. Bartenders almost never asked for identification, as long as you were tall enough to place a quarter on top of the bar. Driving back from Matamoros, however, was a different matter, as the question of citizenship made our return difficult.

Are you an American citizen? The question always rubbed my friends and me the wrong way. Once in a while, we gave wise-crack answers knowing we might be asked to step out of the vehicle. There was one particular time when my friend climbed out of an open car window just to express his irritation. I wondered why we weren't arrested on the spot.

While our antics during border crossings were primarily to poke fun at the customs agents, my friends and I were offended each time we were asked about our citizenship. This was especially true when the agents knew we were from Brownsville. Their robotic questions were asked with guilt, and their expressions were almost apologetic. We understood they were doing their jobs, but we resented the system that made this ritual interrogation part of our everyday lives.

We weren't alone. Traveling from Brownsville in any direction guaranteed stops for everyone. If you were headed to San Antonio or Austin, you could count on it. Twenty-five miles outside of Brownsville at fixed Border Patrol stations, we were required to roll down our windows and answer questions from armed agents. I often wondered how Anglos in Austin or Houston would have felt if they were stopped—sometimes on pure whim—and asked to prove their citizenship.

I have vivid memories of traveling with my family throughout the state as a boy. Whenever we drove into those Border Patrol stations, my heart would race as I nervously wondered if something was going to happen to us or if we had done something wrong. Thankfully, my Father and Mother would calmly and respectfully greet the agents and explain, in perfect English, that every person in the car was an American citizen. My parents acted as if these stops were normal, and their demeanor was surely intended to keep their six children calm and reassured. Sometimes an agent would peer into the back seats and ask us children, "Are you Americans?"

"Yes, sir," we would answer politely. When my Father finally drove away, my heartbeat would slow down, relieved once again that nothing bad had happened.

I gradually became accustomed to these roadside stops. But I also became indignant and insulted. Our trips were interrupted by law enforcement officials in ways most Texans would never experience. As a teenager, I understood that South Texas citizens were treated differently than people who lived in other parts of the state. The fact that my family traced its roots back almost a century before Texas became a state made the matter more disturbing. In not-so-subtle ways, Hispanics in general were thought of as second-class citizens in Texas, regardless of where they were born or how long their families had lived in the U.S. Only later would I realize this was true in other states, not just in the one I called home.

Other than the times we had to endure the checkpoints, my years in Brownsville were wonderful. I thrived at Saint Joseph Academy, the all-boys Catholic school my brothers and I attended through high school while my sister, Ana, attended the all-girls Catholic school called Villa Maria.

I began playing baseball at nine years old for a team sponsored by Burton Auto Supply Company of Brownsville. I fell in love with the game and quickly became a solid player with keen sight. At age twelve, I led the league in home runs and was looking forward to playing in the All-Star tournament. Like many boys my age, I fantasized about playing in the major leagues and imagined that winning the All-Star games would launch my baseball career.

1959, Federico kneeling second from left with Burton Auto Supply team.
Photo courtesy of the Peña Family Archives.

In the last game of the regular season, I crashed into a second baseman and tore the ligaments and cartilage in my right knee and had to have surgery. I assumed that when my cast was cut off six weeks later, I would be back on the field. But when I saw my atrophied muscle drooping from my very visible thighbone, I cried with all the despair a boy that age can feel. My life had come to an end, my dream of big-league baseball evaporated.

At such a young age, I could not accept that God had cursed my baseball career. I was angry about my injury, which worsened later in life. Rehabilitation in the 1960s wasn't the science it is today. I guess common sense wasn't a priority in Texas high school sports then either, because when I entered St. Joseph Academy, I ended up playing for their football team, the Fighting Bloodhounds. It seems ironic, but I am glad I played sports because I met Coach Gus Zavaleta, the man who would have a deep and life-long impact on my life. Coach Gus was a former Marine who coached every sport at Saint Joseph's—baseball, basketball, football, and track. A big man, he played fullback and defensive end for the Marines football team, the Leathernecks. Though tough and demanding, he inspired us by focusing on character building. I felt like a Marine recruit during those hot and humid days practicing in South Texas.

1964, Federico as a "Fighting Bloodhound".
Photo courtesy of the Peña Family Archives.

Our football field was mostly weeds and was plagued with "stickers," nettlesome thorny nubs that stuck to the skin and stung. We attempted to irrigate the field's "grass" by lifting and connecting heavy pipes to spray water from the *resacas*—nearby depressions in the land that, when full, formed pools of water. Though our efforts were pretty much in vain, we did manage to coax some measure of color onto a field that, if looked at from the right angle, seemed somewhat green.

Coach Gus was old school, and at times denied us the water we needed more than the never-growing grass. We'd nearly faint under the relentless sun, and all he would offer was dismissive advice to "just take some salt tablets." When injured, we were ordered to "run it off."

I was a running back, though I weighed a diminutive 135 pounds. In a feeble attempt to intimidate our opponents, the official football program for my school listed me at 150 pounds. I was never afraid on the football field, although the bruises I nursed the morning after a game always reminded me that I wasn't built to play such a sport. But I was proud of my endurance and tenacity, and adapted easily to the strain I put on my body.

At the end of my junior year, I felt my knee cartilage go loose again soon after making the varsity football team. I was blindsided by a terrible hit to my already injured knee while playing defensive end. It seemed I was going to have to quit another sport I loved. But Coach Gus had other designs.

"Fred," he said, using my nickname, "I have an idea. We'll tape your knee, and you can alternate as quarterback with Westerkom, Gonzalez, and Wilson, the more experienced players. You won't have to run too much." He paused for a moment, then added, "I mostly need you to help lead the team."

I appreciated that Coach was asking for my help and at first thought this was a great idea—except that I couldn't throw well. Still, before every practice that summer, our Team Manager would circle rolls of tape around my knee, then secure it with a steel knee brace. And off onto the field I would run.

Coach Gus's plan seemed to work well for a while. Then, a couple of weeks before our first game, two other players and I were injured on the same day. The three of us jumped onto the hood of a friend's car for a ride from the school building to the athletic field. We thought A.J., the driver, could see where he was going, and he thought we were guiding him. Neither was the case, and the car crashed hard into a flat-bed trailer, sending the three of us flying into the air. My feet hit the pavement, and I found myself running at full speed for a second before the momentum overcame me and I was thrown to the ground. We ended up in the hospital with road rash on our hands, elbows, chests, and backs.

But someone had to play in the opening game of the season. So, in addition to wearing a steel brace on my already mangled knee, I taped a foam pad to my left hand to cover my wound so I could take snaps from the center. The ball, of course, kept bouncing off my hand when it slammed against the pad, but I kept trying.

Whenever the center was able to get the ball into my hands, I would raise my right arm to throw a pass. The first time we tried this, I opened a slow-healing elbow wound and blood was everywhere. Somehow, I, along with my fellow wounded teammates, survived a tough senior year. We were, after all, the Fighting Bloodhounds.

Looking back to those memorable days at St. Joseph, I marvel at what the Marists—the Catholic brothers who ran the Academy—allowed Coach Gus to do. Each winter, if an athlete wanted to be in the Bloodhounds Club, which every jock aspired to join, he was initiated with a wooden paddle riddled with holes. I remember having to pull a huge rope across the football field and through the freezing waters of the *resacas*. We had to crawl through mud and were degraded and humiliated by the upperclassmen.

Though considered back then to be rites of passage into

manhood, these rituals were nothing less than hazing. I wondered what Saint Joseph himself would think of our crazy, youthful antics. I knew if my two older brothers, Gus and Oscar, had survived it, then surely, I could too.

Despite the torture, I admired and respected Coach Gus. I learned from him the importance of pushing myself to physical and emotional extremes, working hard, following through, and leading a team. Looking back, I believe Coach Gus was preparing us for life's challenges. As he often said, "I want to build men of character!"

When Coach Gus died fifty years later, his former players returned to carry his casket across the football field. The young boys he treated as Marines and helped guide into manhood came back to honor him on his former field of glory. They carried more than his body that day, of course; they bore a legacy of grit and determination that we'll all carry as long as we live.

Whatever leadership skills Coach Gus saw in me were apparently evident to my classmates, who elected me to offices in high school I did not seek. At graduation, they selected me "Most Likely to Succeed."

3. Roots That Run Deep

On May 15, 1755, Coronél Tomás Sánchez established the frontier post of Laredo on the Rio Grande in what was then part of Spain, decades before the signing of the Declaration of Independence. I am an eighth-generation descendant of Sánchez on my Mother's side of the family. He is my fifth Great-Grandfather.

Tomás Sánchez hailed from families who sailed in galleons from Spain during the sixteenth century. He was born in 1709 in Nuevo Leon, which was the part of New Spain that today includes Mexico, Central America, Florida, and the southwestern United States. Sánchez served in the Army, managed a large ranch, and later joined an expedition organized by the Spanish. They were to explore and colonize Nuevo Santander, a province that then included the northeastern part of today's Mexico and a portion of what is now Texas. The expedition reached the Rio Grande, where Sánchez petitioned for permission to begin a new settlement using his own resources.

To this semi-arid, barely inhabitable land that routinely registers some of the hottest temperatures in the hemisphere,

Sánchez brought three courageous families. In addition to the at times inhospitable climate, they encountered Lipan Apaches and the Comanche nation. Sánchez and his small band prevailed. By 1767, they had built enough of a town that the Governor of Sierra Gorda christened the Sánchez villa with the name of a town in Santander, Spain: *San Agustín de Laredo*.

As the ranking military officer, Coronél Tomás Sánchez became Laredo's first *alcalde* (Mayor or Magistrate), setting in motion the mayoral genetic makeup passed on to future generations. Some would face eerily similar challenges to those I faced as Mayor of Denver. Sánchez and his successors had to grow their city—often against virulent opposition. My ancestors contributed to South Texas history through the eighteenth and nineteenth centuries by building and protecting their communities, homes, and enterprises, especially during and after the Mexican-American and Civil Wars. Their valiant and historic achievements are part of my story and highlight but one Hispanic family's impact on our nation. All families have historical anomalies, and it is ironic that during the Civil War my ancestors fought for the Confederacy, which stood for much of what I have always opposed. While most Latinos from California and the Southwest supported the Union, some supported the Confederacy.

Three of Tomás Sánchez's progeny—Santos, Refugio, and their half-brother Cristóbal Benavides—fought in the Civil War on behalf of the South. Santos Benavides—the half-brother of my Great-Grandmother, achieved the rank of colonel, and was the highest-ranking Tejano in the Confederate Army.

The role of Hispanics in the Civil War, while largely untold, is significant. Laredo was strategically important to the Confederacy, as it allowed cotton to be smuggled into Mexico for sale to international markets. The Benavides family defended it in the Battle of Laredo.

Santos Benavides, a rancher and merchant, served as Mayor of Laredo in 1856 and remained a strong community leader.

Following the vote for secession in 1861, he established Confederate dominance in Laredo and in the Rio Grande Valley, extending all the way to Brownsville.

Texas Confederate Governor Edward Clark, impressed by Benavides and his defense of the border, honored him with an engraved pistol. The commitment of the Benavides brothers to the Confederacy moved the Texas legislature on March 6, 1863, to pass a joint resolution commending them "for their vigilance, energy, and gallantry in pursuing and chastising the banditti infesting the Rio Grande frontier."

1882, Coronél Santos Benavides with his wife Agustina.
Photo courtesy of the Peña Family Archives.

At the same time, two prominent Union leaders in Texas, Edmund Davis and John Haynes, recognized Laredo's strategic value and offered Benavides a general's commission in the Union Army. Santos respectfully declined and instead became a Confederate colonel. Just weeks later, what might have been a decisive moment in the war occurred.

Precious shipments of southern cotton were stacking up in San Agustín Plaza in downtown Laredo. Under no circumstances could the plaza or the cotton fall into the hands of Union soldiers who were stationed outside the town.

Colonel Santos Benavides and his troops courageously defended the Plaza, repelled the Union attacks, and saved the cotton. On May 24, 1864, the Texas legislature congratulated Benavides and his forces. He later served three terms in the Texas Legistlature from 1879 to 1885.

The following year, in 1865, General Robert E. Lee surrendered at Appomattox.

The story of Santos Benavides is indicative of the historical involvement of my family, which has been here for more than 450 years, beginning with the arrival of Captain Juan de Faría from Spain in 1566.

My family's history—and the family histories of Hispanics in the U.S.—is an integral part of the tapestry that is woven into the American story. In painful and jagged ways, the arc of history for Hispanics is far different from the one recited incompletely in our nation's classrooms.

The story of my family is more than business, war, and politics. With our Spanish and Mexican blood, we are rooted in the land with a long history in what is now southern Texas. We have always been part of these United States. This history and the ethics and values instilled by my parents are imprinted in me. Together they nurtured a sense of confidence and responsibility that made me who I am.

A few months ago, as I was walking in downtown Denver wearing a suit and tie, a young man approached me and yelled, "You fucking Mexican! You spic! You greaser! Go back to Mexico!" I was startled. And then I was angered. For a split second, I wanted to confront him. Thankfully, my better sense prevailed, and I continued walking home. Ironically, I had just attended the swearing-in ceremony of Denver's new Chief of Police, who happens to share my Latino heritage.

"Go back to Mexico" is a racist slur hurled at Latinos by those who do not understand that we never "left" Mexico. Instead, much of Mexico became the United States. So, it wasn't surprising that on a recent visit to Ellis Island, my wife and I could not find our ancestors' names in the registry. They came from Spain and Portugal as early as the 1500s, long before there was an Ellis Island, or were already part of the "discovered land." Ours is a different "immigrant" experience. My ancestors in North America intermarried with indigenous people and settled lands that today are known as the American Southwest. Other families settled lands that became California, Nevada, Arizona, New Mexico, and Colorado. The insulting demand that we "should go back to Mexico" shows ignorance of our history and contributions to this country.

June, 2009, At Farias Elementary School, dedicated to Federico's ancestor in Laredo, Texas. Left to right, Federico, Alfredo, Mom, Gustavo and Ana. Photo of the Peña Family Archives.

The courage and determination it took Tomás Sánchez to build a city were characteristics he passed on through the bloodlines of his family. Not far to the south of Denver, where I continued my family's legacy of public service, rise the headwaters of the Rio Grande. For Tomás Sánchez, the Rio Grande was in many ways uncharted. Yet he was brave enough to cross north, to land that would eventually become part of the United States, to stake his claim on the future. Tomás Sánchez bequeathed a legacy of leadership I have always strived to honor.

This legacy of courageous men and women who dared to create a life where there was so little to be found, who took risks and fought to protect their land, has given me the desire to meet life's challenges.

For these reasons, I have rarely felt overwhelmed or inadequate. Like most who have served in public office, I have faced many challenges. Some I met well; others I did not. But I have always been buttressed with the knowledge that my ancestors persevered, contributed, and prospered. Likewise, Americans today must trust in the work and values of our ancestors to create an even greater nation. Our business, civic, and political leaders can learn from the centuries-old accomplishments of Hispanic families and appreciate our extraordinary potential as we forge into the twenty-first century. After all, our roots do run deep.

Circa 1900, Fabián Farías (Federico's Grandfather) standing on the far left, in front of Farías Grocery Store, Laredo Texas. Photo courtesy of the Peña Family Archives.

4. Two Cities: So Close...So Far Apart

There was something out of balance in Brownsville. It didn't matter that we were actively participating in many facets of community life; we weren't always seen that way. As a teen, I began to feel the differences between Brownsville and upstream Laredo.

Although not raised in Laredo, I felt at home there during my frequent visits. Maybe it was because I knew of my family's role in founding and developing the city. Most Hispanic families in Laredo enjoyed a sense of belonging in a way that Latino families in Brownsville did not.

The differences were palpable, uncomfortable. The paradox was evident: while 90 percent of Brownsville's population was Latino, most of the business, civic, and political leaders there were Anglo. Incredibly, it wasn't until 1960 that the first Latino Mayor was elected. Laredo had Hispanic Mayors much earlier. Even the Anglo Mayors spoke Spanish.

This tale of two cities became emblematic for me. I began to understand that, while Laredo was where my storied ancestors made history, Brownsville was more representative of the real world. Hispanics in Brownsville were marginalized. This affected my view of the world and laid the groundwork for the disillusionment that later nearly broke my faith in my country.

Brownsville was as small as Laredo, with about 30,000 mostly Catholic Latino souls, most of whom were impoverished by fate and lack of fortune. Laredo itself was not nirvana, but it had distinct economic, social, cultural, and political differences noticeable to a young boy.

Unlike their Anglo counterparts, most Latinos in Brownsville were chronically uneducated and underemployed. Although they worked hard and kept the economy buzzing, it hardly seemed to benefit them. Over time, I realized that the disparities between the two cultures were pervasive.

Most Anglos in Brownsville did not bother to learn Spanish, while those in Laredo were more often bilingual. As soon as children in Brownsville went to school, names were changed; José became Joe, Roberto became Bob, and of course, Federico became Fred. We understood English was the official language—a point literally driven home by rules that prohibited us from speaking Spanish at school. This war against the Spanish language was ubiquitous and made it clear that in Brownsville, citizens were viewed differently based on their ethnicity.

I did not fully comprehend that I was going through a defining moment, as were many Hispanics in the U.S. The pressure to be anglicized greatly affected our social, economic, and political development. Why was my family's history ignored? I didn't ask this of my parents, and it wasn't discussed with my friends. Instead, people inexplicably acquiesced. We accepted the world around us with a tradition of humility that discouraged us from rocking the boat. For the time being. As we matured, we began to question this treatment. Occasionally, my friends would utter quietly, *"Pinche Americanos."*

At the center of the city was Fort Brown. Built along the Rio Grande around 1845, the fort saw its first action during the Mexican-American War. The war was the turning point between the two countries that would affect everyone on both sides of the border. Today it remains a source of cultural contention and confusion. Stories abound about who started the war. In her book, *The Wicked War*, historian Amy Greenberg describes how President James Polk coveted war with Mexico as part of the "Manifest Destiny" movement of the 1840s. Polk sent General Zachary Taylor to Corpus Christi, Texas with orders to cross into Mexican territory. This provoked Mexico's response, which gave Polk the excuse to invade. After the war, the U.S. confiscated more than half of Mexico—525,000 square miles—including parts of present-day Arizona, California, New Mexico, Texas, Colorado, Nevada, and Utah. 3,000 Mexicans, after paying a fee, became American citizens.

Following the Mexican-American War, Anglos made up more than half of Brownsville's population, owned most of the land, and held most of the well-paying jobs and government offices, according to historian Gilberto Hinojosa. From that point on, the Mexican population in Brownsville lost much power and was left to perform menial labor. They were looked down upon by the Anglos, who deemed the Hispanics in their midst as lazy good-for-nothings who drank, danced, and gambled too much. Most irksome is that Hispanics were also considered to be docile and weak according to Hinojosa.

After the war, the Rio Grande became the official but anti-historical border between the two countries, separating families and creating two disparate societies. The human separations caused by this new river boundary formed a social and cultural border within Brownsville itself: one for the wealthy few and another for the poverty-stricken majority. I could still see the difference one hundred years later.

In Laredo, Latinos had a different experience. Although my ancestors founded Laredo on behalf of Spain and led its development for decades, their circumstances changed when Mexico emerged as an independent country. Mexico did not have an effective, competent government to properly administer her outlying regions. Consequently, many Mexican families, especially in the regions closest to the developing United States, chafed under the rule of Mexico City. In 1836, both English- and Spanish-speaking families, including my ancestors, joined together in a revolt against Mexico to carve away land that became a new republic they named Texas. The revolution in Texas set off a series of events, many of them painful, that had a dramatic effect on our country's history. To complicate matters, another republic formed within the newly proclaimed Republic of Texas—the Republic of the Rio Grande, whose flag flew over Laredo for a brief eleven months in the year 1840.

The creation of the Republic of the Rio Grande sprang from the same anti-Mexico City sentiments that ignited the Texas revolution. Juan Francisco Farías, one of my Mother's ancestors, served as Secretary of the new Republic of the Rio Grande.

However brave and determined its supporters, the Laredo Republic was attacked by the Mexican Army under the command of General Mariano Artista. The fight was hardly a match, and a brief 283 days after its founding, the Republic of the Rio Grande came to an inglorious end.

One hundred and fifty years later, on February 17, 1994, while serving as U.S. Secretary of Transportation, I was invited to visit Laredo to celebrate the birthday of the Republic of the Rio Grande. The Mayor of Laredo appointed me the republic's honorary president "with all the rights and privileges appertaining thereto and with the duty of assisting in the defense of the Republic against any who might become its enemies and the preservation of the history, boundaries, and natural resources indigenous thereto." I couldn't help but think of my ancestors who had defended the feisty republic so many years ago against the Mexican Army.

In 1848, the Mexican-American War ended. It forever changed the destinies of both countries—and of my family. People were confused as to whether Laredo would remain part of Mexico. Ultimately the town would fall within the U.S. border, and suddenly everyone would have to choose between the two countries. My ancestor, Juan Francisco Farías, opted to stay in the U.S. to protect the land originally settled by our family. For a five dollar fee, he applied for U.S. citizenship on April 29, 1857, and remained in Laredo.

Notwithstanding this painful history, it is amazing to watch Laredoans demonstrate their loyalty to the United States. Since 1898, they have shown their patriotism by embracing the most American of holidays—George Washington's birthday—while celebrating their city's bicultural identity. The Washington Day festivities in Laredo still feature a ceremony on the International Bridge attended by Mexican and American citizens and dignitaries. Two children from each country meet in the middle of the bridge and give each other an *abrazo,* or embrace, symbolizing the amity and understanding between the nations. "Two Laredos beating with one heart," as the locals say. The notion today of building a "Great Wall" to separate these communities is anathema to most Laredoans. I wonder how many Americans know that this patriotic tradition is maintained today by this largely Hispanic border town? It is a manifestation of the confidence and mutual respect of both Latinos and Anglos.

Unlike Brownsville in the late 1800s, there was integration of families in Laredo. Perhaps that facilitated the Farías and Peña families to be successful ranchers, businessmen, and civic leaders. My closest connection to that lineage was my Grandfather, Eduardo Peña.

Reflecting the integration of Laredo's families, my Grandfather married Clementina Merriweather, my Grandmother, whose family was of Scottish descent. She was perfectly bilingual. I admired my grandparents. My Grandmother was involved in the George Washington organization and volunteered at the city hospital. The homemade baked goods sold at the family's grocery were from her kitchen. Thinking back, I am impressed by my Grandfather's business acumen—he owned two grocery stores—and his civic engagement—he was an alderman for twenty years. Like my Father, he worked until he was eighty years old.

Decades later, I revisited Laredo's City Hall and wondered if my Grandfather would have been as successful in Brownsville as he was in Laredo. Would the unspoken and subtle obstacles that pervaded aspects of Brownsville life defeated him back in the early 1930s and 1940s?

When my family visited Laredo for Washington Day celebrations, the six Peña children were distributed among different relatives with homes on both sides of the river. I grew to understand that both Nuevo Laredo, Mexico and Laredo, Texas were deeply connected. Experiencing this gave me pride and purpose as an American Latino with deep roots.

I have often wondered how my life would have unfolded had I been raised in Laredo, where things just seemed more balanced and the differences between Anglos and Mexican Americans were not only respected but accepted. Would I have felt so connected and comfortable in Laredo that I never would have left? Were the sometime negative experiences in Brownsville subliminally pushing me to leave? The question of why Brownsville and Laredo evolved so differently lingered during my high school days. Eventually, the answer would lead to an erosion of my belief in the American system of governance and drive me to become a civil rights lawyer to defend Latinos.

But first, it was time to go to college.

5. The Texican

It was early 1964, and in a few months, I would graduate from St. Joseph Academy. There was no doubt that I would go to college. Moreover, I was expected to follow my two older brothers, Gustavo and Oscar, to Texas A&M where they were enrolled. And why not? My Father, his two brothers, and other relatives from Laredo were all Aggies.

The South Texas economy was dependent on agriculture—my Father was, after all, a cotton broker, and the military was in our veins. The *A* and the *M* in Texas A&M were not small letters to us. Though the *m* stands for *mechanical,* it could have stood for *military* since the university produced over 20,000 combat troops, and more officers, during World War II than our military academies. My family was centered with discipline, organization, and obedience, thanks to my Father's upbringing and military training at A&M.

Aggies are famously, and fiercely, devoted to the university and its traditions, and my Father was a true Aggie. Sometimes our family of eight would pack into Dad's station wagon and drive seven hours to College Station. We would arrive on

Thanksgiving Eve to watch the Aggie student body light their giant bonfire, a thrill for a young man. The next day, the entire family would enjoy the annual rivalry with A&M's nemesis, the University of Texas, at an outdoor picnic.

Texas A&M's traditions were woven into my family's soul. As children we knew "The Aggie War Hymn" by heart. We were awed when the Aggie marching band, led onto the field by the seniors in their knee-high leather boots, stepped up to form a perfect square in the end zone. For a moment the crowd would quiet, and then bugles would begin the school song. As the crowd exploded, chills would race through my body. Then pure excitement swept down from the stands as the first grandiose notes sounded from the country's most impressive military marching band. Soon enough, the raucous rallying cry of "Hullabaloo! Caneck! Caneck!" would fill the stadium.

After years of indoctrination, it seemed natural that I would follow the Peña men and become a part of Aggieland. I wanted to belong there, to pledge lifelong fealty to school and tradition as thoroughly as my Father. Several of my high school classmates and I were excited about getting buzz cuts, joining the corps, and earning our leather boots. My Father, however, had other designs, ones that would be life changing.

On a late March evening in 1964, as he was sitting in the living room reading in his favorite armchair, he asked me to join him. I sat down, wondering what was on his mind. He began by asking me how serious I was about becoming a lawyer. He questioned me about my plans. I do not remember what I must have mumbled, but I do remember what he said. It was the unthinkable. "If you want to be a lawyer, you should attend the University of Texas since it has a good law school and A&M has none." My jaw dropped. I had not realized A&M, the heretofore perfect university, had such a striking deficiency. My heart sank.

Why was my Father—the Aggie of all Aggies—discouraging me so late in the application process from becoming an Aggie and suggesting instead that I attend the University of Texas?

In Austin, of all places? What would I tell my friends? We had plans!

I sat there, numbed by my Father's sudden upending of my plans. But that was my Father. Instead of thinking that my desire to be a lawyer would pass in time, he selflessly and pragmatically set aside his own desires for his son to graduate from his alma mater.

The thought of one of his sons attending Texas must have bothered him. But he knew that the University at Austin was the state's largest institution of higher learning. From its ranks came many of the state's leaders in business, government, commerce, and the arts. In fact, the campus hosted Texas Boys' State, the student leadership development program for high school youth, which I had attended years earlier. Still, Austin was foreign to me. Misgivings aside, I was soon on my way to start the magnificent journey that would become my life beyond Brownsville. The student body of the University of Texas, or simply "The University," as our haughty school sweatshirts proclaimed, numbered 33,000—more than the population of Brownsville. I drove the 350 miles north to Austin with a couple of older students. They regaled me with stories to convince me of how much I would love Austin, and my excitement grew as we neared the city. We cheered when we crossed the Colorado River and caught sight of the University Tower, the campus landmark rising imperiously 300 feet over the landscape.

Then I saw the majestic state capitol, the symbol of Texas power. However central A&M had been to my family, it was located in College Station, a somewhat isolated town compared to Austin. Almost instantly everything changed, made sense, and smothered any interest I once had in attending A&M. After all, I was a *Texan* living in one of the largest states in the Union. My ancestors had helped its formation. One of them, Santos Benavides, had traveled here by horseback from Laredo as a member of the territorial legislature. Presidents and national leaders sprang from the university here. And, back then, Texas had a much better football team! I was full of hopeful expectations, although a bit apprehensive about what to expect.

It took a few years for me to realize that the number of students with Spanish surnames was less than 3 percent of the entire university. That appeared to be several hundred out of 33,000! The difference from Brownsville couldn't have been more profound. My initial enchantment with the university waned quickly as this reality sank in. It wasn't until the spring of that year that the Board of Regents voted to remove all racial barriers, integrate student housing, and hire the first Black faculty member.

Some days I could walk across the entire forty-acre campus and not exchange a single word with anyone. I knew only a handful of people at UT who hailed from South Texas. And I was somewhat shy. It was easy to feel very lonely. I felt wistful remembering the cordial and plentiful "howdies" at A&M that students extended to every visitor.

I felt odd in a way I could not quite understand. I was in many respects a foreigner in the state my ancestors founded. Aside from my private musings about Brownsville, I had never experienced this feeling of isolation. But I endured, unlike others who could not adjust to the demands of college life and dropped out.

The money I had saved for years was not enough. Though I received some modest support from home, I earned my meals washing dishes in the Kinsolving women's dormitory near my own dorm. I never actually came face-to-face with the mostly Anglo girls who lived at Kinsolving. After finishing their meals, they would place their trays into a chute that led to a conveyor belt that brought me the dirty dishes. All I saw were their hands. It became apparent to the Black and Hispanic dishwashers that only Anglo students were assigned to serve the coeds face-to-face on the food-serving lines.

In class and elsewhere on campus, I kept my head down, confident that my upbringing would help me navigate the unwelcoming environment on campus. But I was naïve. When a professor of English returned one of my essays with the note, "*C+... Not bad for a South Texas boy,*" at first, I smiled. (Maybe he was surprised I could write in English.) Only later did it dawn on me that he had not meant this as a compliment. Instead, he had resorted to the automatic, routine condescension exhibited by so many. It hardly mattered; I had learned from my parents not to hold a grudge. Plus, I was finally in a classroom with girls!

A green oasis of springs, rivers, hills, and lakes, Austin was magical in the spring. I came to love the city and decided to remain there for a summer to work and take extra classes. I was looking forward to an invigorating and fun three months. It wasn't long before the world changed.

Concern over the country's involvement in Vietnam had been growing. On August 1, 1966, I witnessed a new kind of madness that is unfortunately not as shocking now as it was back then.

It was nearly noon and I was flipping hamburgers at a restaurant near Guadalupe Street, the school's main drag that ran close to the University Tower. Suddenly, I heard sounds that, for a South Texas boy long-used to hunting, were unmistakably familiar. *Rifle shots.* Soon gunfire was raining down all over campus from atop the tower. Charles Whitman, an engineering student and former Marine, had climbed to the tower's observation deck and was shooting at the defenseless people below with lethal accuracy.

In the end, Whitman killed seventeen people and wounded another thirty-two. He was stopped when an officer shot him. An autopsy found a tumor in his brain. Little did I know that day in August would usher in a new age of violence whose long shadow would fall on campuses throughout the country.

For such violence to explode from the University Tower was unthinkable. The tower was part of my life. I spent days and long nights in that building, which housed the main library. I loved the smell of its books, ancient manuscripts, and newspapers.

The desecration of the University Tower by one disturbed young man's senseless violence was very hard to bear. The Observation Deck at the top of the tower was subsequently closed for years.

Eventually, campus life returned to some sense of normalcy, and the ensuing semester brought forth the annual ritual—student body elections.

A group of students from South Texas decided to mock the student elections by running a candidate for president they thought best represented student government: Mickey Mouse. These students, known as "independents" who resented that fraternities and sororities controlled campus elections, constructed a papier-mâché head of Mickey himself. They successfully petitioned him onto the ballot. Mickey became the nominee of the Aroused Political Association to Help You, or APATHY. I joined the group, as I endorsed their satirical message about campus elections. During the campaign, we took turns donning Mickey's head and campaigned around campus accompanied by a ragtime band. The days I transformed myself into Mickey, I wanted to be as authentic as possible, so I also dressed as Mickey would by wearing a blue blazer, white pants, and white gloves. I even mimicked Mickey's voice.

1966, Mickey Mouse campaigning for University
of Texas Student Body President.
Photo from The Daily Texan, courtesy of the Peña Family Archives.

In the end we shocked ourselves. Mickey finished third in the balloting, garnering 12 percent of the vote—a respectable showing indeed for a rodent made from parchment. We had made our point: student government was a bit of a farce.

Despite my cynical participation in promoting a mouse for higher office, I remained a serious student. By the end of 1968, I received my undergraduate degree in political science with a minor in international affairs. It was time to actualize my dream to attend law school, an undertaking that quickly proved to be more challenging than expected.

I feared, since standardized tests were my bane, that I would bomb the LSAT, the entrance test to law school. I was not surprised by the dismal results, but I was disappointed when the University of Texas School of Law initially denied me admission. But I wanted to get in so badly I decided to pay a visit to the school's Assistant Dean.

Not a minute into our meeting, the hesitant Assistant Dean explained that I probably would not be accepted. "Your poor LSAT results suggest you cannot handle the school's demanding curriculum," he said carefully, adding that I might not be able to pass the Texas bar exam since I don't perform well on such tests.

"But I really want to be a lawyer, and I'll work hard," I responded.

"We'll see," he replied politely, clearly not wanting to hurt my feelings.

I was crushed, but something inside of me—perhaps the audacity of my pioneering ancestors or the tenacity drilled into me by Coach Gus, or a combination of both—propelled me to persevere.

Over the next few weeks, I called the Assistant Dean's office inquiring about my status. I was pestering him by day and praying by night. Which stratagem worked, I do not know, but my name was included on the final list of those admitted by the University of Texas School of Law in 1968. Perhaps the Assistant Dean was impressed with my determination and concluded it might be enough to sustain me through the rigorous law school curriculum.

To this day I don't know whether divine intervention or human grit prevailed for me, but I remain certain of the pitfalls of standardized testing. I believe it is unwise to place exclusive emphasis on standardized tests to assess the innate abilities of students. I am pleased to be a poster child for the poor test taker who can succeed. Today, Hispanics are becoming prominent lawyers and judges across the country but remain hugely underrepresented in the profession. According to the Hispanic National Bar Association, while Hispanics make up 18 percent of the U.S. population, they comprise only about 4 percent of U.S. lawyers. I believe that standardized test scores, the enormous expense of school, and inadequate law school recruitment account for the shortage of Hispanic attorneys across the country. It does not help to hear a president inappropriately criticize a distinguished Hispanic federal judge. Nevertheless, there are thousands of Latinos who have the drive and ability to succeed in the legal profession if only they are provided an opportunity to excel.

Life has its ironies. I was recognized as a "Distinguished Alumnus" of the University of Texas more than twenty years after barely being admitted to the UT Law School. Imagine, that same south Texas boy who received the patronizing "not bad" on an English composition, became a Distinguished Alum. And the Law School, which originally hesitated in admitting me, invited me to address its "Sunflower" graduation ceremony, where I was made an honorary member of the "Order of the Coif." Today, my portrait hangs on its walls among prominent law school graduates.

These experiences introduced me to the real world beyond Brownsville. They prepared me for future challenges presented by people and institutions that did not understand or appreciate the Latino experience in America. But I also realized that I could not only persevere but also succeed by committing myself to hard work, sacrifice, and never abandoning a dream. I credit my parents, their commitment to their children and our education, and to the self-determination of my ancestors who helped settle our nation.

6. Civil Unrest 101

One summer when I worked for prominent Brownsville attorney John Black, my dream of practicing law became more real. I was preparing depositions and observing trials. I witnessed a legal system that was accessible only to some. I became more and more aware of how unjust, insensitive, and cruel our society can be to the poor, innocent, and defenseless. In the evolving rhetoric of the 60s, these victims were being crushed by *the system.*

The system was everything and everyone who, for whatever reason, made life worse for the "underclass." The system included aggressive police officers, insensitive educators, unresponsive public officials, and landlords without scruples. It permitted faceless corporations to underpay their workers, endanger their safety, and pollute the environment—all things hostile to fundamental fairness and decency.

Then there was the war in Vietnam. Many in my generation were angry over the senseless deaths, the questionable mission, and the mistruths foisted on the American people about our "victories" there.

Taken together, these disturbing systemic conditions ignited my generation's concern and compassion, galvanizing a sense of mission and purpose. We had to end the war. Fight injustice. Protect the poor. Safeguard the environment. We at the Law School—who would one day be responsible for the laws that governed society and the change it required—considered ourselves the vanguards of the Age of Aquarius.

Students at UT and across the country protested the Vietnam War, committing acts of civil disobedience and staging demonstrations against the *establishment* that sustained the system. During one of my final exams, a bomb threat forced us to evacuate the Law School.

1970, Federico at UT protesting the Vietnam War.
Photo courtesy of the Peña Family Archives.

The rage growing throughout America reached its apex when the Ohio National Guard shot and killed four students in May 1970 at Kent State University. Campuses throughout the nation exploded with protests. In Austin, anti-war student leaders called for a sit-in in the middle of campus. I abandoned my law books at the library and joined the rest of the anti-war students streaming in the direction of the University Tower.

What started as an afternoon demonstration actually lasted several days. Along with thousands of other students, I ended up sleeping on the campus grounds. While I was worried about missing class, I was more concerned about the armed Texas National Guard surrounding us, and I sensed that we would likely march to the seat of Texas government a mere six blocks away.

After several days of peaceful protests, our skin scorched to leather by the sun, we decided that it was indeed time to march to the capitol. But we needed a parade license, and city officials were not accommodating. They were solidly in the camp of President Johnson, who at one time represented Austin in Congress and was now in charge of prosecuting the war.

Without a license, we had to stay on the sidewalks three abreast as we marched from campus. This restriction increased the possibility that outright violence on the scale of Kent State would occur. Surely the 20,000 marchers who were about to take to the sidewalks would spill into the streets, compelling the police, the state guard, and state troopers to react.

One of the law students assisting local attorneys to secure an injunction against the city pleaded with me to help hold up the march. I told him it was too late, that we were going to take our chances.

Miraculously, only minutes before the march was to begin, the legal team won an order from the courts allowing us to abandon the sidewalks and take to the streets.

Emboldened, we occupied the full width of the street. It was an extraordinary moment. A mass of humanity marched in the direction of the capitol, and our numbers swelled in size as office workers and downtown shoppers joined us. Our chants against the war were loud and irreverent, especially for conservative Texas in the 1970s. Onlookers looked aghast when they heard us yell, "One, two, three, four, we don't want your fucking war." The march was one of the largest in the country and was covered extensively by the media. We were proof that Texas, the home state of the President, was turning against the war. The painful irony for many of us was that we supported President Johnson's other war, the war on poverty. When he was only twenty, Johnson had taught in an impoverished school of Mexican American students in Cotulla, Texas, seventy miles northeast of Laredo. I was proud that a U.S. president from my home state was responsible for an avalanche of legislation that promoted better schools and protected the civil rights and social security of the nation. But I could not support his stance on Vietnam.

After several days of protest, I returned to the library to find my books exactly where I had left them. My career in law awaited, books and all. Perhaps I was learning that no matter how much I protested the established order, the courts would still be there—a centuries-old system fashioned to provide remedy and stability in times of turmoil and unrest. And, indeed, the Supreme Court was in the process of overturning discriminatory laws and was actively checking the president's powers. The court was a glimmer of hope, I thought, that perhaps could fix a broken system. And after more years of protest, and the election of new political leaders, the Vietnam War finally came to an inglorious end in 1975.

This is a great lesson for us today. We had a president (Trump) with a dictatorial attitude who attempted to stymie Congress, threatened the press, and manipulated the courts all to thwart any check and balance on his power. He behaved as though he was above the law. But in the face of these egregious actions and their aftermath, we must continue to engage and bring change in every creative way we can. We can protest peacefully. We can participate in civil disobedience, and accept the civil penalties. We can appeal to the courts based on our constitutional rights. We can vigorously exercise our right to vote and elect more responsive leaders. And we can run for office ourselves.

These are the strategies we see today as millions demonstrate around the world to protest police brutality and demand reform of our criminal justice system. We can elect leaders who will address climate change, correct income inequality, and safeguard our right to vote. We must keep hope alive. And we must believe that our democratic institutions can provide checks and balances when used properly and strategically. It may take time, but change comes when we fight for it.

My passion surfaced during school breaks when I returned home to visit family. I found myself in heated discussions with my Father, the former Army Captain whose sympathies were with the war. I believed the war was wrong and that Vietnam would not tumble "like dominoes" into the web of communism that many feared was spreading throughout Southeast Asia. I believed we were wasting blood and treasure in a distant land instead of focusing on the challenges at home. Though our disagreements were passionate, they would prove to be very important in the long run. My Father, despite his views, pressed me to find answers and not just complain about problems. I recall one painful conversation when he raised his voice and said, "If you're so smart, what's your answer to halting the spread of Communism?" I did not respond at first, but the question caused me to think about my position. I don't remember if I had a profound answer. Many others of my generation were having similar, difficult conversations with family and friends. Over time, more Americans came to see the war as wrong, including my Father, who eventually developed misgivings about it.

Unfortunately, I wasted years during which my Father and I rarely spoke. I regret that I could not find a more pragmatic approach and a deeper understanding of his experience and that of the Peña brothers' courage during WWII. Such was the shortcoming of my youth and immaturity, deficiencies I sometimes see in some of the violent protests of today. Over time, as my hair got longer, it became even more difficult for me to go home. My parents disapproved of my disheveled appearance, given the conservative culture of the Peña home and local community. Still, by pressing me for answers, my Father helped me find my center and identify exactly what needed to be addressed, a skill that would prove to serve me well. He taught me that it was not enough to identify a problem or complain about a condition. I needed to develop an answer, a solution better than the status quo. Decades later, as a State Legislator, Mayor, and Cabinet Secretary, I would need to offer innovative strategies to remedy a problem or achieve an objective. It is never enough to simply complain or criticize.

Along with protesting the war, I was driven to fight for equal rights for the country's minority population, of which I knew I was a member. Dr. Martin Luther King Jr. and the civil rights movement symbolized the chasm that existed between people of color and the rest of the nation.

I became engrossed in civil rights issues as I watched news of marchers in Alabama attacked with fire hoses and dogs under the direction of "Bull" Conner, the State's Commissioner of Public Safety. The problems inherent in our country's military campaign in Southeast Asia continued to impassion me as I learned of friends returning from Vietnam injured or maimed— or worse, dead in steel caskets.

As my frustrations grew, the local government, the State of Texas, the Democratic Party, the University of Texas, and the courts themselves seemed too slow to respond. Appearing incapable of providing relief, they instead stifled—even opposed— legitimate discourse and disagreement.

My faith in the very system I was working so hard to participate in was taking a beating. Fortunately, the Supreme Court, led by Chief Justice Earl Warren, remained a beacon of hope for those of us struggling to maintain our fading idealism. The federal courts became the forum in which citizens could seek redress against racism, sexism, and other societal maladies. It served as a genuine "check and balance" wisely imbedded in our Constitution.

There were moments, however, when I entertained the idea of pursuing a more traditional law practice. I was intrigued by the idea of practicing criminal law, and I interned for the District Attorney in Houston as part of my criminal law course. My vacillation between the type of law to follow notwithstanding, my letters home revealed that I was on my way to becoming a civil rights or public law attorney.

But my anger at the injustice I saw overwhelmed any sense of equilibrium. I have a feeling that many Americans are similarly frustrated today. Issues like global warming, criminal justice reform, income inequality, anti-Semitism, police reform, and ethnic and racial discrimination have propelled demonstrations once again onto the streets.

I wrote letters to my parents expressing my feelings about the need for change. I came across these letters recently after my parents' deaths, and could feel the passion of the times rise up from the discolored pages. Each letter gives me great remorse for the alarm my parents must have felt when they read my screeds. They must have caused them sleepless nights. One, written during the summer of 1970 while I interned for the Mexican American Legal Defense Fund, was the most telling. MALDEF was founded in San Antonio as a national civil rights organization to spearhead the drive for justice for Latinos. My work involved meeting with parents, students, and other Latino activists who had the courage to speak up in defense of their civil rights. I wrote home about one such meeting at a local elementary school with Hispanic parents who were upset about the school board's dismissal of a popular principal. I described the termination as "a bad deal" for both the principal and the parents, but we could not justify a legal claim against the school board.

The day after my meeting with those parents, as noted in my letter, I drove 160 miles from San Antonio to Uvalde to work on another school board case. *"We are asking the Board,"* I wrote to my parents, *"to allow the students to make up their missed classes and enable them to pass, as the Board has ordered all teachers to flunk the protesters...about 500. At the hearing of the teacher, the Texas Rangers were present, armed, and ready for trouble. I hope tomorrow's session won't be too heated. I don't know how much you know about Uvalde, but it's really the home of the Anglo."*

The idea that I was going to a meeting with armed members of the Texas Rangers, an outfit which has a notoriously anti-Latino past, must have made my parents deeply afraid. And my reference to the "home of the Anglo" was a kind of polemical rhetoric and sentiment not usually heard in our household. My Father, who had several Anglo friends, would never speak in disparaging terms about Anglos. And since he did not fully support my civil rights work, he might have felt that I was wasting my talents and education on matters best left to others. He was still hoping I would practice more traditional law. But it was becoming clear to me that it was my responsibility to use my legal skills to break the cycle of unequal treatment of minorities.

I relished the fight. It was invigorating to work with other young MALDEF lawyers who shared my passion for addressing the plight of Latinos across the country. We worked late hours but also played hard. We engaged in endless political discussions over steaming bowls of *caldo de res,* a Mexican beef stew that was a specialty at Beto's Restaurant, located a few blocks from our office. On weekends, my Tío Fabián would take me to local taverns and restaurants to meet his friends on the west side of San Antonio. I sensed that many of them were thankful I was engaged in the fight for civil rights.

The short three months I worked for MALDEF were emotionally draining, yet exhilarating. We found some success in the court. We won a decision in a federal case in New Mexico— *Serna v. Portales Municipal Schools*—in which the court ordered the school district to provide bilingual education to Hispanic students. But the progress was too slow, and I was becoming impatient and disillusioned.

Back at school later that year, I updated my parents, not by telling them about my law school studies, but about my work with a local Latino lawyer who was representing seven Latino youngsters who'd been arrested for interfering with an arrest.

"This is an especially important case," I wrote, *"because of recent Austin happenings: knifing of a policeman at the coliseum by Chicanos, throwing of bricks and bottles at police at the carnival by Blacks, and the various shots at police in East Austin by Blacks. People are trying to keep these events quiet to prevent racial trouble, but at the same time they want to really crack down. That's why this Mayo case is really going to be tough to beat. I don't think it can be questioned that Austin will be experiencing racial troubles within some months, and neither the city nor the people really care to seriously try and solve the causes of unrest."*

I imagine my parents' angst equaled my anger, but I was exasperated by the racial and ethnic tensions in Texas. I was beginning to abandon hope that city and state leaders would resolve these problems in a fair or meaningful fashion, confirming my suspicion that the institutions and safeguards of our political system were failing.

My parents, meanwhile, had reached their own conclusion: it was time to get me out of Texas. They sent me news clippings about the wonders of San Francisco, gingerly suggesting a move to the West Coast. I was apparently indifferent to their concerns or their hints, as I next wrote on November 15, 1970: *"Life continues along and I'm thankful that there are enough revolting conditions which help me continue toward my destiny."* My Mother probably covered her mouth with her hands; my Father likely shook his head at my celebrating the "*revolting condi-tions*" that were inspiring my "destiny." And still I went further: "*I hope it doesn't embarrass you much, but I'm becoming firmly committed to this movement.*" I had not even a small inkling of the psychological and emotional impact I was having on my parents. I had developed a callousness and indifference to everything but the "cause." Such was my mental state that I had no intention of attending my imminent law school graduation ceremony, much less inviting my parents to the commencement. Not all of their virtues had been lost on me, however. My loyalty to family needled my conscience enough to remember how important my graduation was. I am thankful that I came to my senses. As it turned out, it was so important to my parents that they drove 200 miles to Laredo to pick up my grandparents, Eduardo and Clementina, to bring them to the ceremony. My Grandfather acknowledged my achievement by presenting me with a Velasquez Spanish dictionary with the inscription: *Para el talentoso licienciado, Federico Peña, con todo cariño, un recuerdo de su abuelo que lo admire y quiere mucho.* For the talented lawyer, Federico Peña, with much love, a remembrance from your Grandfather who admires and loves you greatly. Ironically, the parchment I had so longed to acquire still remains rolled up in its original cardboard tube.

The year before my law school graduation, I had my first real involvement in politics, helping to manage a gubernatorial campaign. Frances "Cissy" Farenthold was running for Governor of Texas against the conservative Dolph Briscoe. Ironically, Briscoe was from Uvalde, the town where I had met up with the Texas Rangers. Unlike the Mickey Mouse campaign at UT, this election was a deadly serious matter, and my entire family was involved. We challenged the rules of political engagement in Cameron County. We refused to pay off the *politiqueras*, women who promised votes for pay. They would come to our campaign office and say, "*Queremos ayudar a la Senora Cissy, pero necesitamos gasolina y llantas."* We want to help Ms. Sissy, but we need gasoline and tires.

"No," I would respond, *"si quieren elejir el mejor candidato, deben assistir sin pagos y solo con tus corazones."*

I told them that if they believed in Ms. Farenthold, they should drive people to vote out of the goodness of their hearts, without being paid. It might have been the first time in Brownsville politics that many became engaged for the right reasons. Our determined efforts helped Farenthold win our county, though unfortunately she lost statewide. The effort gave me a taste of how elections can be won and the negative consequences that happen when they are lost. Decades later in Denver, when I visited high schools, I would share that sentiment by telling students, "The political system rewards those who participate and punishes those who do not." One cannot be a bystander.

After graduating from law school in 1972, I passed the Texas bar exam on my first attempt and was officially sanctioned to work as a Texas attorney. I realized my dream of becoming the first attorney in my family. Once licensed, I became a Reginald Herbert Smith Community Lawyer Fellow (REGGIE) sponsored by Howard University in Washington, D.C. The REGGIE required me to move to El Paso to assist in a legal aid office. I was excited to go. For a $12,000 annual salary, my job included community organizing and bringing class action litigation against various governmental institutions that were discriminating against minority citizens.

My parents were proud of my achievement and perhaps pleased to see the influence this had on my two younger brothers, who later became lawyers. But deep down, I believe they must have hoped that the principles of hard work, civic leadership, and family honor would eventually move me toward more traditional legal work.

Six months into the position at El Paso Legal Aid, I began to realize that the board and the lawyers had different expectations as to the scope of my work. While I was focused on civil rights, they expected my work to center around divorces, evictions, and other traditional cases. I lasted less than a year, and so lost my first job almost immediately out of law school. Disappointed by my firing, I decided to visit my younger brother Alfredo in Colorado, where he was attending the University of Denver Sturm College of Law. Alfredo would become the third lawyer in our family, following his triplet brother, Alberto. I had no definite plans, but after so much tumult in becoming a lawyer, I felt hardened, serious, and ready for battle as I headed to Colorado. Little did I know what awaited me there.

Part Two: Denver (1974–1982)

7. Fighting the Good Fight

Denver was supposed to be a stopover. I intended to visit my brother for just a few weeks and then pursue an invitation to join a friend at California Rural Legal Aid in San Francisco to work with farm workers.

Driving up from El Paso on Interstate 25, I passed through Albuquerque where, in 1988, I would eventually marry, and where in 1992 I would receive a life-transforming phone call. Just thirty-five miles west of the freeway I was traveling on sat Los Alamos National Laboratory. One day I would oversee Los Alamos as Secretary of Energy, where serious charges of espionage would surface against one of its scientists during my tenure.

I drove innocently north on Interstate 25, car packed with my meager belongings, listening to a radio station broadcasting in what I assumed was the Navajo language. Past Santa Fe, I would need my holy faith as I began the climb up Ratón Pass en route from New Mexico into Colorado. The original Santa Fe Trail was laid through Ratón Pass in 1821. It would later serve as the entry point for American troops into what was Mexico during the Mexican-American War.

I knew little about northern New Mexico's history and even less about the pass. At an elevation of nearly 8,000 feet above sea level, treacherous winter weather can churn up in an instant, bringing extremely dangerous driving conditions. Sure enough, as my car climbed the pass, light snow began to fall. I wondered why vehicles were parked on the shoulders of the road...and soon had my answer. A blinding, furious snowstorm whipped around me and I could feel my car lift at times against the wind. The few snowfalls I'd witnessed in Austin had not prepared me for a snowstorm so intense. I mistakenly turned on my car's headlights and flicked on its high beams, compounding my blindness.

Mesmerized by the snow, I continued driving blindly, making the curves by sheer guesswork. I still believe that some form of divine intervention kept the howling wind and snow from sending me careening off that mountain. Otherwise, I have no idea how I crossed into Colorado in one piece.

Once the snow cleared and I returned to lower elevations, I was awed by the beautiful scenery. I could smell the fresh scent of pine when I opened my car window. I imagined hiking in these woods and exploring the roaring rivers. It was amazing. I found it hard to believe such a place existed. Brownsville this was not; Austin, even with its green hills, could barely compare. I wondered how I could transfer my two-year REGGIE fellowship from El Paso to Colorado.

Arriving in Denver, I was immediately captivated by the city. The mountains beyond it were truly majestic. Their snow-capped peaks were magical. I decided that until word came from Washington about the fellowship, I would sleep on my brother's couch and explore Colorado. After all, in Spanish the state's name "Colorado" was apt: the beautiful state was, in fact, painted in color.

I had never seen anything like it. Every mountain, hill, and stream reflected light that seemed to change by the hour. I woke up excited every day, invigorated by new views and color-ful landscapes. And I liked that the state's roots ran as deep as those of Laredo and Texas. I explored places like Alamosa, San Luis, Antonito, Pueblo, Trinidad, Cañon City—Spanish-named cities in Spanish-named counties like Conejos (rabbits), Huer-fano (orphan), and Costilla (rib) that each shared a connection, like I did, to the Rio Grande.

On one of my trips exploring the state, I stood a few feet away from the headwaters of the Rio Grande in southern Colo-rado. In the mountains, the river's waters were clear and blue—far different from the dank river in Laredo. By the time the river arrived in Brownsville 1,900 miles from the Sangre de Cristo Mountains in Colorado, its waters were danker still. Though bedazzled by Colorado, I proudly recalled that these lands, like my ancestral home of southern Texas, were once settled by Spaniards, and later Mexicans, while keenly aware of the cliff dwellings in Southwestern Colorado that bore witness to Native Americans as the original inhabitants.

When Colorado and New Mexico became separate entities, long-standing Hispanic families like the Bacas, Mondragons, Salazars, Lujans, Romeros, and many others were separated, diminishing their political and economic clout. Over time, through new legalisms and outright chicanery, many of these families lost original Spanish and Mexican land grants that they believed were protected by the Treaty of Guadalupe Hidalgo, signed by Mexico and the United States.

While exploring Colorado, I finally received notice that my REGGIE fellowship had been transferred to the Denver office of the Mexican American Legal Defense Fund (MALDEF) head-quartered in San Antonio. I was now working as an attorney for the same civil rights organization for which I had clerked years earlier as a law student in San Antonio.

I was excited about staying in Denver, where I was quickly welcomed by my brother's friends. I met interesting young pro-fessionals also drawn to the State Capital. These people would help form an important coalition that would elect me the city's Mayor a decade later. They came from around the country, visiting and never leaving, forming the continuous influx of intellectual capital that would eventually make Denver the second highest college-educated community, per capita, in the country.

I passed the Colorado bar exam as easily as I had passed the Texas bar, and plunged into my work. The Denver MALDEF office was immersed in the intensifying politics of the city, which were enflamed by the Crusade for Justice headed by the fiery Rodolfo "Corky" González. Corky was one of several activists across the country leading Latinos to assert their rights and reclaim their heritage. Corky helped establish a new Hispanic identity, which he personified in a poem, "Yo Soy Joaquín." Corky's exploits made some conservative Hispanics across the country uneasy, but he energized me as I went to work in the courtroom. I recall the conversations we had about his early boxing career, his participation in the Democratic Party, and his eventual disillusionment with the inability of Denver's civic and political institutions to combat discrimination. I soon began marching in the streets of Denver with him and his followers. We were part of a new movement that demanded fair treatment of Hispanics, and I was prepared and willing to use my legal skills to defend our civil rights and to promote social, political, and economic advancement.

My growing awareness of the discrimination that existed in the U.S. against Hispanics and other minorities was changing me. I was acquiring a new perspective about who I was, so much so that I finally dropped the moniker "Fred" and reclaimed the name given to me at birth—Federico.

When I think about my decision to use "Federico" instead of "Fred," I realize it was the result of the complex personal, political, and cultural journey I had been on since childhood. I had long accepted the name "Fred," because subconsciously I assumed it would ease my journey as a young man in a college and law school with few Hispanics. But that journey was over and I began to feel more genuine, more grounded. This was especially important to my psyche because I was prosecuting cases involving the very issues of social injustice, discrimination, and inequality that burdened so many in our nation's Hispanic community.

One of my cases generated intense public interest. I took over a lawsuit that MALDEF had previously filed against the Denver Police Department. The lawsuit sought penalties against the police for their behavior during a celebration at the local Platte Valley Action Center, the home of a Hispanic community organization. A disturbance had occurred, police responded, and somehow the incident erupted into a shootout. It was not clear how the conflict started, but a number of people were injured and arrested by the police. The court had already proved unsympathetic to the lawsuit. Shortly after taking the case, one court hearing rekindled my old anger and disillusionment. I spent weeks researching a lengthy Motion of Discovery that was accompanied by an even more complex and detailed Memorandum, in order to obtain police documents. As the hearing opened, however, it became apparent that the judge had not read my Memorandum. The attorneys representing the City of Denver had only to make a simple objection to my motion for the judge to readily and summarily reject it. I was livid. My clients and a case of critical importance to the community would not be receiving a fair hearing. I walked out of the courtroom in disbelief. The case dragged on through the Colorado state courts for years, ironically resurfacing ten years later when my name was later substituted as the defendant in my capacity as the new Mayor of Denver. Thankfully it was finally settled when my City Attorney concluded that this lingering case had some merit and that it was time to move past old conflicts.

Another case of importance I helped litigate involved discrimination in Denver's public schools. Many school districts across America continued to discriminate against minority students despite the mandate of *Brown v. Board of Education,* the Supreme Court decision that outlawed school segregation in 1954. The Denver public school system was no exception. I joined the fray as part of the legal team representing Hispanic students and teachers in the first tri-ethnic school desegregation case in the country.

Keyes v. School District No. 1, Denver, Colorado, which originally focused on segregated Black students, soon included complaints from Hispanic parents and students. We argued that Hispanic teachers were not being hired by the school district and that Hispanic students were not being offered appropriate education programs or equal resources as other students.

Keyes was one of the first cases to conclude that schools could not classify Hispanics as "white" for the purpose of meeting integration standards. Thus, commingling Hispanic and Black students was not "integration," as the school administration argued. *Keyes* was twice appealed to the Supreme Court, which finally ordered the implementation of a plan that would bus students in order to better balance school enrollments.

The decision provoked a violent backlash. Denver school board members received menacing threats. School buses were burned, and angry exchanges erupted among school board members who were divided over bussing. Ultimately, bilingual education classes were funded, and a plan to hire Hispanic teachers and administrators was implemented. *Keyes* would continue to affect the city of Denver in an unexpected fashion— white flight to the suburbs.

While pursuing this lawsuit against the Denver public school district, I also challenged the composition of a Federal Grand Jury in the State of Colorado. In one case, U.S. District Judge Fred Winner impaneled a Grand Jury to investigate the deaths of several Hispanic activists killed when their car exploded in Chautauqua Park in Boulder. When it became clear that the Grand Jury did not include minorities on the panel, we filed a complaint that Judge Winner rejected.

After the hearing on our motion, I went outside the courthouse and spoke to several hundred demonstrators to explain the court's decision. I stood on a concrete bench with a bullhorn in hand to address the audience. A photographer captured an image of me with my long hair and mustache, an image that appeared the next day in *The Denver Post*. That picture would be used against me years later in an attempt to scare voters when I ran for Mayor.

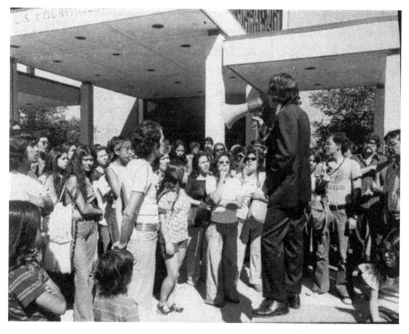

1974, Federico explaining Federal Grand Jury legal challenge to
Latino community members. Photo by Juan Espinosa, El Diario de la Gente.

I learned that when one is fighting injustice, your actions can be later used against you in ways you might never anticipate. I did not care then, nor do I today, how others might judge me when fighting for a cause I believe in. I believe in following one's conscience and acting on one's beliefs, even when many others disagree.

I thrived on the hard work and long hours as a MALDEF lawyer, fighting the good fight. I worked almost seven days a week for an annual salary of $12,500. Almost every legal dispute I litigated was highly charged and politicized— for good reason. I was enmeshed in the contentious civil rights issues of the day as I fought against discrimination, police misconduct, and insensitive school boards or administrators. As I spoke to other REGGIE lawyers across the country, I realized we were all following the same strategy: introducing innovative and groundbreaking arguments in the federal courts in the hope that our clients would ultimately prevail and bring peaceful, progressive, and necessary change to a country in turmoil. And we are still in turmoil as we face police misconduct, systemic racism, reemerging white supremacist groups, immigrant detention centers, and more. The list is long twenty years into this new century. No wonder the Trump era, which gave a voice to these kinds of ideologies, created such strong emotional backlash in people. Black Lives Matter is a reaction to police brutality and racially motivated violence. Deadly assaults on Hispanics and Asian American are resurfacing.

I was running full tilt within the maelstrom sweeping the nation, and I was relishing it. But I was also losing something of myself in the process, which I admitted to my parents in a three-page, single-spaced letter written in May 1973.

"I am beginning to realize my uprootedness in light of my failure to recall Mom's birthday and, until I received your latest letter, Oscar's birthday. I never seem to forget those dates, but for reasons which are becoming clearer to me, that is occurring. I somehow feel that I am growing in respects which I had neglected in Texas and only time will tell if that growth is in the proper direction. Speaking of direction, I do not know when I will be returning to Texas. The inner attraction still remains but I wonder if the fluidity of our society is working against that and I wonder if that fluidity is healthy. I do know that I am enjoying the State of Colorado and the City of Denver and I guess those are important to anyone's life."

Clearly, I was worried about the suffocating effects of my

work and about the disconcerting impact it was having on my relationship with my parents and family. I was beginning to accept that returning to Texas might not be in my future. My original goals of attending law school, of pleasing my parents, of establishing a legal practice had, like me, become something else. I was forgetting important family birthdates, forgetting the importance of family itself.

I wondered what my parents thought and how they felt about my disengagement and looming estrangement. It was challenging enough for them to accept the political and philosophical distance their son was putting between them and other members of the family, but a permanent, physical separation was another matter.

That same letter, though, did reflect concern for my Father. I was worried about him and his business. He had worked all his life for the Longoria family, and now I sensed that the partnership was stressed following the death of the patriarch who had held the family business together:

"I appreciate, Pop, your concern in not having us worry about that issue, but I think we are mature enough to [be] informed and have some knowledge about your business. As you both often told us when we were younger, 'It's better to tell us than to have us read about it in the paper.' Well, if you never actually said that, it seems you said something akin to that statement."

I was twenty-six years old when I wrote that letter, and I am certain that my concern about his business must have startled this otherwise stoic and proud man. I ended my letter pensively:

"There are so many problems and so little time, energy, and brains to solve them. Working with disadvantaged groups can have a schizophrenic effect on one; there are acute ups and downs and they seem to turn one inside out, and then outside in. At any rate, it keeps you alert."

I was being pulled apart. I was passionate about my work in Colorado, but I also wanted to make sure I did not sever or damage my familial roots in Texas.

Noticeably absent from these letters is any reference to personal relationships. Consumed by my work, I had little time for socializing, and my friends were primarily fellow civil rights attorneys. My entire life was my work, and I was being carried away by the currents of the nation's civil rights movement.

Across the country, valiant Latino leaders like César Chávez were emerging, and political activity was taking place in ways never before seen. Chávez was leading penniless California farmworkers against the powerful agricultural interests of that state by organizing strikes and a national boycott of grapes and Gallo wines. I was honored to meet him years later along with several Hispanic State Legislators in Colorado. I was deeply moved by his humility and inspired by his passion for social justice. We assured him of our support and encouraged him to extend his political impact across the nation. Chavez taught us that we could bring extraordinary change by engaging in peaceful civil disobedience. This is a lesson that still applies today.

In Texas, Hispanics were giving rise to a new political party—La Raza Unida Party. In New Mexico, Reyes Tijerina formed an organization called Alianza to restore usurped land grants to the descendants of the original Spanish and Mexican inhabitants of the Southwest. When authorities in Rio Arriba County in northern New Mexico arrested and jailed members of Alianza, Tijerina led an armed raid on the Tierra Amarilla courthouse to free his associates.

Of all the challenges facing Hispanics in the 1970s, however, educational inequality concerned me the most. One of the more active organizations in Colorado on this front was the Chicano Education Project (CEP). When my REGGIE fellowship with MALDEF was ending, CEP co-founder Bill Rosser—who years later would lobby me at Don Quijote's—approached me, accompanied by his co-director, Gil Cisneros. They were aware of my work and asked me to serve as the organization's attorney. After some thoughtful consideration, I took the job.

The Chicano Education Project was actively organizing Latino parents and students in Colorado to challenge discriminatory educational practices across the state. In school district after school district, Spanish-surnamed students were being disproportionately suspended or disciplined by teachers and principals, and too many were dropping out. These students often came from Spanish-speaking homes, and their schools were failing to teach them in a linguistically relevant manner to succeed academically.

I was sometimes the only attorney willing to venture into small, rural communities whose political leaders had little sympathy for *outside agitators*—the classic epithet that was meant to stir up public opinion against those of us who dared disrupt decades of outdated thinking. My friends called me "the Equalizer," a reference to a TV character who took up difficult causes. Many of the challenges were daunting, especially the hateful stares from school board members and administrators in places where the Latino community had never before had a voice.

Often, I represented parents and students making their first-ever presentations to their elected school boards. Many were uncomfortable speaking to powerful business and civic leaders, and most had never attended a school board meeting. Yet there they were, with me alongside, to argue for better education for their children. When necessary, I would speak for them, armed with data demonstrating how poorly Latino children were performing, showing the inadequacy of the curriculum, and highlighting the absence of Latino teachers in the schools.

In Center, Colorado, I worked with courageous parents like Jenny Sánchez and Adeline Sánchez. Thankfully, attorney Norm Aaronson of Colorado Rural Legal Aid provided additional support, since he lived in nearby Alamosa. It was clear that the potato growers of the region did not prioritize Hispanic students getting an education that could lead them to college rather than jobs picking prized Red McClure potatoes. The start of the school's fall semester was sometimes dependent on the timing of the annual potato harvest. School administrators emblazoned *The Home of the Red McClure* on the school's official stationery.

When I stood with Jenny and Adeline to demand that the school board provide better instruction to Hispanic students, board members made it clear that they did not see any need for change. In response, Hispanics in Center organized politically and registered to vote. They elected their own to the school board and over time some progress was made. Today, four of the five board members in the Center, Colorado school district are Hispanic. But it was a hard slog and required years of hard work. I was impressed with the strength, courage, and determination of many Latino parents who risked their jobs and reputations by standing up to the powerful interests in their community.

1976, The three lawyers who worked on the Grand Junction school case. Left to right are José Márquez, Federico Peña, and Art Lucero. Photo courtesy of the Peña Family Archives.

In Grand Junction, students and parents filed a federal discrimination case against school officials. Together with Rural Legal Services attorneys José "Larry" Marquez and Art Lucero, we presented voluminous data and testimony of discrimination over a two-week trial but did not prevail. I was angry that we lost because I sensed the judge was biased against our case, and

I felt we'd let the Latino parents and students down. How were they going to continue to attend classes? How were their parents going to be treated in a small town that did not take kindly to the litigation? The only conciliation was that some of the parents remained involved politically, and Larry eventually became a Colorado appellate judge. But the loss rattled my confidence in the federal courts of Colorado.

Years later, when I was running for Mayor, some of these same Latino parents and students drove many miles to campaign for me in Denver. I was moved to learn that many even mailed their hard-earned dollars to support me. I did not realize the impact I had, even when we lost their cases.

However much I enjoyed meeting and working with parents and students across Colorado, my civil rights work came with a price. I viewed politicians, governmental agencies, school boards, and almost anyone in authority with suspicion, and sometimes instant distrust. I lost much of my faith in the political institutions I was taught to revere. The more I worked with citizens enduring discrimination, or ignored by government bureaucrats, the more distressed I became. Although I believed the only venue to secure justice and bring about positive social change was in the courtroom, I was jaded and cynical. And for the first time in my life, I was easy to antagonize. I was depressed and began to doubt my own legal ability. Was I smart enough to present cases in federal court? Maybe I was the problem...not the institutions I was attempting to navigate.

How did I arrive at this place in my life? Hadn't I worked at a prominent law firm in Brownsville and for the prestigious District Attorney's office in Houston? What happened to the hope I felt when Cissy Farenthold ran for Governor of Texas and nearly changed history?

Back then, with my neatly cut hair and my immaculately laundered shirts and pants, I embraced the fundamental soundness of our democracy. I believed anyone could succeed in America with hard work, sacrifice, and education. But my days of short hair, always-shined shoes, nice coats, and coordinated ties had ended. Something had happened to me. Something had happened to America. I now saw the world as it actually was. And I did not like it. I was compelled to challenge authority in every form I thought disregarded defenseless people and communities of color.

It was time for people to get out of my way.

8. Rekindled Hope

I was a product of angry times, part of the tsunami of American youth launching broadsides against the established order. We were challenging social and cultural mores. I could not tolerate the mistreatment of citizens, in Colorado or anywhere else in the country.

Notwithstanding the subtle discrimination in Brownsville, my character was shaped by a disciplined family with strong values and a strong sense of pride in its roots. This fortified me later in life against the struggles and conflicts around me. It was not until I emerged from the protective wings of my parents that I felt the brunt of the systemic injustice in our nation and understood its historical depth. As my youthful naiveté gradually gave way, I took on the look, clothes, and bearing of the lawyer-warriors who were fighting to ensure that the future of our country would be better than the past.

The strength I inherited from my parents and ancestors led others to take note of me. I found myself leading meetings of attorneys, community leaders, and activists. They sought my opinion and looked to me to provide counsel.

My first real opportunity to lead came in 1975 at the Chicano Education Project when our team had an epiphany about our work. Why was I the only staff attorney suing individual school districts across Colorado for failing to provide quality education for Hispanic students? Why not convince the Colorado Legislature to enact a statewide bilingual education law to cover all 181 school districts in Colorado? There were already supportive legislators in key positions. Paul Sandoval, a Chicano Education Project board member, was in the state Senate, and Rubén Valdéz had become Speaker of the Democratic-controlled Colorado House of Representatives. Passing this controversial legislation would be difficult at any time, but with these two formidable supporters on our side, at least we stood a fighting chance.

We spent months gathering evidence, seeking advice, and organizing testimony from educators, administrators, parents, students, and citizens across the state. I learned more about the deep frustrations of students and their parents concerning insensitive school administrators through dozens of meetings across Colorado. Their perspectives and guidance were incorporated into early drafts of the proposed legislation. We undertook a genuine grassroots, bottoms-up approach to writing the Colorado Bilingual Bicultural Education Act of 1975. If it passed, it would become the most extensive and comprehensive bilingual education law in the country.

Unfortunately, the proposed law was pure controversy and it provoked heated reactions. It resembled the nasty rhetoric of immigration debates today. Prospects looked especially grim in the state Senate, which was controlled by Republicans. Nonetheless, we lobbied hard with persuasive testimony. Our work paid off in the House, where the bill passed with the strong support of Speaker Valdéz and Democratic legislators. It then moved to the Republican-controlled Senate, where passage was anything but guaranteed.

Keeping the bill alive through various Senate committees was a parliamentary challenge. Senator Sandoval succeeded brilliantly in securing funding for the program. Paul taught me the power of negotiation. I watched as he crafted a political compromise with the Republican chairman of the Joint Budget Committee. Paul adroitly demonstrated how to "give and take" in a political environment and how to find common ground without compromising one's values. This honorable skill seems to have disappeared from national politics today. It is disappointing that Senate Majority Leader Mitch McConnell held up more than 400 bills passed by the House of Representatives. These bills languished in the Senate without any opportunity for debate or negotiation.

Having survived the committee process, our measure went before the full Colorado Senate, which brought robust debate that drew countless amendments. The heated arguments continued for days before a packed gallery. With the final vote still in doubt, a decisive moment came when Senator Roger Cisneros, a veteran of World War II who had served in Okinawa, rose to speak. His fellow Senators were immediately intrigued. A polite and genial lawyer from Denver, Roger Cisneros was not prone to showboating and seldom took to the floor.

He approached the podium and in a deliberate and calm voice began to tell the story of his impoverished upbringing in New Mexico. The entire Chamber was silent. He talked about his family and the difficult lives they led. He described his wartime service to his country.

To a rapt audience, he recounted the struggle of working by day and attending law school at night. He talked about how difficult it was for Hispanic children to succeed in public schools because of discrimination. "I remember," he said, "seeing signs when I was growing up in Colorado that read, 'No Dogs or Mexicans Allowed.'" After letting his remark linger, he concluded, "I have served my country and I have sacrificed long and hard, and this law must pass so that future generations will be spared these injustices." The galleries above him erupted in applause.

The voting began, and as the tally in favor of our bill rose, a profound realization dawned on me—*institutions are no better, or worse, than the people in them.* When the final vote was counted, we had won. It was historic. The Senate passed our bill and Governor Richard Lamm signed it into law. Political observers, editorial writers, educators across the state, and the Hispanic community were all amazed. But no one was more amazed than me. The democratic process had worked for an issue that was deeply important to me.

In working through the challenging legislative process, I had the extraordinarily positive experience of interacting with both Democratic and Republican legislators I had previously and summarily disparaged as being part of *the system.* To my surprise, they did not have horns after all. Most were caring, thoughtful, and courageous. I was energized and uplifted by them. Almost overnight, my faith in the legislative process—at least in the Colorado legislature—was restored. It seemed government could work, after all.

My cynicism gave way to a new understanding—that many lawmakers were good and well-intentioned people who operated in an imperfect system. They brought values, prejudices, and perspectives based on their background, religious exposure, and personal experience. But that did not make them evil. Like me, they were well intentioned. They were democratically elected by their constituents and expected to reflect their values. Just because they had different points of view did not make them wicked. We simply had to have honest discussions and work to reach a respectful understanding. Naive? Maybe. But perhaps government was salvageable! Perhaps it could work fairly, equally, and with justice for all people just as I'd once been taught.

Encouraged by this win, I returned to representing Colorado families in their battles with local boards of education. Shortly afterward, I helped initiate the high-profile case *Lujan v. Colorado State Board of Education.* Students from sixteen low-wealth districts contended that the state's school finance system had deprived them of an education equal to those enjoyed by students in wealthier districts. According to 1976 public data, certain school districts were receiving more than $3,000 per pupil per year, while others received one-third of that amount. The *Lujan* case was not ultimately successful in the courts, but it did help pave the way for the passage of the 1988 Public School Finance Act, which was supposed to ensure uniform funding of public education throughout the state. Sadly, the Colorado legislature is still struggling to enact fairer funding strategies, because wide discrepancies remain among school districts.

Although I lost a number of legal cases during my time with the Chicano Education Project, there were people who believed I was ready to serve the public in a bigger role. While attending a routine meeting at the state capitol, I was surprised when a group of legislators asked for a meeting.

Senators Paul Sandoval, Dick Soash, and Don Sandoval, and Representatives Wayne Knox and Richard Castro wasted no time suggesting that I run for a vacant legislative seat in northwest Denver. The district's representative, Speaker Rubén Valdéz, was running for Lieutenant Governor and his seat was open. They argued that I had proven myself during the fight to pass the 1975 bilingual education bill. One said my legal skills were needed in the legislature; another said I was thoughtful and would make an attractive candidate. They had obviously talked beforehand. They made sure to tell me that I would soon need to move to North Denver to satisfy state residency requirements.

I was stunned. I had not given any thought to running for office. It seemed awfully far-fetched. I had lived in Denver for just a short time, and my brief stint in the capitol made me painfully aware of the political pecking order. Undaunted, the lawmakers pressed me to run. It was obvious, they emphasized, that I was prepared to serve and join their ranks.

Perhaps I was undervaluing myself. Perhaps my colleagues saw me relate to hundreds of people from across the state. Perhaps they sensed that I was fulfilled by helping newly empowered citizens successfully engage in the democratic process. Perhaps I reflected the courteous ways of my Grandfather, Eduardo, who served the people of Laredo as an alderman for so many years. Perhaps I was changing again. Perhaps my hope and faith in America was being rekindled!

Soon I trimmed my hair, shaved my scraggly beard, and moved into Speaker Valdez's former district in North Denver. I rented a small house on Navajo Street across from Pagliacci's Italian restaurant and parked my car in a vacant lot next door. These were politically turbulent times in Denver and there was tension among political groups. Old families dominated politics and were not pleased to see Hispanics grow in clout. Some community activists made it clear that they considered me an outright interloper. Some said I had not "paid my dues." And at least one person was dead set on deterring me from running.

While I expected opposition, I never dreamed I'd be on the receiving end of a violent message. One night, tired from a long day, I was awakened from a deep sleep by an explosion outside my bedroom window. Someone had thrown a gasoline bomb at my trusty Volvo. Luckily, they missed and merely set the nearby grass on fire. I quickly dressed, ran outside, and put out the flames. After some thought, I opted not to call the police or the fire department, as there was really nothing they could do. I decided not to call home either.

Though I was shaken, anger soon overtook my fear. The idea that thugs, perhaps driven by racial motives, would try to intimidate me from running for public office erased any doubt that remained about my decision. I was going to do it, come hell or high water. At least I hadn't been shot at like my friend Representative Richard Castro had been during his first campaign in West Denver! A small fire bomb was nothing!

I campaigned vigorously, walking door to door for several months, across the entire six-square-mile district of approximately 35,000 people. I worked at my law office until 5:00 p.m.

and then canvassed for several hours until after dark. My hard work paid off and I handily defeated a long-time community leader who had probably never expected an unknown lawyer, barely thirty years old (and from Texas), could beat him in his own backyard.

In January of 1979, I took the oath of office to become a member of the kind of governmental institution I had wanted to challenge not long before. My new roots in Colorado grew deeper, and Texas receded further into the past.

9. To the Statehouse

I was excited to join the Colorado House of Representatives. While the Democratic Party was in the minority in both Chambers, Governor Richard Lamm was a Democrat. And though only a freshman legislator, I took on the complex challenge of reforming the state's obtuse school finance system. My understanding of the intricacies of school funding came from the *Lujan* case. And while I worked with Republicans and Democrats on other issues, only a few legislators understood school finance. Republican Senator Al Meiklejohn from Arvada proved to be a helpful ally on this front. Also an attorney, Al cared deeply about education. We developed a mutual respect as we worked to improve the state's financial support of public schools, funding that already consumed a large part of the state's budget. We shared the understanding that the quality of schools fundamentally determined our state's future. All school districts deserved equal funding if Colorado's students were to compete in a global economy. Sadly, funding disparities exist today across our nation, and American students do not compete well with foreign students in science and math.

At the end of my first session, I was exhausted but pleasantly surprised when *The Denver Post* rated me as one of the ten most effective legislators, a recognition unusual for a freshman.

When I won re-election the following year, some Democratic legislators approached me to challenge our caucus leader. They asked if I would be interested in running against the long-tenured incumbent, whom some believed was not aggressively representing the views of the caucus.

1980, Colorado Hispanic Legislators with César Chávez, President of National Farm Workers Association. Left to right are Federico Peña, George Chávez, Rubén Valdéz, César Chávez, Polly Baca, and Richard Castro. Photo by James Baca.

We'd lost our majority in the previous election, and many members thought our Democratic Leader was not willing to sufficiently challenge the new Republican majority. They wanted someone they believed more accurately reflected the liberal to moderate views of the caucus. Representatives Jerry Kopel and Wayne Knox, among others, suggested I take the idea seriously. They promised to lobby on my behalf and garner sufficient votes for me to win the leadership fight. Here I was once again listening as a group of legislators suggested I take on a new responsibility I would not have considered on my own.

As a one-term legislator, I felt honored and humbled by my peers' confidence in me to lead the caucus, but I was hesitant to, in effect, lead a coup. I did agree, however, that something had to be done. I insisted that Representative Richard Castro be approached first. Castro was a friend, a mentor, and an ally. He was also the incumbent assistant leader and next in line for the leadership position. Consultations with Rich, however, revealed that he would not have the votes to win, and so the revolt proceeded. At the age of thirty-three, I became the Democratic minority leader of the Colorado House of Representatives.

My election caused a stir in the Republican majority caucus. A newspaper account reported that Republicans feared I was going to be a firebrand and decided they needed someone to go "toe-to-toe" with me. They selected Ron Strahle, a veteran legislator, as their majority leader. Evidently, his job was to spar with me.

1981, Photo of Federico Peña (left) standing next to
Representative Ron Strahle on House Floor.
Photo courtesy of the Peña Family Archives.

But most political observers did not know me very well. I grew to like and respect Ron Strahle. We understood that while we each had a job to do, we could be friendly and maintain a mutually respectful relationship while vigorously supporting our caucuses. There was no need to burn down the Chamber. After the session, Ron was very generous with compliments. He said he had "learned that Federico is a gentleman. He was absolutely trustworthy—and that's the most important attribute a legislator can have."

It was the only way I knew to behave. I followed in the footsteps of my parents and grandparents. A veteran reporter wrote: "When Federico was elected minority leader, a lot of people said he would be combative, obstinate, and obstructive. He was none of those...His debates at the microphone were good and fun to listen to because neither [leader] would argue with emotion. They were like two champion debaters."

The leadership role allowed me to listen to and appreciate the views of fellow legislators representing every region of the state. I practiced the art of compromise, never held grudges, and worked to conduct myself with integrity. My word was my bond, and I voted my convictions. I was the lone vote, for example, against a bill to increase criminal penalties for juveniles. I believed that in pandering to the movement "to be tough on crime," we were too often increasing penalties with knee-jerk abandon for youngsters who should have the chance to reform their lives. Every Democrat and Republican supported the legislation. With a lone red light flashing next to my name on the electronic voting board, I wanted to make a point that we should be more thoughtful. My lone vote against the bill would be used against me years later.

Given my growing legislative role and increased visibility, it was only a matter of time before I would be thrust into national politics. In 1980, when President Jimmy Carter was seeking his second term ahead of the Reagan landslide, Colorado Democrats elected me to attend the National Democratic Convention in New York as an "uncommitted" delegate. This meant that I, and the other uncommitted delegates, Mo Siegel and Sheila

Carrigan, were not obligated to vote for Mr. Carter on the first ballot at the convention.

We were young and passionate about our politics. Mo went on to become a prominent businessman founding the Celestial Seasonings tea company, and Sheila, the daughter of a federal judge, became a prosecuting attorney in Boulder.

I respected President Carter for his intelligence, integrity, and hard work, but I did not believe he could win re-election. Inflation was unacceptably high, Iran was holding fifty-two Americans hostage, and there were hours-long lines at the gas pump caused by the Arab oil embargo. Carter's poll numbers spelled disaster for the whole Democratic ticket. We needed a stronger nominee to lead a united party into the elections. But the convention became one of the most bitter in recent history.

A vicious battle ensued for the presidential nomination between President Carter and Senator Edward Kennedy. Both had fallen short of the votes needed to win outright. Once the first roll call of delegates started, the chairman of the Colorado delegation pressured the three of us "uncommitteds" to vote for Carter. He wanted to announce on national television that Colorado, an early voting state, was unanimous in supporting Carter.

Huddled off to one side by ourselves, Mo, Sheila, and I agreed to remain uncommitted through the first round of balloting. We wanted to see whether Kennedy or someone like Wisconsin Senator William Proxmire or Washington Senator Scoop Jackson might gain traction. I was flabbergasted when a senior Democratic leader threatened me, as if in a gangster movie. "If you do not change your vote," he growled, "your political career in Colorado will be over." I was taken aback, but my surprise quickly turned to anger and then indignation. The three of us held fast. The official record of the convention should reflect that the three delegates elected by the Democrats of Colorado to vote "uncommitted" in the first round of balloting did exactly that. In the end, with no alternative to President Carter materializing, we voted for him in subsequent rounds.

I mailed a postcard featuring Madison Square Garden, the site of the convention, to my parents on August 12, 1980. I wrote: "This is the place where we're doing our fighting. I'm not too pleased how things are developing. It's tough to support a president you don't believe in." I ended with a sigh of relief: "Glad the hurricane missed you," I wrote, referring to Hurricane Allen, which had raked Texas that year.

Unfortunately for Carter, the political hurricane spun by Ronald Reagan tossed him out of office. For me, though, my obstinate refusal to buckle under pressure from party bosses burnished my reputation as someone who could not be bullied. I would stay true to my word.

Although President Carter was not re-elected, my respect for him grew after he left office. My admiration for him and his wonderful wife, Rosalynn, has expanded through the years. No other ex-president and First Lady have strapped on a tool belt and hardhat to build homes for the poor as the Carters have done with Habitat for Humanity. Their work through the Carter Center in Atlanta has garnered respect around the globe and has been instrumental in bringing democracy to millions through the monitoring of elections worldwide.

I entered my fourth year in the Colorado House of Representatives in 1982. I did not believe that politics was a life-long career, and I wanted to practice law with my brother, Alfredo. I watched politicians who stayed in office too long. Some lost their energy, ability to think creatively, and connection to their constituents. So, I announced my retirement from politics.

Little did I know that once again others had a different plan for me, a quixotic one at that, as I discovered at Don Quijote's restaurant, where I was persuaded to run for Mayor of Denver.

Part Three: Still in Denver (1983–1992)

10. The Campaign: From Imagination to Action

D enver in the early 1980s in many ways resembled America today. She was uncertain of her vision for the future. Citizens were frustrated with City Hall. Viaducts were crumbling, air pollution was worsening, neighborhood leaders felt ignored, the airport was congested, and historic structures were being razed. There were doubts about how to address the many challenges the city faced.

Yet, I believed that Denver was positioned to prosper beyond what anyone thought possible. I was convinced we could harness the energies and talents of our citizens to remake the future. So, on a cold December day in 1982, I stood on the steps of the Denver City and County Building and, with little media present, announced my candidacy for Mayor.

The Denver City and County Building—majestically poised across from the state's iconic golden-domed capitol—shone resplendent that day. Its construction had marked the end of the City Beautiful era in Denver and now before it, standing in its glory, I called on citizens to embark on another grand adventure. I did not simply envision a good or better city. I dreamed of a great city, and I called on citizens to imagine it with me.

Speaking to the small crowd gathered that day, I was nervous about the path I was about to take, one that led me away from practicing law and deeper into the world of city politics. But, like an athlete before a race, my anxiety stoked within me a confidence that I could win.

As supporters cheered my speech, I sensed that they too embraced the mission before them, almost with a sense of glee. They understood the undercurrents of discontent in our city. That knowledge made them believers and advocates in the cause to steer Denver into a new future. It would take their deep passion to pull off one of the greatest political upsets in the city's history.

Our quest was soon tagged by political pundits with disparaging monikers like *Mission: Impossible*. Eventually, there were seven candidates in the race: Mayor McNichols, District Attorney Dale Tooley, two former cabinet members from Governor Lamm's administration, two civic activists, and me. If none of the candidates in the non-partisan election received more than 50 percent of the vote, the top two would meet in a runoff election.

I was already considered a liberal State Legislator by those who recalled my work as a long-haired lawyer working for the controversial Chicano Education Project, and especially for supporting the Colorado Bilingual Bicultural Education Act of 1975. Some Republicans and conservative lawmakers opposed my work. I supported neighborhood activism, investments in underserved communities, reducing air pollution, and job training for disenfranchised workers. I opposed the death penalty and supported a woman's right to choose. And I supported equal opportunities in education, having invested much time in reforming the state school finance law.

The Rocky Mountain News—one of Denver's two newspapers—tagged me as the dark horse candidate. Other political commentators were less flattering, and they were not alone.

Some close friends speculated that the mile-high altitude of Denver had deprived me of the oxygen essential to my brain's normal function. One friend, a prominent banker, told me, "Federico, I am sorry, but Denver is not ready for a Hispanic Mayor."

I listened soberly to these sincere voices of caution and pessimism. Perhaps my young age fostered a naiveté that immunized me from these naysayers—I was thirty-six. Perhaps the tenacity of my ancestors steadied me and gave me solace. Maybe it was a combination of both. Whatever it was, I moved forward with confidence and a hardy and equally passionate group of supporters and advisors.

Tom Nussbaum, who months earlier had been part of that cabal at Don Quijote's, volunteered to be my Campaign Manager. The campaign team initially included progressive thinker John Parr, Westword Newspaper co-founder Sandy Widener, urban policy expert Tom Gougeon, and environmentalist Tony Massaro, attorney Sherry Seiber, and school administrator Katherine Archuleta. Other political pros like Governor Lamm's general counsel, David Greenberg, and Pat Schroeder's advisor, Arnie Grossman, joined the team.

I started to greet people at shopping centers, churches, Denver Broncos football games, and community and neighborhood meetings. I enjoyed meeting people and working with wonderful volunteers. I don't remember ever being tired during the campaign. It was the same when I worked long hours as a civil rights lawyer and a State Legislator. I found that being passionate about my work numbed me from exhaustion. Tired or not, I didn't always receive a warm welcome. It was tough seeing my campaign literature discarded and walked on, but I accepted rejection with grace, an essential trait I had inherited from my Mother.

No longer having to report to one place for work, I was free to roam every part of the city. One evening I visited the headquarters of the Capitol Hill Neighborhood Association, one of the most powerful civic groups in Denver. I introduced myself as a candidate for Mayor. The somber members were respectful but seemed perplexed by my presence. Elsewhere in the building, I strode into a meeting of hot air balloonists and introduced myself. There, too, I was courteously, though not excitedly, received. I entered another room and found a third group discussing park issues, and they too quietly suffered through my self-introduction. Often at these early meetings, people would look at me blankly.

The most common response to my candidacy was "Federico who?"—an editorial comment with justified skepticism. Hearing this remark and pursuing my sometimes-fruitless forays to seek out voters did not dampen my enthusiasm, however. On the contrary, I became intrigued to find so many citizens— from hot air balloonists to neighborhood activists—gathering to pursue their interests with great passion. The city was alive and teeming with activity, although mostly out of public view. Denver was not the sleepy cow town some considered it to be.

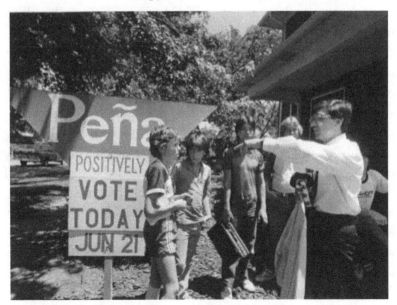

1983, Candidate Peña speaking with young people about the Mayor's race.
Photo courtesy of the Peña Family Archives.

Undaunted by the early cynicism that greeted my campaign, I forged ahead, meeting with union leaders, women's groups, environmentalists, and every ethnic and racial group in the city. I shocked the established order by campaigning in gay bars, something most mayoral candidates in America in the 1980s would never have considered.

The idea of aggressively reaching out to the gay community (the term LGBT was not used then) came from one of my paid campaign staff members. Early on, she said she needed to tell me something that might be a problem for my candidacy if made public. We met in a quiet room and I asked what the issue was. She told me she was lesbian and worried it might jeopardize my campaign. Then she offered to resign. I told her to forget it. She was not to leave, but instead keep doing the great job she had been doing from the start. Over time, she became more public about her sexuality and took me along to gay bars and meetings of gay activists. Later in the campaign, I was the only candidate to support a city ordinance banning discrimination against gays. And gay voters rallied to my side. I was breaking new ground.

People noticed that my campaign was about something new, and soon this became my theme. Our television commercials were emblematic of change. Instead of trying to mainstream my surname with its distinctive spelling, we seized on it to separate my commercials from the blur of other political ads. The *eñe* over the "n" in Peña would fly out in our ads and land boldly over my name. In the same vein, I rejected the suggestion of some of my advisors that I resurrect my old nickname, Fred.

I was not driven to be the first "Hispanic" Mayor of Denver. I was running as an individual who cared deeply about people, who had a vision, new ideas, and energy to propel our city forward. I was proud of my heritage, but that was not my driving force for wanting to serve our community.

The initial response of the Hispanic community to my campaign was ambivalence. I knew I was starting with a reasonably good base of support among Latinos in Northwest Denver. I had, after all, won two elections to represent that part of Denver in the legislature. But others doubted I could win a citywide election. Maybe they were conditioned to a way of thinking that was not in my DNA. I was flabbergasted when the head of the local Spanish-language radio station announced he could not support me. Curiously, he too said Denver was not ready for a Hispanic Mayor.

Many older Hispanics and Denver natives supported Mayor McNichols out of allegiance to him. They had doubts about Dale Tooley, who had run twice against McNichols, and they naturally believed that the Mayor would win again. I lacked citywide name recognition and many Hispanics saw me as too young and inexperienced, not to mention an unknown from Texas. It was reasonable for them to not want to waste their vote, so they maintained their support for McNichols. While I was disappointed with this mixed reception, I never gave up seeking their support.

Hispanics were only 8 percent of the city's registered voters. Denver was not Albuquerque, San Antonio, or Santa Fe—cities that had recently elected Latino Mayors. Obviously, I had to appeal to the broader electorate. I felt comfortable in reaching out to complete strangers, but periodically I received harsh responses, which were discouraging. Inspired by the warm response from others, I soldiered on.

I did not shy away from my ethnicity and continued to visit all parts of the city. Though dismayed that promised campaign funds were not materializing, I began to feel that my campaign was penetrating the public's consciousness. It didn't take long for an avalanche of support to start coming my way. It grew from week-to-week. Within months, what had been hatched as an implausible adventure morphed into something more.

The "Peña movement," as it would be called, expanded to an army of 3,000 volunteers. The progressive growth of my broad-based, grassroots campaign gave me immense confidence. My

brother Alfredo selflessly suspended his law practice and oversaw our ever-growing number of campaign workers. We rented
a large vacant building that once housed Jake's Auto Parts.
Soon we had a full-fledged campaign organization, including
an impressive manufacturing operation in the basement where
thousands of triangular wooden signs, painted blue and white
and emblazoned with the slogan "Peña for Denver," were made.
An energetic young volunteer named Jeep Campbell ran the
effort. Visitors were amazed when they entered our basement;
no one had ever seen such an operation in a political campaign.

The unique wooden signs and their tactical use became a
topic of conversation among election observers and political
pundits. A sophisticated targeting system distributed the signs
throughout the city, effectively maximizing the political presence of the campaign. The signs sprung up like wildflowers
across every neighborhood, feeding the campaign's momentum.
Every time I spotted them, I was moved by the thought that
people who did not even know me were willing to divot their
lawns to showcase my campaign. I was excited, but mostly humbled, by their support.

Periodically, volunteers changed the signs' messages by
hanging a rectangle board on our triangular signs. Some read
"Vote on May 17," and following the primary, others read "Thank
you." Like the old Burma Shave billboards, we changed our
messages to maintain attention. Our strategy was to deepen
and broaden interest in the campaign to spur the large turnout
we needed. Our volunteers included young professionals, labor
activists, environmentalists, women's rights supporters, gays,
neighborhood activists, Latinos, Asians, African Americans,
small business owners, and others who represented every part
of the city. Some enthusiastically made phone calls every day
and night, while others kept our enormous offices clean. Still
others religiously installed our campaign signs in front yards,
on sides of buildings, and even on rooftops all over town. One
volunteer, Leo Rodriguez, crisscrossed the city cheerfully deliv-

ering hundreds of yard signs to scores of neighborhoods.

Once I started to see the diversity of our support, I knew that we were developing the broad base we needed to win. I sensed that my message of new ideas, vigorous leadership, and the willingness to tackle tough issues was starting to resonate.

My respect for voters was deep. While my opponents handed out flyers that short-handed their positions, thanks to the expertise of Tom Gougeon, we produced two pages on each of the twenty-five major issues affecting the city. The campaign office gave out specific position papers on air pollution, crime, neighborhood revitalization, and other major challenges facing Denver. There were no computers, internet service, cell phones, Facebook, or any kind of social media. I wanted to reach voters personally, appealing to their intellect with our positions, and I was blessed with unexpected support as a result. A prominent Republican businessman, Lee Ambrose, came forward to endorse me. When Dan Hoffman, the former Manager of Public Safety and Dean of the University of Denver College of Law, announced his endorsement, he brought important credibility and attention. The most unexpected and impactful endorsement came from the conservative *Rocky Mountain News*, the paper that had labeled me the "dark horse" candidate just a few months before. And I gained the endorsement of a popular weekly publication called *Westword* with Sandy Widiner's support. These endorsements provided the proof many voters needed that mine was a serious campaign to not just win an election, but to dramatically improve their city.

I always felt we were going to win. Everywhere I went, I sensed victory. The campaign had blossomed and seemed to be on its way to a victory—until Election Day arrived with a bluster.

11. An Election for the History Books

On May 17, 1983, the day we had hoped to make history, the city was buried by a huge, late spring snowstorm. Our campaign signs, which we'd worked hard to plant in dozens of neighborhoods, were blanketed with snow. The fifty-four mile an hour winds didn't help. Together the snow and the wind threatened to wipe out months of hard work. I was surprised like everyone else by the wet and heavy snowfall. Weather forecasters were notorious for misreading impending storms. Some local television stations lost their signals, and operations were disrupted at Stapleton Airport, causing cancellations and delayed flights. At some polling places, voting got underway by the power of candlelight and flashlights.

Undeterred, I plowed, literally, through the day visiting phone banks and encouraging volunteers at campaign headquarters. Despite the storm, they needed little encouragement. They came by the hundreds through the snow to pick up their election-day voter lists to make sure people found their way to the polls. We all knew that without a large turnout we could not win.

1983, Snow on election day.
Photo courtesy of the Peña Family Archives.

I made as many stops as I could. The city seemed to be moving in slow motion. And yet I saw hundreds of supporters standing against the wind on dozens of street corners. Shivering, they waved "Peña for Denver" signs. Seeing this army of bundled-up believers, I was deeply moved and could not fathom letting them down. I had a lump in my throat as I watched so many people show such an immense outpouring of support, especially in wintry conditions. Driving past each corner, I rolled down my car window and shouted, "Thank you for your support!" They smiled, cheered, and waved their signs back at me. All I could think was: INCREDIBLE!

That day passed in a flurry of activity until the polls closed at 7:00 p.m., when our poll watchers started to call in results from each precinct.

In those days, voting machines were opened at the end of the day and poll watchers could look over the shoulder of the precinct judges to record the votes. Our poll watchers either called in the results from a pay phone or drove quickly to our headquarters with their findings. David Greenberg and Tom

Nussbaum tallied the votes on a chalkboard, with results tabu-
lated quicker than the city's news organizations.

When we realized we had done well in the conservative
parts of town, we sensed that if our base precincts voted in large
numbers, we would win the primary. We heard reports that
working-class voters, who typically vote after 5:00 p.m., were
standing in lines beyond the 7:00 p.m. deadline.

The night before, a local reporter had dutifully called to ask
my opinion of how the election would unfold. When I told him I
believed we would come in first place, he paused and snickered
audibly. Inside polling, he said, suggested I would finish fifth.

Like so many other observers, this reporter had no way of
knowing how motivated our volunteers would be on election
day. As they returned to campaign headquarters from their
last-minute get-out-the-vote assignments, our volunteers were
excited about the long lines they had seen at the polls. They
knew they had achieved something historic, and just hearing
the thrill in their voices convinced me that we would have the
high turnout we needed to win.

We were right. Instead of dispiriting my supporters, the
unusual May snowstorm and had galvanized them. They generated a 63 percent voter turnout, a record for a mayoral primary
election in Denver.

Just before 9:00 p.m., aware that Mayor McNichols would
not make the runoff, I went to his headquarters with one of my
advisors, civic activist Sandy Drew, to congratulate him on his
campaign. He and his supporters were surprised but received
me warmly, apparently appreciative that I showed the Mayor
the respect he was due. McNichols was one of the last big city
Mayors who had been part of the American political landscape
for decades. Across the country, these titans were being replaced
by a new breed of young, vigorous, and creative leaders. To
borrow a term made popular from a bestselling 1982 book, we
were living one of the "Megatrends" that would forge the future.

On my way back to headquarters, I learned the incumbent

Mayor had formally conceded, triggering a wild celebration among my supporters. Our crowd had become so large that the fire marshal restricted additional volunteers. Many well-wishers had to stand outside in the cold.

I was exhilarated with the results and could hardly breathe. I thought I was in a dream. While I felt we would win, my supporters' jubilance made clear that they were even more convinced that we would be victorious. We had come in first place with 37 percent of the vote. Dale Tooley was second with 31 percent. The runoff election was three weeks away, set for June 21, and we went back to work early the next day. Tom, my Campaign Director, discovered that the election code allowed citizens to register during a small, three-day window after a primary election. And, of course, he had a plan to take full advantage of this fact.

Overnight our team produced radio ads reminding people who had not voted, and others who were skeptical that I could win, that they could still register and vote in the runoff election. During the next three days we registered 6,000 new voters—previously unheard of in Denver elections. Citizens stood for hours in registration lines winding around the block outside City Hall. One elderly lady, Mrs. Ayon had never voted in her life. When at last she reached the registrar's desk and was asked her party affiliation, she seemed flustered but then innocently responded, "The Peña Party." When her story made the front pages of the newspaper, I immediately called her to thank her for waiting so long in line to register. She told me her son was a Denver policeman and that she was excited that for the first time in her life she had been motivated to vote. Mrs. Ayon was in her 80's.

The media and other political observers were astounded by the passion and intensity of these new voters. The truth is that thousands had simply not believed I could win the primary against both McNichols and Tooley. My primary win erased the preconceptions they held, and they were rocketed out of complacency to register. Several elderly Hispanic individuals told me, "I never thought someone like you would be elected Mayor in my lifetime."

People across the state started to believe I could win. My work throughout Colorado as a civil rights lawyer fighting for better schools had made me many friends. They swarmed to Denver from across the state to help. Busloads came from towns like Center, Del Norte, and Alamosa in the San Luis Valley to canvass, make phone calls, and do whatever it took to get me elected. Fundraisers were held in Pueblo, the San Luis Valley, Boulder, and northern Colorado. These supporters understood that, while they could not vote for me, they would benefit when Denver, their capital city, became a great city. And they imagined it, too. So did the elderly ladies who contributed a few of their hard-earned dollars, sometimes delivered in small envelopes with moving, personal messages of prayer and hope for our success.

The national media took notice and reported on the campaign, and soon assistance came from outside the state as well. Governor Toney Anaya flew in from Santa Fe, and Mayor Henry Cisneros arrived from San Antonio. More than a few checks, almost always for small amounts, appeared unsolicited at our campaign headquarters with addresses from outside Colorado. And my family, of course, came up from Texas.

1983, Mayor Henry Cisneros campaigning with Federico in North Denver.
Photo courtesy of the Peña Family Archives.

I was humbled by the great sacrifices made by so many of my supporters, particularly those who could not cast a vote in Denver. And I was thankful my supporters did not fall for some of the-bizarre rumors and fear mongering that emerged as my campaign grew stronger.

Out of nowhere came tales that the Mexican mafia was financing my campaign, that I was gay, that I had fathered two illegitimate children in Texas. According to the highly efficient and productive rumor mill, it was said I would appoint a leftist public defender as City Attorney and an outsider as Chief of Police. "Law and order in Denver is at stake," these sources implied, or flatly stated. Meanwhile, the few prominent business and civic leaders who supported me shared ugly comments made in private by members of prominent families. These comments told of a general belief that the election of an ethnic Mayor would cause businesses to flee the city, resulting in the collapse of the city's economy, and leaving Denver in ruins.

1983, Candidate Peña on the way to the Denver Botanic Gardens for a mayoral debate.
Photo courtesy of the Peña Family Archives.

These rumors and innuendos made the three weeks between the primary and the runoff election feel like things were exploding around me. As Mr. Tooley and I engaged in face-to-face debates, the accusations and criticisms became more outlandish. Though Tooley was older and a more seasoned campaigner, he seemed surprised when I kept the message and tone of my campaign civil. Our debates attracted large audiences. And while it was generally expected that Tooley would outperform his thirty-six-year-old opponent on stage, I held my own and countered his attacks with equal force.

The media and other political observers reacted positively to me as the debates continued, but the lead that I had developed in the primary began to narrow. In the final stretch we braced for a close election, though our volunteer base continued to grow and a number of prominent businesspeople provided essential financial support that made our campaign more competitive.

The race was close until Tooley's New York pollster made a critical mistake. Dick Morris would go on to play a significant role in national politics, and his reputation as a hardball political operative is well-deserved. But when it leaked that Morris was asking voters about my background and reminding them of my Hispanic roots, the newspapers and other media pounced.

Moderate voters and many McNichols supporters, offended by this tactic, joined our campaign and contributed enough for me to battle Tooley dollar for dollar. By the end, we had raised $750,000, an unfathomable amount considering the fact that we had started with next to nothing.

The day of the June runoff did not dawn with a snowstorm, thank goodness. And by 9:00 p.m. that night, we knew we had won, though narrowly. In the largest electoral turnout in the city's history, almost 73 percent of registered voters went to the polls, and 51 percent of them voted for me. The windmill had been slain! At thirty-six years old, I was now the Mayor-Elect of Denver.

As our victory that evening became apparent to the jubilant crowd gathered at our campaign headquarters, I gave Tom Nussbaum a huge bear hug. "We did it!" I shouted. Hugs then went to Katherine Archuleta, John Parr, Sandy Drew, David

Greenberg, Tony Massaro, my brother Alfredo, and my closest campaign members. Some were so happy that tears poured from their eyes. Despite their exhaustion, they were overcome by joyous adrenaline. I was thrilled by the support of the thousands of Denverites who believed in our vision. I knew we had made history, and I could not wait to start implementing our vision of creating a great city.

I couldn't wait to get to Currigan Exhibition Hall and I was excited to start to celebrate our historic victory with a throng of 10,000 cheering citizens. As we were leaving for Currigan, a security team from the Denver Police Department grabbed me and rushed me outside to a waiting van parked in the middle of the sidewalk. Inside the van, guards pushed me to the floor. Death threats had been phoned into our headquarters by people who were not at all happy about my victory, and my safety was suddenly an issue. I turned to my top guard, police officer Joe Garcia and asked, "Is this necessary?"

Joe nodded. "Mayor," he said soberly, "we now have to take your security seriously, and these threats are very real."

The realization that someone was angry enough to threaten my life was shocking—I thought I had run a straightforward campaign on issues affecting all citizens. Unlike mayoral campaigns in other cities where some candidates used racial tactics to stir animosity among the electorate, I deliberately fashioned my message for all Denverites and naively believed that no one would interpret my message otherwise. The threats were a wake-up call, one that I did not easily accept. I was now playing in another league of politics, and I had not prepared well for this aspect of it.

Though shaken, I regained my composure when I entered Currigan Hall. I was welcomed by a huge banner raised across the stage that read "Hall O'Peña." A welcome sense of relief washed over me as I enjoyed the laughter, allowing me to savor my victory for at least a short while.

Thousands gathered in the hall to celebrate. People from

every corner of the city representing the full diversity of Denver sang and danced to the music. The massive turnout crammed people shoulder to shoulder, many with tears. Dale Tooley appeared and graciously congratulated me and asked the community to support my mayoralty. I was thrilled that my parents, siblings, and their children from Texas were in town to celebrate.

1983, Federico's parents standing in the Hall O'Pena on election day.
Photo courtesy of the Peña Family Archives.

Within hours of this exhilarating celebration, however, I experienced firsthand the meaning of the refrain, "It's lonely at the top." As my family and staff members gathered at the Wazee Supper Club, a pizza restaurant in lower downtown Denver, to continue a raucous celebration, Officer Joe Garcia took me home. Concern for my security meant I would miss my own post-election party.

"I guess it's just the two of us," I said to Joe as we walked into my house.

"Sorry, boss," he replied, also exasperated by this turn of events.

"Hell," I said, heading to the kitchen, "let's celebrate anyway." I scoured my almost-empty refrigerator and thankfully found tamales my Mother had brought from Brownsville.

Next to the tamales stood a bottle of champagne. And so, on the evening of the biggest day of my life, I shared tamales and a cheap bubbly in my home with my security guard, isolated from the thousands of supporters scattered throughout the city who were celebrating the remarkable, historic feat they had achieved.

Denverites had good reason to celebrate. They demonstrated, nearly forty years ago, that voters could see past a candidate's race or ethnicity even in a community that was predominantly Anglo. Because of hopeful policies and unifying messages, voters came together to support a young Latino, even in the midst of the racists sentiments of some. The other lesson learned, with application today, is that citizen engagement makes a difference. With a 73 percent voter turnout, powerful and traditional politics were overturned. Many of those who lost faith in local government had it restored. Imagine if we had a 73 percent turnout in a presidential election! For me, the election was the ultimate transformation. I recalled that years earlier I had attacked political institutions as being unjust. Now I would be entrusted to bring the change I had been fighting for.

1983, Election night celebration and congratulations of victory from Dale Tooley. Photo courtesy of the Peña Family Archives.

My closest friends say that I rarely take time to celebrate achievements and that I am reluctant to show my emotions. But that night, I was more excited than I had ever been. In ten days, I would be sworn in as Mayor of Denver. While I could "Imagine a Great City," I could not imagine that would only be the beginning. My journey as a young Mayor would prepare me to serve a decade later in two cabinet seats in the administrations of President Bill Clinton. And one day, I would help a young Senator from Illinois named Barack Obama make his own history.

July, 1983, Thousands celebrating Federico's victory on election night.
Photo by James Baca.

12. The First Term

On July 1, 1983, with my family from Texas in attendance, Colorado Supreme Court Justice Joseph Quinn swore me in as the 41st Mayor of Denver. We stood on the same City Hall steps on which I had announced my candidacy the previous December with only a few friends and minimal media attention. Now a large crowd, said to be the largest ever gathered for a mayoral inauguration, celebrated. People came from every walk of life to revel in what *The Denver Post* observed as "the most dramatic City Hall power shift in thirty-six years." Afterwards, I was flown by helicopter to six parks across the city to greet well-wishers who were unable to attend the packed downtown inauguration. People brought their kids to meet me, and it proved to be the most innovative inauguration in Denver's history. I wanted citizens to know that I would be a Mayor for the entire city, whether a particular neighborhood voted for me or not. I was not about grudges.

I did not need a lengthy inaugural speech. The spirit of change for which the citizens had voted was already in the air. No speech could have lifted them higher. I did reflect, however, that the challenges we faced and the opportunities before us were considerable. "But what we are working toward is not the Denver of tomorrow, but the Denver of decades from tomorrow," I said. "We know we can imagine a great city. Now we must create it." I added that I did not fear the expectations of Denver's citizens, which were immense at this moment. I only feared indifference.

July 1, 1983, Mayor Peña sworn in by Colorado Supreme Court Justice Joseph Quinn. Photo by James Baca.

Indifference was certainly not the attitude of those who, since the night of my election, had been threatening my assassination. The police did not show me the hostile letters, and I never heard the hate-infused messages left on answering machines. But the threats were serious enough that, on that very hot July day, they made me wear a bulletproof vest. No one seemed to notice my bulging chest as I took the oath of office. These precautions were not my choice. I told Officer Joe Garcia, who was in charge of my security team, that their concerns were a bit extreme given the joyous crowds. Joe responded, "Boss, if anything were to happen to you on my watch, I would feel like a complete failure and I could never forgive myself." Gradually, I started to appreciate the enormous stress and self-imposed pressure that security teams place on themselves, however uncomfortable and annoying for the general public.

July 1, 1983, Mayor Peña sworn in on Inauguration Day,
standing with Mayor McNichols.
Photo by James Baca.

Securing the safety of public officials had become a preoccupation of law enforcement since the assassinations of President John Kennedy and Senator Robert Kennedy, and the attempt on the life of President Gerald Ford. Just two years earlier, President Ronald Reagan had barely escaped assassination at the Hilton Hotel in Washington. But these security measures cramped my open and accessible style of community engagement and were criticized for their cost to the taxpayer. (The critics did not care that my predecessor incurred similar costs for his security detail.)

I was not inattentive to the cost of government. In fact, it was very much on my mind. On the day of my inauguration, I knew that the city faced a $20 million budget shortfall —not exactly the best starting point to implement the broad agenda I detailed during the campaign. And Denver would soon face serious and formidable economic headwinds after I took office.

Apart from broad economic pressures, those who had been

working for the city felt marginalized, receiving little encouragement to offer their ideas for improving city services. But I was convinced that in order to succeed, we had to harness the untapped talent and intellectual capital of our citizens. People were eager to provide their innovative ideas to address our challenges and they were anxious to serve. Several thousand resumes came poring in and I had to create screening committees to review and help interview the applicants excited to join my administration.

July 1, 1983, Record crowd attended Federico's Inauguration Day ceremony before the City and County Building. Photo by James Baca.

I did not want to make the mistake of assuming that only those who helped elect me could serve our new administration. I understood that winning an election was different from running a city government.

During my campaign, I marveled at the extraordinary caliber of talent hidden throughout the city. Denver had been infused over the years with energetic, creative, and well-educated professionals who had emigrated from other states. Unfortunately, no one had invited these newcomers to participate in the governance of their new city or to think about its future. So, I decided

I would call upon them to do the hard work of adopting the best business practices in City Hall, elevating our planning capability, fighting pollution, revitalizing declining neighborhoods, and advancing the goal of creating a great city.

Many citizens in the metro area felt isolated from their capital city for a variety of reasons. Denver officials rarely acknowledged suburban concerns, and Denver's court-ordered cross-town busing program, intended to integrate public schools, offended them.

To symbolize that Denver was open to new ideas, I opened, literally and figuratively, the enormous bronze doors to City Hall, fronted by six ionic columns of granite, which heretofore had been locked. I wanted everyone to know we were serious about sculpting a great city with full transparency. Mayor McNichols represented the last of the big-city Mayors who controlled local politics and rewarded friends. He was said to have compiled a list of contractors over the years who alone would have access to city business. I was having none of that.

July 1, 1983, Federico addressing thousands from May D&F Tower.
Photo by James Baca.

During his tenure, my predecessor had only one person of color working in his entire top administration. I set out to recruit the best and the brightest individuals regardless of their gender, sexual orientation, race, or ethnicity. My goal was to assemble a young, energetic, committed, creative, and diverse staff.

This approach shocked civic leaders in Denver, and the media instantly suggested I was not selecting the most qualified candidates. This mentality stemmed in part from the fact that the public had rarely seen people in high positions other than strait-laced white males. Talented people who did not fit this limited profile had simply never been given the opportunity to serve in city government roles. And they were more than willing and able. By opening the doors of opportunity in Denver's City Hall to citizens from diverse backgrounds, we were breaking new ground in 1983. It was a tough start to my first term, and the critics jumped at the chance to complain, even though I'd campaigned on the notion that city government should reflect the diversity of its constituents. The dramatic changes I brought fueled further opposition from those accustomed to more traditional governance. I knew I had to conduct myself above reproach, keep my composure at all times, and work harder because I was the first Mayor of color. I was even careful with what I wore —suits almost exclusively and rarely causal clothes—as I was keenly aware of the double standard being applied to me. Critics were waiting to pounce at any mistake, however minor.

During one of my many press conferences, a reporter was heard to comment that I was the "IBM Mayor." Asked what that meant, he replied: "The Itty-Bitty Mexican Mayor." This came to the attention of Tom Nussbaum, who called the reporter's employer, and he was terminated. When prominent Denverite Marvin Davis held the Carousel Ball to raise millions for childhood diabetes, I, like all male attendees, wore a black tuxedo. A guest from Los Angeles asked me to get her a drink. A friend approached and said, "Hi, Mayor Peña," and the embarrassed guest became speechless. I offered to help find her a drink nonetheless. She obviously never expected a tuxedo-clad Latino to be the city's Mayor. While I was chagrined by these experiences, I just kept moving forward, realizing that I was going to confront some amount of racism.

Another controversial change was my appointment of committees filled with enthusiastic citizens eager to contribute. I encouraged them to move aggressively, because I did not intend for my administration to simply manage its way through a tough economy. I wanted us all to fix our sights on the century ahead with bold ideas.

Here again critics snickered that I did not have the courage to make decisions and wondered aloud why I had to appoint so many committees. I was surprised by this because I had campaigned on opening government to all citizens. I did not back down. I argued that while these committees might take more time to address critical issues, in the long term, the solutions they proposed would receive broader support than my simply mandating a solution.

I held a strong belief that the core of the country's cities—their downtown areas and established neighborhoods—represented the heart and soul of America. All our cities, including Colorado's capital, needed to be bolstered. I did not simply want to talk about a new inner-city framework; I wanted to invest in a long-term and permanent commitment for future generations. I had seen the demise of some inner cities across our country, and Denver was not going to follow suit.

These messages of change did not go unnoticed. Members of the media, political pundits, and the city's establishment took note—which was exactly the point. I wanted the perception that things were moving at City Hall to permeate all city life and inspire others to get involved, build new businesses, and improve neighborhoods. But I also understood the many obstacles standing in the way.

The smog that hovered over the city threatened the health of everyone, especially residents who had arrived decades earlier to breathe clean air and improve their health. Known locally as "lungers," they now inhaled toxins that one year violated federal carbon monoxide standards on fifty-six days. Imperiled, too, were the mountain views that formed the city's spectacular scenic backdrop. My predecessor had been complacent about the "brown cloud," suggesting it had existed for centuries or, depending on the day, had probably blown in from Seattle.

A serious national recession loomed, ready to hit the mid-section of the country particularly hard. It would push Denver's unemployment rate two percentage points above the national average. To my chagrin, the old *Keyes* school busing order came back to haunt me. It encouraged the flight of middle-class Anglo families out of the city, further weakening the school and the city tax bases. *Keyes* also triggered the passage of the Poundstone Amendment to the Colorado Constitution.

The Poundstone Amendment required Denver to obtain an adjoining county's voter approval for any proposed annexation. This restriction effectively thwarted Denver's geographic expansion and spurred growth outside the city limits, siphoning away essential sales and property taxes. This significant loss of the ability to easily annex new land was ultimately a blessing. It forced us to focus inwardly on downtown, Cherry Creek, and the surrounding neighborhoods and local businesses. Had the Poundstone Amendment not passed, Denver might have grown into a sprawling 300 to 400-square-mile city with a greater focus on its outlying areas. Forcing us to look inward resulted in a more urban-centric agenda designed to improve the quality of life within city boundaries. Pre-COVID-19, this is precisely what occurred in Denver, which became a thriving and bustling inner city of over 700,000 residents.

In the 1980s, Denver's sales tax accounted for half the city's revenue. By the time I took my oath as Mayor, nine years after the passage of the Poundstone Amendment, the city's tax base and revenue were eroding. The police pension fund was significantly underfunded, a liability we had to address immediately. Downtown office buildings would soon become 30 percent vacant. To make matters worse, the Reagan Administration was reducing federal support for many local programs. The city of Denver was not faring well under Reaganomics.

Many aspects of the city's quality of life deteriorated under the strain. Gang activity and violence were increasing. Bridges and viaducts were crumbling. I had to close one deteriorated bridge a few months after taking office. A number of our viaducts had dangerous engineering sufficiency ratings. An outdated convention center and a constrained airport continued to hamstring growth. Historic buildings were falling to the wrecking ball, further degrading the unique character of our inner city.

My first four years were not a cakewalk. I had to confront the damage that tornadoes inflicted on the Park Hill community and in southwest Denver. My team had to make a decision in the middle of the night on how to save the landmark Masonic Building, almost all of which was consumed by a downtown mall fire. A major airline crash at Stapleton Airport brought agony to the families and friends of loved ones who had suddenly lost their lives. I was heartbroken by this tragedy.

I had to battle some on City Council and a City Auditor who coveted my desk. In order to eliminate the impending deficit, I had to cut many programs. I took ten days furlough without pay, as did my staff and cabinet. I visited city employees at their work sites to explain they would need to take five days off in order to prevent the terminations of many of their coworkers. They were unhappy, but they appreciated that I met with them personally to explain the painful options that confronted our city.

During my first term, many lost faith, and I sometimes contributed to their despair. I made some bad personnel decisions and other mistakes, especially when managing snow removal after two back-to-back storms buried the city in more than two feet of snow. Normally, an eight-to-twelve-inch snowfall was manageable. But two feet? When I huddled with our public works team in the Emergency Operations Center, I was shocked to learn that our antiquated technologies could not track our snowplow drivers. When I asked how many major arterials were cleared, someone gave me an envelope with street names written on the back. City administrators had no way of communicating with their crews. We had to wait for plow drivers to finish an arterial, find a pay phone, and call in completed assignments, street by street. I knew we were in for a rough week as the criticism came pouring in. To make matters worse, a local TV reporter followed a few drivers and found them slacking on their jobs. I was beginning to wonder whether a poor blizzard response was going to blunt our progress on other issues; I was sensing disappointment among my supporters.

Turnarounds are never easy, as I have learned in business. In hindsight, I focused too much on large economic projects that I believed were essential to rebuild Denver's economy. Unfortunately, these projects did not create jobs quickly enough. I prioritized building a new convention center, airport, and shopping mall, and revitalizing the Central Platte Valley, a depressed area of 600 acres adjacent to downtown, instead of short-term necessities. None of these longer initiatives would be completed in my first term. Citizens expected quick change, and the national recession was slow to recede. I believed my ideas would work for Denver in the long term, but I belatedly realized there was a desperate need for short-term improvements. I grew to appreciate the difference.

When people voiced their frustrations that my long-term vision was not producing immediate and concrete results, the City Auditor—who considered himself a future mayoral candidate—labeled us as "Freddy and the Dreamers" after the 1960s rock group. Local media amplified his critique. But my team turned the tables on these critics. During one press conference, my staff wore T-shirts that read, "We are the Dreamers." And they handed me one that read, "I am Freddy."

1983, Federico with Congresswoman Patricia Schroder laughing about Freddy and the Dreamers. Photo courtesy of the Peña Family Archives.

Citizens who embraced our dreams rallied to my defense, and even Congresswoman Pat Schroeder weighed in. She sent me a note in February 1984 attached to Freddy and the Dreamer's 45 RPM record, reminding me that their big hit was, "I'm Telling You Now." Soon my staff was singing the lyrics: "I'm telling you now, I'm telling you right away, I'll be staying for many a day." With her typical humor, Schroeder ended the note, "You now have a theme song."

I put my commitments to civil rights and social justice principles to work when I boycotted the popular St. Patrick's Day Parade. The gay and lesbian community—as it was known then—wanted to march in the parade but was denied permission. I announced that I disagreed with what I believed to be a discriminatory decision, and boycotted the parade. I was inundated with hate mail and angry calls, but I did not back down. I still feel strongly about this type of discrimination. I had sought the support of the community and appointed gay and lesbian members to my mayoral staff. I was not about to abandon them. Thankfully, they were allowed to join the parade the following year and have continued to participate ever since.

It is not easy to be in public office. Its politics affect your entire life, at home and in the office. When the second "100-Year Blizzard" hit the city the following year, something unheard of in Denver, we worked doubly hard to clear the streets. I thought we were past the worst and that my team had control. I flew to a Mexican beach to get some rest, as I was physically and emotionally exhausted. Unexpectedly, the weather worsened and a deep freeze hardened the melting snow. My staff learned that a TV crew was planning to find me and record me resting on the sand while city residents were stuck in their neighborhoods. One of my key staff members, Katherine Archuleta, was tasked to call me and explain that I needed to get on the next plane back to Denver. It was a tough call for Katherine, but she was right, and I flew home immediately. My recuperation would have to wait.

But it was not all serious business. When a local sports promoter and friend, Bill Michaels, suggested we organize a citywide marathon to encourage citizens toward good health, I thought it was a great idea. I had been a reasonable athlete as a young man, and later in life enjoyed exercise mostly to stay in shape and work out my frustrations. I ran my first marathon in 1978 and was still running short races. I loved the idea of a marathon through The Mile High City because it would reflect the healthy environs of Denver and give the Chamber of Commerce another marketing tool. If New York and Boston could each hold a marathon, so could Denver. We decided the winner would be awarded the Mayor's Cup. While I did not win the inaugural race, I improved my time to three hours and eighteen minutes, while in the process inspiring others to get off their couches, hit the parks, and improve their health.

1984, Federico finishing marathon race with trainer Nick Kripakov (right).
Photo courtesy of the Peña Family Archives.

Still, the criticism I endured during my first term took its toll. My supporters were beginning to lose faith in our ability to create a "Great City." The economy continued to deteriorate. And with two major newspapers battling it out for survival, I sometimes felt like a *piñata* being batted back and forth between competing reporters. Some wondered how I weathered the fierce storms. Even in the face of criticism and political opposition, I tried not to hold grudges. I had seen too much valuable energy sapped from people who kept score. While I disliked and was demoralized by negative media coverage, I understood this was part of being a public figure. To preserve my sanity, I refrained from reading many of the negative news accounts. Thankfully, I had a great and supportive team who picked up my spirits when I was dejected. Persistence had been bred into the extended Peña-Farias families throughout the decades, and I was not about to become an exception.

13. The Second Term

The growing pains of a new administration working to reinvent a city will naturally breed critics. After deciding to seek re-election, I was not surprised to learn *The Rocky Mountain News* and *The Denver Post* opposed me, endorsing my opponent. I was disappointed, of course, especially since the *Rocky* had supported my first campaign. But the voters of Denver again proved they had faith in the future, and I won my second term in a run-off.

I ran against six opponents, but this time I was the target. I felt like I was facing a firing squad and I had provided them with the ammunition.

The campaign was so challenging that I came in second place in the primary to prominent attorney Don Bain. I was almost eighteen points behind Mr. Bain in the polls, and many believed I could not make up the gap in the three weeks leading up to the run-off. Both papers ran negative news stories about me, but our campaign team worked harder than before and we squeaked out a victory on election night. I always believed that voters would do the right thing, and thankfully in 1987 most still believed in me.

I was exhausted. After having won my second election by only a few thousand votes, the battle continued. A group of dismayed citizens immediately announced they would launch a recall petition. Because I had made serious budget cuts in light of declining sales tax revenue, they argued that I was mismanaging the city's finances. Privately, I believed they were unhappy that I had won my re-election, and some were distressed that someone of my ethnicity would be Mayor for another four years. Publicly, I confidently declared that I would not be distracted by their effort and would continue to run the city. *The Denver Post's* March 20, 1988, headline screamed: "Recall cinched, Peña Foes Say." My supporters took the lead in refuting the recall effort. Eventually, it failed when it fell short of the necessary signatures. While I maintained a public profile of confidence and remained focused on my agenda for my second term, I felt betrayed by the recall proponents, some of whom I had known for years.

My second term as Mayor of Denver was an acceleration of the first. We made progress in some of the same areas as in the first term, but we'd heard from the voters it was time to double-down on our approach. The goal was to demonstrate visible progress on the major projects that were the centerpiece of my administration. We were motivated by a very bleak economy, stubbornly high unemployment, and struggling small businesses.

"Thinking outside the box" was the new refrain of the times. Across the country, leaders of businesses, government, and institutions of all kinds had to contend with a world that was speeding toward globalization...along with President Ronald Reagan's conceptually honest but impractical ideas involving government.

President Reagan's belief that government could not play an elemental role in turning around the fortunes of a city—or a nation, for that matter—would soon be disproved. He famously stated: "In this present crisis, government is not the solution to our problem, government IS the problem." Reagan did not understand that during the recession that was hitting full force, business and civic leaders were not telling my administration that we were "the problem." Rather, I was being exhorted by the business establishment—and by unions and entrepreneurs—to act more quickly to re-ignite the economy with my first-term strategies. They wanted government to be "the solution" to our recession and to lead the way.

I was willing to experiment with out-of-the box concepts and apply new techniques and approaches, some truly novel. We partnered with metropolitan leaders and business, labor, and civic groups to dramatically reduce our harmful carbon monoxide levels. By experimenting with "no drive" days based on license plate numbers, banning wood-burning stoves, supporting alternative fuels in winter months, and using other measures, we reduced the fifty-six days we'd violated federal standards down to one day. We worked with neighborhood groups by providing them direct funds—not clearly permitted by city law—to buy brooms, paint, and other tools to remove graffiti and clean up alleys. A citizen provided horses for police to start a horse patrol downtown. I appointed a husband-and-wife team, Don and Carolyn Etter, to co-lead the Department of Parks and Recreation, proving that an organization can have two, co-equal leaders. I supported City Attorney Patricia Wells, who was pregnant, in her quest to work from home with a newly-installed communications system—an unconventional idea for the time without internet, Zoom, or video-conferencing in the 1980s. I also appointed talented team members to lead challenging projects by bringing unique and fresh leadership. Anne Bormolini, my Chief of Staff, lead the planning and construction for a major addition to the Central Public Library. City Attorney Steve Kaplan oversaw the construction of the new Convention Center. In each case we "thought outside the box" to ensure a timely completion of major projects.

I understood that new partnerships were needed with labor and business groups, ethnic and racial minorities, women, and gays and lesbians in order to leverage every available resource.

We partnered with a labor union that committed part of its pension fund to help finance the renovation of the iconic downtown Denver Dry building, which had been vacant for years. The union wanted jobs, and we wanted business activity and redevelopment, so everyone won in the end. The Denver Dry building today houses retail stores, offices, and lofts on the 16th Street Mall. It became the home of the Denver Urban Renewal Authority, which transformed itself from an entity that demolished historic structures to one of the most significant preservation actors in the region under its visionary Director, Susan Powers.

1990, the new Colorado Convention Center.
Photo courtesy of the Peña Family Archives.

In the 1980s, Denver's downtown was dying, burdened with a 30 percent office vacancy rate, and retail stores that were closing. A central part of our revitalization was building a new and larger convention center. Major cities were benefitting enormously from visitor spending and were hoping to host national and international conventions. Unfortunately, our City could not finance and rebuild a new center on its own and had to request state aid. To encourage state support, we committed to purchasing stone and other resources native to rural Colorado for the building's construction, providing immediate economic relief to outlying communities. Many were elated when we celebrated the opening of the new convention center in 1990. When I helped cut the ribbon, I had one arm in a sling from surgery, perhaps symbolizing the strenuous effort that had been required. But my joy of completing this significant project overcame any pain from the injury. Thousands of new visitors have since flocked to Denver, supporting the downtown economy. The convention center was expanded again in 2004 under Mayor Wellington Webb, and it resides near the exquisite Denver Center for the Performing Arts complex, the nation's second-largest after New York's Lincoln Center.

June 1990, The Colorado Convention Center Opening.
Photo courtesy of the Peña Family Archives.

Although many today recall my support of multi-billion-dollar projects, I always understood that small businesses were critical to our city. Since local banks were wary of extending credit in the midst of a recession, the city's Office of Economic Development provided millions of dollars in small business loans to hundreds of Denver's entrepreneurs. These city loans incentivized private sector co-investments and created 2,300 new jobs in zones we designated as Neighborhood Business Revitalization Districts. The neighborhood activist in me was gratified. We demonstrated that small businesses were truly the backbone of our economy. Contrary to ultra-conservative critics, we proved that city government could be a responsible lender, especially when traditional banks were reluctant to lend.

The Mayan Theatre.
Photo courtesy of Denver Public Library.

One memorable example of our small business support was our collaboration with a neighborhood group to save the historic Mayan Theatre in the near-west side—now called the Baker District. The Mayan, like many movie theaters of its era, was struggling. It was built in 1930 in the Art Deco Mayan Revival style but had been recently sold to the adjacent Union Bank, which intended to demolish it and redevelop the entire block. The Mayan was not only an important landmark in the neighborhood, but it was also only one of three theaters of this style remaining in the country. Residents of the area formed the Friends of the Mayan to save the building. The City Council designated it a Denver landmark, but that only delayed a demolition permit for ninety days. On the ninety-first day, fences were up and a wrecking ball was on site. I called Pat Bowlen, owner of the Denver Broncos, who had a relationship with the Canadian-owned Union Bank. Upon my prodding, Bowlen connected us with the head of the ownership group, Dick Landon, who in turn gave the city more time to submit a redevelopment proposal.

The compromise proposal, negotiated with the city's planning department under its Creative Director Bill Lamont, provided additional incentives and avigation—air and space—rights to the bank in exchange for preserving the Mayan. The partnership saved the Mayan, and it remains a popular destination today, serving a critical role in the economic revitalization along South Broadway. This relatively small project gave me much greater joy than many of the other infrastructure investments we made because it immediately improved the quality of life for citizens in the neighborhood.

One of our more notable small business loans went to geologist John Hickenlooper, who was unemployed due to the energy downturn in the 1980s. Hickenlooper switched careers and opened a brew pub in lower downtown named the Wynkoop Brewery. I participated in the ribbon-cutting ceremony. Eventually, Hickenlooper went on to sit at my old desk in the Mayor's office before being elected Governor of Colorado in 2010. And who would have ever guessed that a city loan would help propel a young entrepreneur to later become a presidential candidate? He was elected Colorado's latest Senator in 2020.

The small business loans the city made were overwhelmingly successful and were almost entirely repaid. There were many who believed, and still believe today, that this form of government involvement in assisting the private sector interferes with the traditional forces of a market-based economy. They were wrong then and are wrong today.

I strongly believe there is an appropriate role for government to play, especially when a city, or a nation, is in recession. Consider the extraordinary and essential government response to the coronavirus we are witnessing today. We need strategic government involvement, partnering with the private sector, unions, foundations, investment firms, and other civic organizations at the national level to ignite our economy, rebuild our infrastructure, and invest in innovative technologies allowing the U.S. to better compete in the global economy. There are lessons to be learned from the Denver experience.

Another challenge Denver faced was the decline in the retail sector. Before I came into office, Denver could claim few of the top fifteen retail centers in the metropolitan area, as most of the newer centers were built outside the city. Denverites—almost half a million in population—had to make their way to the suburbs to shop. This was problematic given the city's heavy dependence on sales tax revenue. So, we began the process of rebuilding yet another languishing part of old Denver.

The nationally famous Denver architect, Temple Buell, developed the city's first merchandising mecca in Cherry Creek on land that had once been a garbage dump. For decades, Buell struggled to achieve his dream of redeveloping the Cherry Creek Center into a gigantic three-million-square-foot complex. Recognizing my administration was willing to implement new ideas to revive the city's economy, he tried again. Buell's proposal triggered an enormous neighborhood battle. Ultimately, his idea floundered, but a new developer from Michigan, the Taubman Company, entered the fray.

Nearby homeowners who ringed the site opposed the project's original size. I listened to long hours of debate over the proposal, but I knew that a strategically-located retail mall near the center of the city was key to Denver's revitalization. We could have easily walked away, deeming the project more trouble than it was worth. My commitment to engage when possible spurred months of listening and negotiating that resulted in consensus among neighborhood associations, developers, competing retail centers, and warring factions within City Hall. This was an example of a public-private-citizen partnership that worked.

Our compromise called for the construction of a 1.2-million-square-foot enclosed mall anchored by Neiman Marcus, Lord & Taylor, and Saks Fifth Avenue. We were aware that the new retail center could threaten the boutique shops in Cherry Creek North, located across from this huge new mall. So, we supported state legislation that authorized the first Business Improvement District to support those shops, allowing them to raise funds to revitalize Cherry Creek North. The city invested in other infrastructure improvements in the area. In the end, the compromises we reached then for modern-day Denver have been tremendously successful, and the partnerships we forged provide a blueprint for resolving future controversial projects. Throughout the prolonged fight over Cherry Creek—as with other difficult and controversial proposals—I managed to maintain a confidence and conviction that all things were possible. I knew from past experiences that the difference between succeeding and failing was perseverance.

Out of all our work to revitalize our city, the four most compelling enterprises that together would transform Denver were the creation of the historic Lower Downtown, the revitalization of the Central Platte Valley, the construction of Denver International Airport, and the recruitment of a Major League Baseball team. These achievements helped extricate Denver from a crushing recession and positioned it to become the regional economic and cultural leader that it is today.

14. Preserving Our History...Preparing Our Future

Preserving the historic and architectural heritage of Denver was a personal priority. When I looked at historic buildings, I imagined the old train station my Father had leased for his cotton business in Brownsville. And, like my Father, I saw in them real value.

The old, splendid structures of the city—the Denver City and County Building, the Colorado State Capitol, the beautiful Central Bank building, the Brown Palace, the Oxford Hotel, the Greek Amphitheater, Union Station, and many other historic homes and buildings—are enthralling in and of themselves. They are grand testaments to the pioneers who founded Denver and who themselves imagined a great city. The City Beautiful movement of the 1890s and 1900s, whose members had wanted to personify moral and civic virtue in architecture, produced monumental grandeur in buildings across America.

Historical structures, whether public edifices, office buildings, or private homes throughout the country, are valuable because they offer a genuine feel for contemporary life as well as tangible ties to a city's past.

It is often easier to plow under magnificent assets rather than spend time in their grand presence and imagine them afresh. When commitment to a neighborhood wanes, imagination disappears and leaves a vacuum. Neglected buildings then become hosts to seedy activity, or are taken over by transient populations, too often attracting drug abuse and crime.

Brownsville Train Station where Federico worked in his Father's cotton business.
Photo courtesy of the Peña Family Archives.

Lower Downtown Denver (LoDo) had become such a place prior to my time as Mayor. Unless we acted, LoDo's extraordinary brick buildings would continue to decay, setting them up for destruction. Once demolished, they would be gone forever. Demolition crews had torn down as much as 20 percent of the buildings in Lower Downtown by the time I assumed office. And the places that remained were endangered, especially during our recession. Plummeting property values were compelling owners to tear down historic buildings and convert them to parking lots.

The transformation of LoDo was about preserving our history. The struggle was sparked when both the National Trust and Historic Denver, led by the remarkable Jennifer Moulton, proposed the creation of a historic district to preserve and revitalize the area, which was threatened by private sector demolition. Little progress was made initially, however, until City Councilwoman Debbie Ortega joined the effort and—with Tom Gougeon, one of my long-time aides—drafted legislation and started to secure votes on the City Council.

We consulted with visionary members of the City Council and developers who saw the potential of the LoDo area. Some suggested a voluntary demolition control ordinance, but since it would not be mandatory, I felt it would be merely symbolic. We were either going to restrict demolition and impose design review rules or do nothing at all. To attract support, we offered to install new streetscapes, sidewalks, and street lighting. We would also extend the 16th Street Mall to Union Station and open a LoDo Business Support Office to make loans to those who wanted to start businesses in the district. It was a public-private-civic transaction once again. Ultimately, an ordinance was drafted to create a historic preservation district. It imposed building height limitations and strict design guidelines for rehabilitation, as well as measures that essentially made it impossible to destroy buildings within the district. I was enthusiastic about the proposed ordinance, but we did not have the required seven votes on the City Council.

The fight over the proposed ordinance was extremely difficult. We faced the challenge of convincing property owners who were suffering through a recession that the ordinance would eventually increase their property values exponentially. Rather than simply destroy extraordinary buildings and replace them with parking lots, we argued it made sense to preserve their integrity and create value. Many remained unconvinced, and they lobbied the City Council strenuously, arguing that the ordinance would constitute an unlawful taking of their property rights. Threats of litigation hung in the air, as did the political careers of some of those who would have to vote for the proposal. The fight caused me to push hard against old friends. It was a painful experience.

On the evening of the vote in March 1988, the City Council engaged in a final debate that went deep into the evening. Finally, Tom Gougeon lumbered exhausted into my office to tell me that the ordinance creating the Lower Downtown Historic District had won by a one-vote margin.

Not even its most ardent supporters who celebrated LoDo's passage could have foreseen its extraordinary impact. The salvation of approximately 127 historic structures within twenty-three city blocks that were converted into mixed-use zoning ignited an explosion of growth. Today, LoDo has become a mother lode of prosperity, hosting family dwellings, restaurants, boutiques, art galleries, bars, coffeehouses, law firms, high-tech businesses, and energy companies. The neighborhood surrounding Coors Field—unlike areas around stadiums of other cities—has remained vibrant, with more than 21,000 people living in its condominiums and apartments. LoDo now boasts some of the most expensive and sought-after properties in Colorado.

The revitalization of LoDo stimulated a build-out of the entire downtown area. And the transformation continues today. Denver, like Brownsville, rescued its railroad station by rejuvenating it in 2014. The historic Union Station public-private partnership boasts new restaurants, retail stores, offices, and the Crawford Hotel while co-locating with Amtrak. It anchors a new multi-modal transportation hub including the Greyhound bus terminal that coordinates light rail lines throughout the region and a commuter rail line to Denver International Airport.

To me, revitalizing LoDo was about the long term, however painful its plans proved to be in the short term. Some property owners were dismayed by our vision for LoDo in the 1980s, but for those who embraced the long-term opportunities—who could see the makings of a great city—their faith and hope were ultimately rewarded.

People from around the country often visit Denver to learn from the LoDo experiment, which proves that the future often lies in what we once were as a community and that the value and worth of the past can endure.

Building for the future can also be found by appreciating the value of the discarded past. This past was buried in the neglected 600 acres of land used primarily by the railroads. Known as the Central Platte Valley, this huge parcel bordering downtown was also adjacent to the South Platte River, which flows south to north, contrary to the flow of most rivers. Over decades, this area had become strewn with trash, weeds, dilapidated cardboard, abandoned mattresses, tires, and broken glass.

When I ran for Mayor, this overlooked land mass was undervalued, except for its transient inhabitants. I vividly remember taping one of my first television campaign ads in the middle of this desolation. The camera, mounted on a narrow-gauge track, followed me as I walked, describing what I saw and describing my vision for redeveloping Denver. As I was speaking to the camera, walking gingerly, I felt a nail shoot through the sole of the shoe on my right foot. Luckily, the nail sliced through the space between two of my toes. "This is going to be a challenging development project," I said disconcertingly to Tom Nussbaum, who was relieved the nail had missed my toe. What an understatement!

Some of the local television viewers who saw that commercial appreciated the image I was trying to paint, however. And once I was in office, my team began to craft a vision and a comprehensive development plan for a series of mixed-use developments for the Central Platte Valley. Few believed we could spark this development, especially in the middle of a recession and with a limited municipal budget. But we were dead set on trying.

The planning office, headed by the strong will of Bill Lamont and supported by architect Ron Straka, jumpstarted the process by convincing the railroad companies to consolidate their tracks in order to free up valuable land. We demonstrated the city's commitment to redevelopment by investing millions in new streets, bridges, and viaducts to connect the rest of the downtown to the valley. We worked with Sandy Guertler, whose family owned and operated the historic Elitch Gardens in North Denver, to move his amusement park into the valley as its first major new tenant.

The comprehensive master plan we developed with the help of hundreds of citizens, as well as members of the City Council, would serve as a blueprint for successive administrations as they, too, worked to further expand the area.

Over time, the entire Central Platte Valley has been re-incorporated into an economically dynamic part of Denver. This once isolated, inner-city wasteland is now home to condominiums, apartments, restaurants, parks, offices, and retail operations. Our initial work was expanded under the leadership of now former Mayors Wellington Webb and John Hickenlooper. The Colorado Ocean Journey Aquarium, the Pepsi Center Arena, plus Commons Park came into existence after I left office. Everything that now fills the formerly forlorn Central Platte Valley stands as a legacy to a vision that many shared—and acted upon—forty years ago. Our vision would also guide two other initiatives that would involve much more than redevelopment of a neglected corner of a city: the building of Denver International Airport and bringing Major League Baseball to Coors Field. Both would require the persistence and stamina I inherited from my ancestors.

15. Federico's Folly

Three weeks after I took office on July 1, 1983, a group of metropolitan leaders and members of the Denver Regional Council of Governments met to finally decide what to do about Stapleton, the city's congested airport. The business and civic communities had been debating for years whether to expand Stapleton or build a new airport.

Built in 1929 by Mayor Ben Stapleton, it was located seven miles from downtown. Back then it was considered to be too far from civilization to be useful to anyone but the wealthy, but Stapleton Airport—coined "Stapleton's Folly" by the *Denver Post*—had served the region well. By 1983, time and the growth of the city had passed it by, and it was now problematic. For one thing, the runways were far closer than the 4,300 feet separation required by the Federal Aviation Administration for simultaneous instrument landings. Stapleton lost half of its capacity during poor visibility conditions because air traffic controllers were forced to ground, cancel, or delay flights. These delays rippled throughout the country because the airport handled thirty to thirty-five million passengers per year and served as one of the nation's major hubs. Media reports of unhappy travelers marooned overnight—many of them first-time visitors or skiers headed to the mountains—prompted competing airports to poke fun at Stapleton. Some flyers avoided going through Denver altogether.

Most of the public embraced the option of expanding Stapleton to the north. The abandoned Rocky Mountain Arsenal, formerly a chemical weapons manufacturing site operated for decades by the Department of the Army, could provide the needed land. During my campaign, I endorsed the northward expansion. Most media outlets and business leaders thought this was the best path forward. It seemed almost everyone was in agreement on how to fix the Stapleton problem.

I not only supported the expansion; I had been frantically lobbying for it ahead of the meeting of the Council of Governments that July. I knew there would be opposition by the communities directly affected by the expansion, particularly Adams County and the cities immediately north of Denver. But I wanted to make sure that the regional council made a decision. No more delays. We had to act.

In the days that preceded the meeting, I called and met with other regional Mayors and County Commissioners to build as large a vote as possible for expansion. During the meeting itself, I listened to the final presentation of the completed research and site analyses, work that had taken years and scarce financial resources to conduct. Media from across the state were present, and they dutifully reported that after heated debate, the vote to expand into the arsenal prevailed by a healthy two-thirds majority. It seemed like a solid win for my first month in office, and I felt I had brought closure to a debate that had lasted too long.

My team and I returned to City Hall to celebrate. Soon, however, we started to contemplate the deeper implications of losing the vote of one-third of the region's leaders and public officials. The representatives of Adams County rejected the proposed site with vehemence. They publicly threatened to launch legal and political obstacles to prevent Denver from moving forward with the plan. Adams County's opposition nagged at me, and further reflection and discussion brought me to a fork in the road: either forge ahead as planned, or—after so many years of contentious debate—devise another strategy.

As hard as I had fought for expansion, I was willing to consider the drag of potential lawsuits and stall tactics that might come from Adams County. Denver, after all, was $20 million in the hole and, being an attorney, I knew the costs of litigation. I also counted the collateral damage of having a determined opponent with its own battery of attorneys. Tom Gougeon, who had developed many of my campaign position papers, began to thoroughly re-evaluate our position. The media, meanwhile, treated the matter as settled.

Within a few weeks, Tom reported back with a startling conclusion: Expanding onto the old arsenal could prove to be a mistake—and a costly one. The Pentagon had left the arsenal riddled with buried and unexploded ordnance. There were chemical weapons and residual contaminations remaining from a Shell Corporation pesticide operation. The land was deteriorating with an unknown number of dirty pools above ground and under, some with biological agents and nerve gas. It could take years and billions of dollars to clean up the land enough to make it safe to use—with no guaranteed federal funding to help. Lengthy litigation—probably more than we had envisioned— would ensue, requiring an untold number of costly and complicated environmental impact statements. There could be no end in sight.

Tom reported that we would have to design the proposed airfield around the contaminated areas, resulting in an unworkable, highly-inefficient airport with long taxi distances.

Based on this information we could only speculate when, if ever, we might actually be able to solve the Stapleton problem. It threatened to derail my grand vision for a great city. Denver could never hope to be a great city without an efficient international airport. As a landlocked city, the airport was our sole gateway to global markets.

As disappointing as Tom's report was, I was confident that it was accurate. I picked up the phone, called the Adams County officials, and suggested I meet them for dinner in their backyard. This was a novelty of its own because, historically, when the region's local governments had anything to discuss concerning Denver, the meetings were always held in Denver. They accepted the invitation and within days Tom and I drove north to the popular Bubba's Restaurant.

After the usual pleasantries preceding steaks and beer, we got down to business. We listened intently to their concerns about noise and safety issues. Once they pled their case, I startled them with my response: "Well, what options do we have?" It did not take long to reach a gentlemen's agreement. Denver, we agreed, would move the airport to a new site several miles to the east of the Rocky Mountain Arsenal, but the new airport would have to remain as part of Denver proper. That meant that Adams County residents would need to vote to approve the necessary land annexation pursuant to the state's Poundstone Amendment. I made it clear to the Adams County delegation that Denver alone would own and manage the airport. The Arsenal expansion plan would be abandoned.

Driving home that evening, I was fully aware of the risks this new plan entailed. Building a new airport is a mammoth undertaking. It had been many years since a new airport had been built in the United States and, while the opportunity seemed breathtaking, its degree of difficulty was equally weighty. For a city facing the stress of a recession and a limited budget, it seemed outlandish to embark on a multi-billion-dollar project, if not downright irresponsible.

The reaction was intense when the news broke.

As expected, the public and the media felt they had been sideswiped. After all, I had campaigned hard for the Arsenal expansion plan, and most political, business, and civic leaders for years had supported this strategy. The media had come to accept the expansion project as a *fait accompli*, especially after the DRCOG vote. Many thought that abandoning this broadly-embraced strategy was foolhardy. It was no surprise that the immediate skeptics labeled our breakthrough proposal "Federico's Folly." As I absorbed the many hits we took on this front, I felt more like the "Peña Piñata."

Many of the attacks were personal, and the enormous public relations problem—generated by the controversy we had brought on ourselves—greatly complicated my first term.

The notion of closing an airport that was only minutes from downtown and building a new one many miles to the east was too much for most residents, City Council members, and other local government officials to entertain. It became even more controversial as it took months of negotiations with Adams County. We finally agreed to move the airport east by twenty-seven miles. The unresolved but critical key to the negotiations was the need for Denver to annex fifty-three square miles of land from Adams County.

The area finally selected was so barren that the proposed airport seemed more than inconvenient—it was beyond comprehension. We began to educate the business community and neighborhood leaders, one-on-one and in groups, about the need to close Stapleton and build Denver International Airport way out on the prairie. Opponents joked that we were building the new airport in Kansas. We argued that Denver's growth would eventually make Stapleton unacceptably congested and that the city needed this new airport to propel it into the next century. The city's growth would eventually snarl traffic around Stapleton and bombard local communities with more airplane noise. In a few decades, Stapleton would face the same challenges that other inner-city airports around the nation were already confronting. The new airport, we said, would allow for expansion as the city's needs grew and give Denver the opportunity to convert the old airport into another extraordinary and beneficial purpose. Today, as the Denver Metro area continues to grow, most agree that our analysis back then was correct.

Slowly, some of the critics opened their minds and began to appreciate the opportunity. The annexation vote was set. To win public backing for the annexation election, I worked closely with the business community, especially the Metro Denver Chamber of Commerce. The Chamber raised millions of dollars to finance campaign advertisements in support of the annexation. It organized hundreds of volunteers to go door to door to drum up support for the election. Former Governor Roy Romer joined, lobbying hard on our behalf. In the end, Adams County voted 55 percent to 45 percent to approve the Denver annexation.

The fight over the airport marked an important change for me personally. I had come full circle from the days when I'd looked at institutions like Chambers of Commerce with skepticism. What a difference from my perspective and attitude in college—this had been no Mickey Mouse campaign. Although many in the Denver Chamber were not supporters during my first election, we became full partners in our crusade to advance a broader economic agenda. The memories of my Father and his fellow businessmen working closely with Brownsville's Mayor resonated with me as I considered this fortunate development.

It was time to build DIA.

1991, DIA construction.
Photo courtesy of the Peña Family Archives.

1990, Presentation of $500 million check for DIA from Federal Government.
Left to right are FAA Administrator James Busey, Governor Roy Romer, DOT
Secretary Samuel Skinner, and Peña. Photo courtesy of the Peña Family Archives.

After years of overcoming an unending set of hurdles, we finally broke ground on a glorious day in 1989. Secretary of Transportation Sam Skinner, who avidly supported the $500 million of federal support we needed to build DIA, flew in from Washington to attend. We drove past farm after farm and hundreds of cars parked alongside a small, dusty road leading up to the site of the shovel ceremony. A large crowd had come to witness history in the making. News helicopters hovered overhead and the national media was present to report on an extraordinary day for Denver and U.S. aviation. Along the way, my thoughts drifted to the numerous disputes I'd had to settle to get to this day.

Building the new airport was not simply another project I could delegate. It was up to me and my close advisors to assemble a sophisticated project management team to work with the incumbent team at Stapleton, including its long-time engineer, William Smith. I recruited a talented and strong-willed Aviation Director, George Doughty, who worked well with my highly-competent advisors, including Tom Gougeon, Bill Lamont, Steve Kaplan, Patricia Wells, Katherine Archuleta, Alan Charnes, Skip Spensely, and Jim Murray. Doughty's task was to plan and construct a new airport while continuing to operate the sixth-busiest airport in the country. I met with my team weekly and was intimately involved in every major aspect of planning, financing, acquiring land, and, finally, constructing what would be called the Denver International Airport. Some of my supporters wanted to name the airport Peña International Airport. Mayor Ben Stapleton's name had replaced the original Denver Municipal Airport and similar mayoral namings of airports were common practice around the country. But several members of City Council vehemently objected and held back their support for reasons never made clear. It was a distracting annoyance.

Nevertheless, we proceeded with the land acquisition, which proved treacherous. Scores of disputes over many parcels arose. We had to stand up to some landowners who attempted to gouge the city for excessive compensation. I had to contend with allegations from opponents that my family owned land near the new site and was personally benefitting. The notion that a family with 200 year old roots in Texas would happen to own the exact land where DIA was to be built was preposterous. The work was endless, and sometimes painful, especially when I visited Eastwood Estates.

Eastwood Estates was a bedroom development of about 500 homes, most built for retirement, not far from the new airport site. I knew the news that Eastwood residents would have to give up their homes would be devastating. Rather than send an airport spokesman, I drove out to meet with the residents personally. I arrived to a packed auditorium. Gazing at them, I was reminded of my own parents. Losing their homes and having to move would be traumatic, so we paid fair value and provided additional financial assistance and psychological counseling to those who requested it. I'll never forget their faces as I spoke to them at that meeting. Some were relieved that a decision was made and that the "limbo" status they had lived under for years, since before my election, was finally resolved. But many more shed tears as the shock took hold. How could they sell their homes? Where would they move? We offered many forms of support, but I wondered how my parents would have reacted had a young Mayor from a nearby city delivered them this message.

Working with labor unions proved less painful. Their members were anxious for the 10,000 jobs the airport would create. With the support of advisor Zeik Saidman and Manager of Public Work John Mrozek, we offered solid wages in an agreement that stipulated they would not strike or provoke any labor strife during construction. We negotiated new flight paths with surrounding cities, the Federal Aviation Administration, and the Pentagon. We had to ensure military operations at nearby Buckley Air Force Base would not be disrupted. Prior to our meeting with the Air Force to negotiate new flight paths around their military satellite tracking domes, a team of electronics experts scoured my office for listening devices to ensure the confidentiality of our discussions. But the next morning, a front-page story in the newspaper fully described the clandestine domes in detail. So much for secrecy.

I was outspoken in my resolve to use American talent to design and build the airport. We initially engaged a variety of design firms to develop the layout—a terminal with three modules—requiring a massive steel structure to handle the high prairie winds. However, one of the local architectural firms, Fentress and Bradburn, proposed switching to a tensile fabric roof structure. They unveiled the now internationally-famous roof design with white Teflon peaks made to represent the snow-capped Rocky Mountains.

While half the City Council embraced the design, the other half looked horror-struck. I immediately embraced the design's innovative reach toward the sky, joined the ranks of its supporters, and was thrust into defending it. The media lampooned and lambasted the design, referring to it as circus tents. Unaware that the material was tough enough to walk on, many suggested the roof would tear easily and disintegrate in the fierce winds that blew across the plains. As often happens, the critics blatantly disregarded the facts and unwittingly insulted the vision, courage, and audacity of our local architect. History proved them wrong, as the innovative design went on to win Fentress architectural contracts around the world. Years later, as Secretary of Transportation, I would support the firm's successful bid to design the impressive Inchon International Airport in Seoul, South Korea.

I thought all the debates had ended and that a historic milestone had been reached. Not only had we annexed the land in order to build one of the world's largest airports, successfully following the strictures of the Poundstone Amendment, but we'd also increased the land mass of our hemmed in city by 30 percent. But to my surprise and dismay, opponents of the new airport contrived a new argument: that Denver citizens also needed to vote for the airport, though such a vote was not legally necessary. So, I conducted dozens of meetings around the city to explain the benefits of a brand-new airport to Denver voters.

After a massive months-long campaign, on May 16, 1989, I celebrated a solid vote of approval from Denver citizens, who approved of the airport by a 63 percent to 37 percent margin. I had confidence that Denver citizens would support our novel proposal once they understood all the facts. Later that year, one of the country's most complicated Environmental Impact Statements was approved by the Federal Aviation Administration. In September, the same agency issued the Record of Decision and approved the final site selection and airport layout plan. Finally, the FAA announced the $500 million grant for DIA, which skeptics never believed would be forthcoming. Thanks to the hard work of Senator Tim Wirth, Senator Hank Brown, and

Congresswoman Pat Schroeder, together with tireless lobbying by business leaders from both political parties, the funds came through.

The challenges, however, were far from over. Ours was the first new hub airport to be built since the deregulation of the airline industry. We were testing a new theory, namely, that we could sell revenue bonds without the backing of airline leases to guarantee revenue. Some airlines had previously used their airport leases to block competition, sit on their capacity, and opportunistically trade lease rights and gates at a profit. Nevertheless, we worked with the airlines early on to gain their support, reaching an agreement in 1985, in which we guaranteed continuous improvements to Stapleton in exchange for their support. Deep down, however, the airlines never believed that we would complete the enormously complicated and controversial project of building DIA. Furthermore, the current Stapleton hub offered little room for new competitors, which suited the existing airlines well. Underlying their tepid support was the belief that Stapleton was theirs, and they behaved accordingly. So, after I was re-elected in 1987, they started to publicly question the need for a new airport.

The inevitable showdown occurred on July 10, just weeks after my re-election. United Airlines sent a letter asking for a "clean slate and a level playing field." Incredibly, they proposed a three-phased planning process—as if nothing had occurred the previous four years—and a new review of the "scope and timing" of a new airport. The airlines wanted to review the "present and potential capacity" of Stapleton and re-examine the "operating efficiencies and financial feasibility of various scenarios involving Stapleton and a new airport." Two years after reaching an agreement with Adams County, gaining the approval of Denver voters, and making improvements at Stapleton, the airlines wanted to start all over.

I was furious at their betrayal. The next day, as officials from United and Continental entered my office, I delivered my written response. The tension was palpable. I was prepared for war. I accused the airlines of publicly exaggerating the costs of the new airport and of falsely accusing my team of excluding the airlines from the planning process. I argued that their new proposal would postpone the airport until 1998 or later, assuming they would ever support one. I lowered the boom. I voided the agreement we reached in 1985 and notified them that their leases would immediately be on a month-to-month basis. All interim improvements at Stapleton were suspended and the new east/west runway they badly desired was cancelled. The cost of the new airport would be recovered through landing fees. We would raise revenue from landside sources like parking and concessions, and airside sources including fuel taxes. We would proceed "expeditiously with land acquisition and put in place the appropriate organizational structure to commence actual construction." All these steps, I stated, were necessary to protect the public interest.

I concluded with the following: "The city has spent a year negotiating the revised version of the New Airport Agreement. Now abruptly reversing themselves, the major airlines have refused to sign the agreement resulting from this good faith effort. The new airport is needed and this project must move forward. We will not allow this effort to be needlessly delayed or held hostage."

The room was silent. The airline representatives were stunned. Their strategy had not only failed; it had backfired. They underestimated my resolve and that of my team. And they finally understood that both Stapleton and the new airport belonged to the people of Denver. It was not theirs to play with. They were not going to bully us.

As they left the meeting, clearly upset, there must have been some on my team who worried we had killed the project. How could we possibly proceed without the airlines' full endorsements? How could we sell hundreds of millions of airport bonds in the public market without backing from the airlines?

As news of the showdown broke, community leaders became alarmed. Some called me questioning my tough stance, worried that we could not complete the new airport without airline support. Opponents found renewed strength when airline traffic at Stapleton began to fall as the recession took its toll and the first Gulf War restricted flying across the country. But our team moved forward aggressively.

Once we celebrated the historic ground breaking in November of 1989, the nation knew that Denver was on the move. Nevertheless, we continued to solicit input from the airlines and others as we planned and designed the massive facility. Finally, conceding that the new airport was going to be built, Continental Airlines signed a new lease. Out of respect, my advisors informed United, the dominant airline at Stapleton, that Continental was likely to sign with proposed "modifications" to the new airport design. United responded smugly that nothing we could do with Continental would affect United's competitive position. United remained uncommitted.

Soon thereafter, we announced that Continental had come to the table, signed leases, and been awarded gates at Concourse A, which were located closest to the terminal. United was outraged, but we had done our best to warn them.

The financial picture was improved when in May 1990 we oversold our first tranche of airport bonds, totaling more than $704 million. But when Continental declared bankruptcy, the FAA reduced its projections for traffic at the new airport, and the airport bonds were downgraded. Doubts emerged yet again about whether the new airport remained feasible. I responded by downsizing the airport somewhat, but I did not back down from the project. Then out of nowhere, a local investment firm, Boettcher & Co., issued an unsolicited report urging the city to mothball the airport for two years. I could not believe the attacks were continuing so late in the process, after construction had begun, and after all the milestones we had achieved over the last seven years. Although I was privately irate at Boettcher, I maintained a confident posture, stating: "Mothballing is not something in my vocabulary... Every six months there is going to be somebody who raises an issue and says this project shouldn't be built. I'm very confident that the day the airport opens, those same critics will be sitting around complaining about the color of the airport."

And I wasn't too far off. Even as some critics were finally won over, others continued to ridicule the roof design. United Airlines finally announced their support in June 1991, a few weeks before the end of my second term.

As I reflect on what we accomplished by building DIA, I could not be more proud of my team, the City Council, metropolitan officials, the voters of Denver and Adams County, and the civic leaders. We were able to bring together—maybe for the first time in Denver's history—business, labor, environmental, neighborhood, and minority leaders. Most importantly, thousands of citizens worked to make it a reality. Years later, critics and naysayers who fought the project with roadblock after roadblock have had to acknowledge the international acclaim and iconic status that Denver International Airport has achieved. I have long since felt satisfied that DIA remains one of the most beautiful, functional, and successful airports in the world. Supported by the Denver Art Program that I established in 1988, 1 percent of the airport's design and construction budget has been invested into art in building DIA. The Wall Street Journal recently rated DIA as the No. 1 airport in the country.

DIA has surpassed its financial, operational, and growth targets. This statement, though, excludes the failed electronic baggage system, which was recommended by United Airlines. Mayor Wellington Webb, who succeeded me, oversaw most of the complex construction, including the overnight closure of Stapleton and the simultaneous opening of DIA. He and his team overcame their own challenges. By the time of the airport's opening, I was U.S. Secretary of Transportation and was on hand to welcome its first passengers.

Economists estimate the annual economic impact to our region from DIA in 2019 alone was over $33 billion, providing 260,000 jobs. Redevelopment of Stapleton, the old airport site, has proved to be an overwhelming success—just as I had hoped. A local entrepreneur and philanthropist, Sam Gary, and his partner Ron Williams funded the Stapleton Reuse Study, which outlined the potential of the proposed redevelopment of the 7.5 acres of Stapleton land. The study led to the formation of a unique partnership with private developer Forrest City that expedited the conversion of the old airport into a nationally-recognized, mixed-use development named Central Park. Today, it consists of 9,400 homes, eighteen new schools, and four million square feet of office, industrial, and retail space. It is supported by $1.1 billion in infrastructure spending amid 1,200 acres of open space. About 32,000 people live there now, with new families moving in every month. It will continue to be built out for years to come. City officials estimate that by 2025, property and sales taxes for the Central Park area will rise to $100 million.

Denver's growth, since the construction of DIA, has triggered the need to expand concourses and runways, just as we had anticipated. New additions, like the Westin Denver International Hotel and the commuter rail between Union Station and DIA, were part of our original plans. I have been honored to participate in their openings. Current Mayor Michael Hancock, after negotiating another controversial development called Airport City and Denver's Aerotropolis, is taking the next steps in developing DIA. Ironically, another vote in Adams County was needed to reach an accommodation for the region. I trust that the leaders and planners who continue to make Denver a great city will ensure that the airport continues to serve as an important part of the city's—and its region's—overall success.

There are many lessons from the DIA success story that can be applied nationally. Bloomberg news recently described DIA as a major economic boon for Colorado and declared: "Denver Airport Is a Model for Biden's Infrastructure Plan", Bloomberg

News, April 29, 2021. Detailing the extraordinary economic impacts to our state, author Mathew Winkler urged Congress to invest more in our nation's infrastructure showcasing DIA's extraordinary success as a model. Our leaders must have the vision and the commitment to resolve large and vexing challenges like immigration, education, and infrastructure reform. While there will always be opponents, obstacles, and challenges, I believe most Americans can be brought together. We did this in Denver, recognizing a great need, and then harnessing the talents and energies of our citizens to accomplish a great deed. We deserve courageous leaders who act with persistence to reach new goals while including the American public in the effort.

Even today, I encounter thankful passengers and workers at DIA. Some admit they thought the notion of a new airport in the 1980s was so delusional that they "regrettably" voted against me in my bid for re-election. But I have also been thanked many times for never abandoning the dream. In turn, I am grateful to the thousands of citizens who made it a reality. I am often asked how I weathered the criticism and overcame unending obstacles while struggling to make DIA a reality. In addition to my great team, there might have been some influence from the courage of my ancestor Tomás Sánchez, who had confidently gazed east across the Rio Grande in 1755 to establish a new city. I too looked east and saw our future.

DIA Today. Photo courtesy of Denver International Airport.

16. Batter Up!

Great cities in American history have had great baseball. Since my Little League and Pony League days in Brownsville, I have always loved the game. I fondly recall looking for my parents in the stands every game I played. I grew up watching Mickey Mantle, Stan Musial, Lou Burdette, Yogi Berra, Warren Spahn, and all the baseball greats of the 1960s. Living in Brownsville we had to drive north to see a Triple A team to experience baseball in person. I enjoyed watching the minor league professional Denver Bears play at Mile High Stadium before becoming Mayor. Eating hot dogs and drinking beer at any game is fun. It's an American tradition. My friends wondered aloud why Denver did not have a major league team. Our beloved Bears were just not enough. For more than a few of us, imagining a great city without a major league team was inconceivable. It is no surprise, then, that soon after I was elected in 1983, my administration launched an eight-year effort to bring Major League Baseball to Denver.

In the 1960s, professional sports in The Mile High City were limited. The Denver Broncos were in the American Football

League, not the more established National Football League. The Nuggets were in the American Basketball Association instead of the superior National Basketball Association. And the Denver Bears baseball team was in the minor rather than the major league. The AFL and the NFL merged in 1966 and, ten years later, the ABA and the NBA merged, elevating the status of the Broncos and Nuggets. Baseball fans in Denver were left to dream about their Bears graduating to the big leagues.

Denver had a rich and colorful baseball tradition dating back to 1862, which culminated in the creation of the Denver Bears—later the Denver Zephyrs—in 1947. Denver served on and off as a farm team for the New York Yankees, Cincinnati Reds, Chicago White Sox, and the Montreal Expos. Billy Martin, Ralph Houk, Tim Raines, Andre Dawson, and Barry Larkin, to name a few, all managed teams or played ball in Denver. And Bob Howsam, famed architect of Cincinnati's Big Red Machine of the 1970s, was the first owner of both the Denver Bears and the Denver Broncos.

From the start, the Bears played at Bears Stadium, later renamed Mile High Stadium. For many years, the Bears and the Broncos shared the facility, which was originally built as a baseball park. Over time, expansions at the stadium were intended to entice Major League Baseball to Denver.

During the 1970s, city officials believed that Marvin Davis, an oil and real estate tycoon, would buy a team and bring it to Denver. Davis did make a number of attempts, but his inability to land a team left fans and the sports media alike to wonder what more could be done. I was among them, and I was not shy about saying so when I ran for Mayor. As a candidate, I committed to leading the effort to bring baseball to Denver, promising not to rely solely on the private sector. I intended to put the power of city government behind the cause so both Major League Baseball and potential owners would know we were serious about supporting a franchise.

Once elected, I invited civic leaders such as Steve Katich,

Dean Bonham, Steve Kaplan, John McHale, Dick Fleming, Roger Kinney, Deb Dowling, Elena Metro Newton, Don Hinchey, and others to come together to create the Denver Baseball Commission. I appointed Steve Katich as Executive Director, and the Commission's Board of Directors immediately developed a game plan.

AT&T initially funded the Commission with a three-year grant. Commissioners lobbied baseball owners and hosted MLB exhibition games, along with the U.S. and Japanese Olympic teams. They generated fan support throughout the Rocky Mountain region. The Commission did all it could to promote the idea, including hosting a two-day Denver Baseball Symposium in May 1984. We met with senior-level baseball executives from the Commissioner's Office and from individual team owners to make a business case for Major League Baseball in Denver. We flew to New York to press our case at the MLB headquarters. We worked with the offices of Commissioner Peter Ueberroth and Fay Vincent and with Bobby Brown and Bart Giamatti, the Presidents of the American and National Leagues. Back in Colorado, I huddled with the Governor, and in Washington I met with our congressional delegation, especially Senator Tim Wirth and Congresswoman Pat Schroeder. We went on to meet with prospective owners and investors. We argued our case to every stakeholder who might someday have a role in awarding a franchise to Denver.

A recurring concern was the perception that Denver was too small a market to support a major league team. To encourage the MLB to expand, Senator Wirth threatened to end its federal anti-trust immunity protection. Denver weighed in by sending Steve Katich to testify before the Senate Antitrust Committee. Colorado was applying a full-court press, a basketball tactic, in order to bring baseball to The Mile High City.

The process frustrated me. It was sluggish and had many blind alleys. Major League Baseball worked too slowly for a city on the move. After years of lobbying, league officials surpris-

ingly announced that Denver needed a "baseball only" stadium. Real estate businessman Neil Macey, an early supporter
of mine, worked with State Representative Kathi Williams and
devised a plan to inject new energy into our efforts. They proposed legislation to create a special taxing district comprised of
the six counties in the Denver area. With voter approval, a sales
tax would fund the construction of a new baseball stadium. The
tax would not go into effect, however, until Major League Baseball awarded Denver a franchise.

The state legislature enacted the legislation, which established a site location committee. I encouraged voters to approve
the sales tax increase, and after passage, served on the site committee.

I pushed for locating the baseball park in Lower Downtown
Denver, believing the new stadium would accelerate LoDo's
development and help transform the rest of downtown. My
financial advisor, Jim Polsfut, conducted the financial analysis
for accommodating a baseball franchise. The new park, known
today as Coors Field, proved to be a success in LoDo. Our strategy served as a model for communities across the country, who
have also built new ballparks in town instead of in the suburbs.

With the guarantee of financing for the new ballpark and
an emerging ownership group, we had done our part. It was
time for the MLB to step up to the plate. And they did. Governor Romer played a key role in assembling the final ownership
group. Denver was awarded an expansion team on July 5, 1991,
five days after I left office. The timing of the announcement was
a disappointment. It was bittersweet. But I was thrilled that
eight years of hard work had finally paid off. After some twists
and turns, a solid team of Colorado investors came to the plate.
We delivered the Colorado Rockies to Denver.

A packed house of 80,000 joyous fans filled Mile High Stadium for Opening Day on April 9, 1993. And what a beginning!
The Rockies' leadoff hitter, it's first-ever batter, Eric Young,
smashed a home run over left field—his only homer that year

until the last day of the season. It was exhilarating, except that my work in Washington prevented me from attending the historic game. I had to read about it and, as only a baseball fan can, got goosebumps.

I returned to Denver in 1998 and was finally able to use season tickets I had owned for several years. I enjoyed taking my young daughters and their friends to the games. As my son Ryan grew older, he developed a love of baseball. I watched him play in Denver's little leagues and later in high school. Thousands of other youngsters have benefitted from the vision that Denver-area citizens embraced in the 1980s. It has been rewarding to see the rise of Latino players in the big leagues. Almost 30 percent of MLB players are Hispanic, and many play under visas for "extraordinary" or "exceptional" ability. Every time I attend a game, I think of my Mom and Dad, who enjoyed watching all of their kids play ball. I still smile when I think about the doubts some had that Denver could maintain the attendance needed to sustain a team or that we could assemble an ownership group. The attendance record set by the Rockies in 1993 was nearly 4.5 million fans with an average of more than 55,000 per game.

2021, Coors Field. Photo courtesy of the Peña Family Archives.

Today, Denverites understand that bringing Major League Baseball to Denver was about more than securing another high-profile sports team for the city. Since its arrival, professional baseball has truly enhanced the confidence, spirit, vibrancy, and quality of life of our community and its families. Still today I know that when citizens unite to imagine a greater tomorrow for their children and grandchildren, any city can hit a home run.

17. Reflections on Mayoralty

While winning a Major League Baseball team as my mayoralty ended was a solid hit, the grand slam has been watching my mayoral team members become leaders in their own right. Many who worked with me in Washington have done the same. They have succeeded in business, elected office, philanthropy, and civic affairs. They took with them a commitment to excellence, a passion for public service, and a commitment to conduct themselves with honesty and integrity. They have been kind to say that the personal and professional growth they experienced in creating a great city influenced who they are today. I am proud to have helped cultivate a generation of leaders.

Thankfully, many of our achievements have been enhanced by subsequent administrations who built upon each other to create the Denver of today. Denver benefits from a remarkable continuity that extends from one mayoral administration to the next in a way that not many cities enjoy. The city has averted the demise of public-private partnerships that are too often severed after an election and a corresponding change of administration.

Denver's private sector partners have come to expect that their roles will continue through a change of Mayors, and Denver is fortunate to have leaders who have understood this.

The Denver Metro Chamber of Commerce has been a consistent partner through many city administrations. Similarly, large economic development projects involving significant input and agreements with neighborhood and civic organizations must continue their agreements from one administration to another. In my experience, political stability can breed success, trust, and confidence as a community moves into the future. We need that stability in our nation's capital today.

People were surprised when I announced that I would not seek a third term. We had made much progress in accomplishing our goals set eight years earlier, and most thought a third election would be my easiest. I did not choreograph my next steps in politics and didn't fall into the political mindset of those who compromise their values with sights on their next election. I did not worry about my political future as I made decisions, especially controversial ones, and I tried not to hold grudges. I simply relied on the values and principles I learned from my parents and tried my best.

Similarly, America must rely on the values and principles that have made our nation great for centuries: aiming high, working together in making tough decisions during difficult times, believing in ourselves, and never giving up. These values served us well as our Republic was founded and as we emerged from a devastating Civil War, survived the Great Depression, fought through major global conflicts, and suffered an attack on our homeland. Just as the people of Denver and I relied on these values and strengths in the 1980s, these same values will help us emerge as an even greater country during today's difficult times.

As we face the challenges of the COVID-19 pandemic, social and racial injustice, income inequality, global warming, and crumbling infrastructure, we Americans will persevere. We can do so much more. Let's "Imagine a Great Public School System" by making this a national goal and priority. We can harness the best technologies, provide resources to improve teacher salaries, and support students and parents with wrap-around services like medical, mental health counseling, and help for children with special needs. We can train principals to be great leaders and share best practices across the nation. We must do this because we are no longer producing the best minds in the world.

We can "Imagine an Energy Secure Country" and "Imagine A Great Nation with Great Infrastructure," which I detail later in this book. By coming together as Americans, as we did when Denver was challenged, we can accomplish great feats. Let us harness the talents, passion, and commitment from a new generation of Americans. We are witnessing the emergence of younger, activist citizens from every walk of life running for elective office, leading non-profit and other grassroots organizations, and moving America forward. As Mayor, I harnessed the energies of citizens from every walk of life, and they were more than willing to help create a great city. We can do the same at the national level.

I have learned that change requires action. Today millions of disillusioned Americans who doubt they can "change the system" must get off their couches and get involved. We have seen courageous young people in Florida secure gun legislation. We have witnessed millions protest police killings of Black Americans and begin the difficult process of bringing reforms to local police departments. We have marveled at those passionate about the survival of our planet lobby legislatures to adopt clean energy policies. Political systems can change for the better if we all take action. We are now taking action to halt the COVID-19 attack, rebuild broken families, educate students who have fallen behind, and restore businesses and stimulate our economy.

Let us decide what kind of future we want and then roll up

our sleeves and get to work. Not everyone will be in agreement or be supportive, but I believe most Americans can visualize a greater America and are willing to engage to build it. If we did it in Denver during a brutal recession, we can do it now as a nation.

My eight years as Mayor of Denver saw years of struggle. Those who enjoy our Great City today may not know of or understand the contributions that were made by so many. I believe they, in turn, have a responsibility to further improve our quality of life by tackling our newest challenges.

Washington can learn from Denver's work and begin with a long-term vision for our country. Our elected leaders must identify needed investments and dedicate themselves to the necessary bipartisan effort to make it happen. The pattern of changing course every four or eight years results in wasted time, energy, and resources and is not productive. The most glaring example of this schizophrenic and damaging pattern is President Trump's attempts to effectively erase the Obama Administration's work, from the Affordable Care Act (which most Americans support), to 54 mpg fuel economy standards (which most auto companies can implement), to the Paris Climate Accords (which millennials across the globe are embracing), to the protection of Dreamers. If we contrast these actions to China's laser-like focus on consistent strategies and its global infrastructure initiative (e.g., One Belt One Road), we can predict the outcome...and it is not a good one for America.

Finally, just as we in Denver built trust among our surrounding metropolitan cities, we in the United States should forge even stronger bonds with our neighbors to the north and south. A stronger North America means a stronger U.S.A. We can synchronize immigration policies, form energy and electric transmission treaties, agree on climate change strategies, and enhance the economies of all three nations for starters. We demonstrated that cooperating as a metropolitan region can lead to great outcomes for our region. We forged a new partnership with Adams County to build DIA and over the years formed several mutually beneficial metropolitan districts: Metro Sewage District; Regional Transportation District; Scientific & Cultural Facilities District; Metropolitan Football Stadium District; and Metropolitan Major League Stadium District. Why can't we form closer relations with our North American neighbors?

Although being Mayor was a demanding job, I had a personal life. I met Ellen Hart during the Mayor's Cup race. In 1988, we were married, and in 1990, we had our first child, Nelia, who was born at our city hospital. Nelia's birth was a celebrated event, as it had been decades since a baby was born to a sitting Denver Mayor. She became a common sight at mayoral events, and I loved the time I spent introducing her to the public. Shortly after I left office in 1992, our second daughter, Cristina, was born. Cristina was a joyful child with a bright smile whom everyone adored.

2021, Luminous Wind Sculpture dedicated to Federico Peña for his years of public service, located off Peña Blvd and Peña Station.
Photo courtesy of the Peña Family Archives.

In late 1991, I formed an asset management firm—Peña Investment Advisors—with a great team and wonderful investors. We managed assets for large companies. And if starting a small business while helping to raise two young children was not challenging enough, a series of unexpected and dramatic events awaited us. We were soon uprooted and moved suddenly to Washington, D.C. where our third child, Ryan, would be born at Georgetown Hospital.

18. Clinton Calls

I knew Alexis Herman from her work with Attorney Ron Brown, the chairman of the Democratic National Committee during the Clinton campaign. And I knew her Southern accent could charm a bobcat.

She was calling, she said in her soft and calming voice, on behalf of President-elect Bill Clinton, who wanted me to chair the presidential transition team on transportation. My experience with the new airport in Denver and work with our regional transportation system, she said, qualified me to lead the group. Since I had management experience and firsthand knowledge about transitions, the new President wanted me to come to Washington and lay the foundation for a seamless induction of the new Secretary of Transportation.

"It will only take a few days," Alexis demurred.

The invitation surprised me. I had met with Clinton and Gore during the 1982 presidential campaign, but I did not know them well, and I did not know that their campaign staffs knew much about me. My first reaction was that I was already consumed by my newly established asset management business and, besides, I would soon be flying to South Texas with my young family for Christmas. But, after thinking about it, spending a few days in December to help the Clinton presidency get started did not seem to be too much to ask.

"Okay, Alexis," I said, "but I want to make it clear that I do not want a job."

"So, I can tell the President-elect you will help?"

"Yes, but no job."

A few days later, I was in Washington looking for temporary housing, landing finally at a place with some friends in the city. I made my way to the transition office and to the room where the transportation work was to take place. It was empty. Not a chair, not a table, not even a paper clip could be found. I was standing there perplexed when a young man bounded in and happily greeted me.

"Hello, Mayor Peña, I'm Peter and I'm here to help. What can I do?"

Peter was a young man with endless energy who was assigned to work with me. "Looks like we have to start from scratch, Peter."

Slowly tables, chairs, computers, and office supplies appeared. The few days Alexis had quoted me became weeks. My calls home were placed very late at night, and I was still working with my asset management team. I assembled a group of more than sixty transportation experts from around the country. They were tasked with evaluating the mission, scope, budget, and structure of the Department of Transportation. Their report would serve as a blueprint for the next Secretary of Transportation.

As I was accustomed to working ten-hour days, seven days a week, I knew what was required to get the job done. Fortunately, members of my mayoral team, including Steve Kaplan, Katherine Archuleta, Ann Bormolini, and David Miller, flew in to assist me and we got to work.

We dissected the department's budget, poured over the

composition and configuration of its ten agencies, conducted innumerable interviews, consulted with transportation policy experts, and worked with Andrew Card, the Republican incumbent Transportation Secretary. Andrew was completely supportive and accommodating, without bitterness about his party's defeat. I could not have been more impressed and relieved. This transition work was difficult, serious, and quite comprehensive, a stark contrast to the Trump approach in 2016. Author Michael Lewis details in his book, *The Fifth Risk*, the incompetence and carelessness with which the Trump team handled the transition from President Obama's administration and describes many of the missteps of the Trump administration's entry into governance.

I met periodically with Warren Christopher and Governor Richard Riley, the two men Clinton had selected to co-lead his transition team. Christopher, an attorney from Los Angeles, had served as Deputy Secretary of State under President Carter and knew Washington. Riley was Governor of South Carolina. Scattered throughout these hectic days were briefings with Clinton and Gore. I didn't know who would be chosen to lead the Department of Transportation, but according to the press, Governor James Blanchard of Michigan and businessman William Daley of Chicago were the primary contenders. I thought either would be an excellent choice.

Finally, the transition work was done and our report was submitted to the President-elect on December 21, 1992. I said my goodbyes and headed to the airport. I flew to Albuquerque to meet my family before flying to Brownsville to spend Christmas with my parents. In the Albuquerque airport, I thought I heard a woman's voice paging me, but I dismissed it. Who would be calling me in Albuquerque? I heard my name a second time and found a white paging telephone.

It was Warren Christopher, whom Clinton had just tapped to be Secretary of State. He informed me that President-elect Clinton was impressed with our transportation report and that the various candidates being considered to lead the department "had not worked out." Then, incredibly, he said that Clinton wanted me to fly to Little Rock, Arkansas to be announced the following morning as his nominee for Secretary of Transportation. I was shocked. In something of a daze, I thanked him for his call and for the President-elect's trust in me, but explained I was not interested. I had just started my investment firm; I had made it clear to everyone that I did not want a position in the administration. I told him my flight was departing. He pressed me to consider the request and asked that I make a decision that evening.

With my world suddenly upside down, I boarded the plane with my family and was soon paralyzed by the realization that the plane was not equipped with a phone. I couldn't call anyone for advice. My emotions were everywhere, but I felt more nervous than excited. I was adjusting to private life, having been out of the Mayor's office for little more than a year. I wondered what my business associates would think, and was nervous about how our investors would react.

After what seemed like an eternity, we landed in Houston and ran to another terminal to make our connecting flight. Again, no phone! I was frantic. Up and back into the clouds we flew, until finally arriving at my childhood home in Brownsville late that afternoon. My parents were waiting, nervous and excited. News had leaked of my appointment while I was in the sky and reporters were calling my parents. It all happened so fast. And then—finally—sitting at the small breakfast table in the kitchen where I was raised, I called my partners, investors, and friends to ask for advice. I am, if anything, a good listener, but my ear actually became sore from holding the phone for so long. And my mind wandered—I genuinely did not want to accept the offer. The timing was not right. I was enjoying my private life and had other commitments. My old reservations about the federal government and D.C. institutions echoed in my head. Just how effective could anyone be in Washington?

I had relished my work as Mayor of Denver, and I loved that I could see firsthand the impact of our efforts. We were able to improve lives, help revitalize neighborhoods, support new businesses, and build streets and bridges—even an international airport. As Mayor, I enjoyed recognizing people for their hard work, seeing a child smile at a school, meeting a grateful senior citizen, hearing the thanks of the workers who were building the new convention center. I questioned whether one could have the same impact in Washington. I worried about the demanding schedule that undoubtedly would take me across the country and around the world—and away from my family. Through the next five hours I heard all there was to hear, mostly that I should be honored that the President-elect wanted me, that I could do a good job, that I had everyone's support, that the country needed me, and that I could not say no.

I called Little Rock around midnight. As I sat at our old breakfast table, a table that was intended to be a door but had been converted, I marveled at how my simple life in Brownsville had become a life thrust onto the national stage.

As I sat pondering my life, the Clinton operation contacted a family friend, Tony Sánchez, an oil and gas and banking entrepreneur in Laredo who owned a private plane. They arranged for him to pick me up in Brownsville at six in the morning and fly me to Little Rock. It was impossible to secure a timely flight out of the small Brownsville airport. I hand wrote my acceptance remarks during the flight, which I later gave to Tony Sánchez as a thank-you for the use of his plane.

Arriving at the Arkansas Governor's mansion, I could see that it was engulfed with staffers, media, and security officers scrambling about in a frenzy. Everyone looked exhausted but driven by the excitement of a new administration. Other cabinet nominees and their families arrived to be announced, and they too joined the melee.

President-elect Clinton introduced me in glowing terms, and in my remarks, I thanked him for the opportunity to serve the country. Then I made my way quickly back to the airport, back to Brownsville, and back to my family for Christmas.

Within a few weeks, we bought a house in Alexandria, Virginia. I reorganized my business, said goodbye to the scores of friends who had helped me through the years, and bid our home in Denver *adios.*

Instead of going west, young man—as the saying goes—I once again turned my sights east, and it did not escape me that others had propelled me once more into a public office I had not sought. I thought of my ancestors who had been called to serve, sometimes looking east, some to found a city, others to war, but always east in service to others.

Part Four: Washington, D.C. (1993–1996)

19. Technology Secretary

The Department of Transportation is generally considered a "second tier" level of the federal government—until people die in exploding trucks and airline crashes. I didn't expect that as Secretary of Transportation I would experience these catastrophes, along with earthquakes, Soviet MiGs, communists, kings, and the introduction of a little-known invention called GPS (Global Positioning System) into the mainstream of American life.

And no one warned me about the "murder boards"—the excruciating first step in the Senate confirmation process—which today's highly partisan politics have made even more painful. Murder boards are about a nominee's entire life. Attorneys raked over every aspect of my life for days on end prior to my hearing. I devoted almost two weeks to completing the required paperwork. I documented every fact and timeline of my life. The attorneys then went to work. They wanted answers to everything—and then some.

I answered questions about my parents, my family, my schooling, my days at the University of Texas, every job I'd ever had, and every organization I'd ever belonged to, my political relationships, my personal life and habits—everything—including, of course, my tax returns, investments, and business relationships. They cross-examined me as if I were on trial. And in a sense, I would be when I sat in front of the Senate committee that would determine my fitness for leading a multi-billion-dollar department and handling national security data.

These sessions were exhausting, and while they were pummeling me with questions, the FBI was in the field doing the same to my parents, friends, associates, critics, and neighbors— even strangers. Knowing the FBI would find nothing, I began to prepare for my confirmation hearing with the oversight of the White House, which went smoothly. In a matter of hours, the members of the Senate Transportation Committee recommended my confirmation, and I was voted in as the twelfth U.S. Secretary of Transportation. I was thrilled by the smooth process and excited to start my new challenge as Secretary of Transportation.

1993, President Clinton and Vice-President Gore after Federico's confirmation as Secretary of Transportation. Photo courtesy of Clinton Presidential Library.

Sadly, the President's critics claimed that his cabinet appointments focused more on "diversity" rather than ability. That criticism had been lodged even with my appointment. I was dismayed that the Beltway mentality was so narrowly focused that it could not accept that I was qualified to head a major department because I was Hispanic. Much of this anti-diversity sentiment, of course, resided in the minds of those with little knowledge of the contributions of Hispanics to our nation. Incredibly, Dr. Lauro Cavazos was the first Latino appointed to the U.S. Cabinet as Secretary of Education in 1988. Mayor Henry Cisneros and I were the next to be appointed by President Clinton, and thus few in Washington had little exposure to Latinos serving in the highest levels of government. It shocked the political establishment to see two Latinos serving simultaneously. Four years later, I would become the first Latino to head two federal departments.

Notwithstanding the criticism, I enjoyed recruiting individuals to the department who came from diverse communities and in fact had the requisite skills and talents. I had done the same in assembling my mayoral cabinet. It has taken decades of pressure for corporate and government entities to accept that diversity and inclusion are needed to be successful. The recent protests of Black Lives Matter, the disproportionate deaths of minorities from the coronavirus, and the discriminatory practices of many organizations compel governmental and corporate organizations to "include" us in major public policy and business decisions. Until we are fully embraced, our country will not fulfill its cultural, social, and economic potential. It is not enough to have us in key positions in government and business; we must be "at the table" when decisions are made. To succeed in business today you have to fully understand the diversity of the marketplace. And that cannot be done without all of us at the proverbial "table."

With my team coming into focus, my next challenge was managing an enormous department. As Mayor, I managed

Denver's $325 million budget and about 10,000 employees. The federal government was another world. The Department of Transportation in 1993 had 110,000 employees and a budget of approximately $35 billion—one hundred times the size of Denver's. Scattered throughout were the operations of the department itself, dozens of regional and international offices, the Federal Aviation Administration (FAA), the Federal Highway Administration (FHWA), the Coast Guard, and every office that monitored any mode of transportation. Despite the vastness of DOT, I was confident that I had the requisite organizational, leadership, and management skills to further the President's agenda. And it helped that I recruited Mort Downey, who previously served as Budget Director of DOT, as my Deputy. Mort's deep transportation experience in New York was invaluable.

Despite my comfort in operating in the D.C. environment, there were times I felt out of place. At my first Presidential White House dinner, I hosted a table with dignitaries from across the country. As I sat at the most formal dinner in my lifetime, with countless pieces of china, crystal, and silver, and delightful military violinists performing, I nearly picked up the finger bowl thinking it was a soup. There were no finger bowls in Brownsville! Thankfully, I noticed another guest dip his fingers in his bowl before reaching for his dinner salad. I was a long way from South Texas.

One thing I learned quickly was that contrary to conventional wisdom, the vast majority of DOT employees worked hard, and the responsibilities they bore were vast. They tackled enormous domestic and international challenges while abiding by a presidential mandate to help eliminate the national deficit inherited from the Bush administration. That meant reducing the size of the department. In under four years, we worked collegially to reduce the departmental workforce by nearly 10 percent, to 99,000 employees—all while continuing to lead the nation and the world in transportation initiatives. I was blessed to work side by side with so many talented and committed indi-

188 | Federico Peña

viduals; many have remained my friends over the years.

President Trump, on the contrary, belittled the dedicated federal employees who love their country. He imagined a "deep state" and lashed out at "leakers." Had he understood and appreciated the talent and commitment of his extraordinary federal workforce, he could have harnessed their skill and energy to move his agenda forward. No leader can lead by undermining his or her team.

I was amazed to learn that our country spent more than $1 trillion a year on transportation services, nearly 17 percent of our gross domestic product. I calculated that a 1 percent gain in efficiency would save the American economy $100 billion over a decade. This was an even better way to help eliminate the deficit. But how to do it?

Most of our work was traditional: funding highways and monitoring their construction, assisting in the development of transit systems, and financing airport projects. In addition, safety in the transportation sector took on a greater priority as we soon experienced tragic airline crashes, Amtrack accidents, rail derailments and truck driving tragedies. Soon we were instituting controversial drug and alcohol testing programs for transportation workers and instituting Positive Train Control and collision avoidance safeguards for railcars. The unusual spate of airline crashes compelled us to host a two-day safety session with airline CEOs, pilots, and mechanics to reenforce their focus on airline safety. The National Highway Safety Administration would push additional safety requirements for the auto industry.

But early on, I knew that I wanted to be known as the "Technology Secretary." I believed that our transportation systems offered the single best arena for harnessing technological advances to respond to the real human needs for safety, convenience, and a cleaner environment.

In my view, transportation technologies in the 1990s had the potential to create new industries to employ American workers, offer good wages, and produce products for both home markets and for export. In addition to providing economic growth, these new technologies could help us overcome the many issues related to traffic congestion and air pollution. Our problems could not be solved with traditional approaches like adding more highway lanes or runways at airports, especially with air quality threatened by our ever-increasing volume of travel.

I wanted the department to be a catalyst to launch innovative, job-creating companies and stimulate economic progress. A crucial role of the department was to set worldwide standards for the development and use of new technologies. This would enable America's intelligent transportation industries to grow at home and secure world leadership.

Speaking on October 7, 1994, at the Transfuture Technology Fair in Washington, I cast a vision for what new transportation technologies could mean to our daily lives. Imagine, I said, a society with information systems that would connect all forms of transportation to the information superhighway that Vice President Gore spoke about so frequently. In this seamless web of information and transportation, a suburban commuter could wake up in the morning, flip on a computer or television, and get real-time reports on the fastest route to work, taking into account real-time road and traffic conditions, weather, and the status of local trains and buses. Many of these advances describe the world we live in today.

If commuters decided to drive their lightweight, near-zero emission cars with onboard navigation, they could manage their commute more efficiently. If their vehicle was involved in an accident—an increasingly unlikely scenario, given new collision avoidance systems and built-in radars—the vehicle itself would immediately and automatically send a call for help, inform emergency services of its exact location, even report the severity of the crash—all using onboard transponders and sensors. These systems, I said over twenty-five years ago, would save billions of hours of time and thousands of lives every year. And for business travelers, these technologies would allow an executive going from Washington to New York to use a single plastic card to ride the metro to the airport, fly to New York, rent a car, drive into town, buy gas, pay for parking, and make an automated-teller transaction. Meanwhile, travelers on Amtrak's high-speed rail to New York could rest assured that intelligent management systems were in place to dramatically reduce the chance of accidents.

In that 1994 speech, I predicted that intelligent transportation systems would bring remarkable changes to commercial vehicle travel and freight shipment. The Manager of a motor carrier or freight company would be able to give thousands of shippers real-time information on the location of their cargo, how it was stored, and when it would get to its destination. These new systems would create advanced just-in-time delivery systems, saving businesses billions of dollars in shipping, inventory, warehousing, and fuel costs, making the economy more productive and competitive. And of course, the ultimate winner would be the consumer.

Transit systems, I added, would be transformed by intelligent transportation technologies, giving commuters greater comfort, safety, and convenience. Interactive kiosks at stations and bus stops would give passengers directions and provide increased security. Buses would be made of lightweight, high-strength composites, powered by fuel cells, natural gas, hydrogen or electric batteries, and equipped to sense and avoid collisions. These buses would emit no fumes and would place much less stress on roads and bridges.

I predicted that, as telecommuting became more common, getting to work for many would no longer mean a ride or a drive, but simply a walk from their bedroom to a virtual office in their home with faxes, modems, and televised conferences with colleagues.

Most importantly, I declared that I would use the department's purchasing power to foster innovative technologies and push for the deployment of high-strength, long-lasting materials for infrastructure construction and repair while encouraging the state agencies we funded to use them as well. All of these technologies could be integrated into an intermodal national transportation system to connect America.

As I look back on my speech in 1994, it is remarkable how much of the technology I referenced we now enjoy. My predictions must have been mystifying. The Department of Transportation was sending a message to American entrepreneurs that their government was ready to facilitate investments in innovative systems to move the nation forward. To accelerate progress, I negotiated with Secretary of Defense Les Aspin to allow the military GPS system to become more available for civilian use. Ultimately, this greatly expanded transportation technologies throughout the country, which we now take for granted.

Today, we see the fruits of that vision from decades ago. It is time for our national leaders to once again partner with entrepreneurs to imagine and create the next generation of transportation technologies. Unfortunately, investment policies change from one administration to another. The 2020 budget proposed by President Trump dramatically cut government investment in new technology. The result will be domination by China or other nations in artificial intelligence, high-speed rail, and more. We learned in Denver that consistent investments over consecutive administrations produced great results—but there must be constancy of purpose and long-term vision. Washington leaders seem unable to adopt such a simple investment philosophy.

In addition to Intelligent Transportation and Global Positioning Systems advancements, we fashioned the Partnership for New Generation Vehicles (PNGV), linking the big three automakers of Detroit with smaller technology firms to develop an emission-free commercial vehicle, three times more fuel efficient than cars of the 1990s. I joined Vice President Gore in meetings with the CEOs of Detroit's Big Three to urge them to invest $1 billion that would be matched by federal laboratories and research institutes.

To reach these goals, I strongly supported experimenting with lightweight materials—like those used on the stealth bomber—so American engineers in Detroit could design new buses and transit vehicles. We experimented with more efficient engines, fuels, and other vehicle technologies. We funded research into sensors that, embedded in roadways, would one day guide driverless vehicles—an idea becoming a reality today.

With the leadership of Vice President Gore and Jack Gibbons, the President's science advisor, progress on this front has been accelerating since the turn of this century, founded on the steps we took at DOT in the early 1990s.

Had Gore won the U.S. presidential election in 2000, the progress in these areas would have been even more remarkable. Instead, many of our transportation partnerships ended, and foreign manufacturers have since outpaced American manufacturers in the development of high-efficiency engines, electric vehicles, and hybrid technology. Still, many of our 1990s' successes survived and will help ensure the U.S. remains a world leader.

As globalization gained momentum, requiring more international travel to new markets, U.S. aviation policy became increasingly more important to the rest of the world, given the dominance of American carriers in the industry. My interest in international relations and treaty negotiations—inspired many years before by my Father's international business experiences—grew as I traveled the world as Mayor. I understood that global trade and international travel were intensifying and that aviation policy needed reform to accommodate this new trend. My experience building the new airport in Denver, with its corresponding demands to learn the rules, regulations, and nuances of international air access, also intensified my interest in liberalizing international commerce.

As the new Transportation Secretary, I learned that the Carter Administration was the last to review the country's international aviation policy. The approach we fashioned in international aviation agreements during my time in the DOT became known as "Open Skies." These treaties liberalized regulations, minimized government intervention, and created a free-market environment for the airline industry.

Canada had the greatest need for reform. The existing U.S.-Canadian aviation agreement weighed down the largest bilateral aviation relationship in the world with the force of an albatross. The old agreement limited the number of flights. The flights it allowed imposed inefficient and contorted routes. President Clinton's own Mother became part of the saga, as the media reported the travails she experienced making her way to Canada from Arkansas.

For years, U.S. and Canadian transportation officials tried, unsuccessfully, to rewrite the old, restrictive arrangement. On the advice of our new ambassador to Canada, James Blanchard—one of the original people mentioned to lead the DOT—I suggested that we appoint new negotiators with Canada and start over.

I recognized that prior negotiations had fallen victim to "negotiator fatigue." I applied a simple lesson I had learned early in my mayoral years: when negotiations stall, it may be time to bring new individuals with fresh perspectives. I appointed General Counsel Steve Kaplan to partner with Canadian Jeffrey Elliot. By breaking through old thinking, they hammered out a new agreement within months that allowed air carriers from both countries to establish direct flights between any pair of cities on either side of the border. My experience with foreign business leaders helped. I related easily to my Canadian counterpart, Minister Doug Young. With a shared goal of reaching an agreement, we negotiated the final details directly.

By the time President Clinton made his first official state visit to Canada in February 1995, the U.S.-Canada Open Skies Agreement was ready to be signed. It was the centerpiece of the trip, and I was proud to receive from President Clinton one of the pens used in the signing of the historic document.

Within three years, passenger traffic between the U.S. and Canada increased a remarkable 37 percent, far in excess of the meager 4.3 percent growth recorded during the final three years of President Bush's second term.

February 1995, Canadian Minister Douglas Young and Secretary Federico Peña sign new Aviation Treaty while Prime Minister Jean Chrétien and President Clinton witness signing.
Photo courtesy Clinton Presidential Library.

The new U.S.-Canada aviation agreement revitalized our country's relationship with Canada and added to the economies of both countries. Today, fourteen million travelers each year fly across our northern border for work or excursions or to visit family. One key lesson I learned in resolving the long-standing impasse with our Canadian neighbor was that personal relationships are essential to reaching new understandings. I developed that rapport with Transportation Minister Doug Young, which facilitated honest but straightforward exchanges of the political, economic, and trade priorities between our two countries and our respective airlines. By negotiating with mutual respect and appreciation of our respective constraints and flexibilities, we were able to produce a win-win for our economies and our competitive airline industries. Sadly, President Trump chose to address Canadian trade issues not by applying diplomatic and creative approaches, but by public bashing and bravado that left little room for thoughtful and meaningful dialogue.

Although I was delighted by our new aviation accord and impressed by the hard work and dedication of our team, the DOT would soon be tested by a sensational safety dispute with General Motors and by the worst earthquake in the history of Los Angeles.

20. Exploding Trucks and the Northridge Earthquake...Improving Our Safety and Infrastructure

On October 1, 1994, I made an initial determination that GM's C-K pickup trucks made between 1973 and 1987 were unsafe. I announced that the Department of Transportation would conduct a public hearing in December to determine if they should be recalled. GM designed these vehicles with two twenty-gallon gas tanks mounted outside the safety frame. The increased fuel capacity was useful in marketing the trucks, but the location of the tanks exposed them to direct impact during collisions. Crash investigations showed that the tanks were exploding and spewing fuel on passengers, causing serious burns and even deaths. According to federal law, DOT was required to conduct a hearing before proceeding with a forced recall.

Under normal circumstances, the National Highway Safety Administration (NHTSA), an entity within the Department of Transportation, would have conducted the investigation and made the determination. Created in 1970 under the Highway Safety Act, NHTSA was established to achieve the highest standards of excellence in motor vehicle and highway safety to protect the traveling public. I appointed an emergency room physician, Dr. Ricardo Martinez, to head NHTSA. However, because of his prior private sector work reviewing several associated truck crashes, he recused himself. As a result, the NHTSA staff came directly to me for final decisions.

This safety controversy began when both the Center for Auto Safety and the nonprofit advocacy group Public Citizen filed a recall petition against these GM trucks during the Bush Administration. On December 8, 1992, the agency announced it would officially investigate the crashes. I took office in early 1993, and on April 9 of that year, NHTSA called on GM to voluntarily recall more than six million C-K pickups with side-saddle fuel tanks. GM refused, declaring that the trucks met all applicable federal vehicle safety standards. After additional investigation by NHTSA, I asked for their best data and evidence supporting a case both for and against a recall. The staff was split and presented the two options, along with their reasoning behind each.

1994, Secretary Peña supporting seat belt use with DOT Crash Test Dummies.
Daughters Nelia (Bottom Left) and Cristina (Bottom Right).
Photo courtesy of the Peña Family Archives.

After careful review of the reports, I determined that the GM pickups had a safety defect and called for a public hearing. I noted that the side-saddle fuel tank design was originally selected for marketing reasons and had not changed in fourteen years. We had evidence that GM was aware—possibly as early as the mid-1970s—that C-K pickups were more vulnerable to fires when involved in side-impact crashes.

GM and its supporters were ferocious, and their personal attacks on me and on the DOT were unprecedented. A congressman from Michigan called on the DOT's inspector general to investigate my decision. In November, GM sued me, arguing that because the pickups had met the safety standards in place in the early 1970s, when the trucks were introduced, I was engaging in retroactive rule-making. GM hired the powerful law firm of Kirkland & Ellis, and its lobbyists went to work on the White House, members of Congress, and the Justice Department. All three major automakers—GM, Ford, and Chrysler—wrote directly to President Clinton, asking him to intervene to "address the intolerable state of regulatory uncertainty that will otherwise result from Secretary Peña's decision." They argued that my decision "would have an adverse financial impact on each of the companies."

General Motors knew that the NHTSA staff was struggling with voluminous amounts of data and tactically besieged the agency with even more. The strategy of overwhelming the team was effective in convincing NHTSA, based on the new statistical analyses, that I could not justify my decision in a court of law.

Although our attorneys were examining the case, the Justice Department had ultimate authority in deciding whether to sue GM to force a recall. They were not willing to chance a legal battle of that magnitude, especially with uncertain data from NHTSA staff. So, after much political pressure and legal uncertainty, the Justice Department and DOT lawyers settled the dispute by requiring GM to pay $51 million for safety research, including $8 million for child safety seats for low-income families, $11 million for public education about drunk driving and seat belt use, $10 million for a fire safety lab, and $5 million for burn and trauma research.

At times I wondered if I should have resigned over the vicious and poisonous political environment this case created. However, I firmly believe that when government is entrusted with public safety, even in the face of difficult legal and political environments, it should err on the side of the public.

Today, astute corporations, when confronted with a potentially damaging crisis, take action to protect consumers because it is the right thing to do and because customer loyalty is paramount. GM's new management team appears to have done this in its more recent ignition safety recall. Contrary to some who clamor for shrinking the size of the federal government, NHTSA is an agency that needs more firepower to continue to foster traffic safety. I believe that Congress should fully fund NHTSA because consumers expect an independent and objective entity to monitor the safety of products that can endanger lives when not built properly. With increased production of electric vehicles and trucks, NHTSA must have the resources to ensure their safety, particularly with further innovations in battery technology. In addition, the Department of Transportation's attorneys, not the Justice Department, should decide whether legal actions should be taken against manufacturers of defective vehicles, as they have the expertise in this arena.

There were, however, other times when government responded magnificently to dangers confronting the public. On January 17, 1994, I was representing President Clinton at a Dr. Martin Luther King, Jr. celebration in Birmingham, Alabama. I received an emergency call advising that the faults under Los Angeles had given way at 4:30 that morning. The Northridge earthquake set off seismic waves that rolled and rocked the ground. The impact of the 6.7 quake was still being assessed when I learned that large and critical parts of Interstate 10, Interstate 210, and various interchanges in and around the city had collapsed. The damage was extensive, especially in Northridge, located in the San Fernando Valley, and air and rail service to L.A. had been affected.

I completed my remarks to the gathering in Birmingham, apologized for my need to depart, and flew to California. I arrived four hours later and helped lead the federal interdepartmental team that addressed the disaster, which spread across 2,000 square miles.

Critical infrastructure was destroyed, and thousands of homes, hospitals, schools, and businesses were damaged—some beyond repair. My mayoral experience with tornadoes, snowstorms, and major fires prepared me for some disasters, but the damage inflicted by this earthquake was at a very different level.

The transportation disruption and economic loss from the Northridge earthquake required an innovative approach to accelerate the reconstruction of the area's downed and damaged freeways. Doing business the old way would cause a year and a half of delays to make repairs. That timeframe was unacceptable for a city the size of Los Angeles. Mayor Richard Reardon worked closely with us on a new approach to address the devastation. Together we devised a brilliant solution: pay contractors a bonus for completing their projects ahead of their expected completion dates. These incentives were expensive, but they spurred record-time reconstruction of the freeways and overpasses flattened by the quake. The financial savings to the regional economy far surpassed the additional expense for incentivizing the contractors' accelerated work.

A few months later, when the first of the rebuilt highways was scheduled to re-open, Vice President Al Gore and I were in Los Angeles to celebrate the occasion. To my dismay, California's leaders indicated that Gore was not welcome as they did not want to give credit to the Federal Government's role. I was dumbfounded. He was the Vice President of the United States! In retrospect, I saw this insult as an indication of the highly personal politics that were beginning to take hold in our country.

Only I, as Secretary of Transportation, was grudgingly allowed to attend.

The sour note left by the attitude of state officials dissipated later that evening to some degree when hundreds of vehicles lined up, revving their engines in anticipation of driving on the rebuilt freeways. As they passed us, honking in delight, the drivers waved at the camera crews recording the joyous moment. We reopened the freeways in record time, just eight months after the tragedy. Most of the remaining projects were finished weeks earlier than expected.

The Northridge earthquake brought out the best in most of us, a spirit I tried to embody in daily interactions with citizens across the country. The Clinton Administration's response was comprehensive and immediate when disaster struck. Many administrations lose public support when they fail to effectively respond to emergencies. President George W. Bush mishandled Katrina, and Trump did the same with Hurricane Maria when it devastated Puerto Rico, and more recently the coronavirus pandemic. The American people expect that the federal government will adroitly respond to emergencies, fulfilling this fundamental responsibility. President Clinton understood this and in the 1990s created a professional team in FEMA to successfully coordinate federal departments and agencies during every emergency.

In rebuilding Los Angeles, I saw firsthand the need to invest in our nation's infrastructure. During the 1990s, the nation's massive infrastructure was being repaired, maintained, and built anew, and thousands were put to work at good-paying jobs. Our economy, in the midst of recession, was being stimulated.

Unfortunately, the politics of Washington have ground progress to a halt, and Congress has been slow to meaningfully invest in new transportation infrastructure critical to the expansion of our economy. Ports need to be expanded, as global trade will continue to grow. Airports need to be improved, as aviation traffic is increasing each day. Meanwhile, our highways are deteriorating—65 percent of them are rated as "poor"—while the number of vehicles on our roads keeps growing. High-speed trains remain on the drawing board, while other countries zoom past us into the future. New technology needs to be incorporated into infrastructure to generate additional transportation efficiencies. Across the country, more than 100,000 bridges needed to be replaced years ago. Backlogged transit projects are estimated to total $86 billion. According to the Texas A&M Transportation Institute, traffic congestion costs consumers $121 billion annually, or about $800 per vehicle each year. Commercial truck drivers alone waste time and diesel fuel to the tune of $27 billion annually.

In spite of these urgent needs, Congress wasted seven years (2008–2015) by passing short-term measures (twenty-seven bills in all) to maintain the status quo. In the meantime, a number of states have been forced to institute new tolls, and many courageously increased state gasoline taxes or turned to some form of privatization for financing new construction.

Congress finally enacted a new transportation measure in 2015, ironically called the FAST ACT, which provided $300 billion over five years. In typical "smoke and mirrors" fashion, FAST ACT was financed with a hodgepodge of funding sources: selling oil from the Strategic Petroleum Reserve; using surplus funds from the Federal Reserve; and borrowing billions from the General Fund. But the federal gas tax, the long-established source of the Highway Users Trust Fund, was not increased. Congress kicked the proverbial can down the road so that in 2021 alone, there will be an additional $113 billion shortfall. Perhaps this short-sighted congressional action is another reason so many Americans have lost confidence in Washington D.C.

We can do better. America can rise to face this challenge. What is needed today is for our leaders to demonstrate what President Kennedy called "profiles in courage." We have seen that courage before when Lincoln led the transcontinental rail lines, when Teddy Roosevelt built the Panama Canal, and when

Eisenhower enacted the Interstate Highway System.

As Secretary of Transportation, with the leadership of Highway Administrator Rodney Slater, and with bipartisan support from Congress, we enacted the six-year Transportation and Equity Act for the 21st Century (TEA-21). The bill provided $218 billion—a 40 percent increase over the previous six years—for major construction projects. This bill did more than provide funding. It encouraged state and local authorities to plan and invest in America's roads, bridges, transit, and airport systems to benefit the traveling public. And we had the courage to increase the federal gas tax. It has not been increased in almost twenty-five years!

President Trump wanted to invest $2 trillion in infrastructure projects. While I was in agreement, he never offered legislation, and nothing was accomplished during four years of promises.

As my Father taught me years ago, it is not enough to complain about a problem; I should offer a solution. We can begin by increasing the taxes on federal gas and diesel. Though controversial, they have not been increased since 1993. Had they been indexed to the consumer price index, the current 18.4 cent per gallon tax would now be thirty cents, and the current diesel tax of 24.4 cents per gallon would be about forty cents. We can also institute a new vehicle per-mile tax, which would vary according to the weight and type of vehicle and/or the damage to roadways. The use of tax-exempt bonds, private activity bonds, or tax credit bonds to raise revenue at the state and local level can be expanded. We know how to implement these initiatives.

Private sector dollars can be raised by partnering with private equity infrastructure funds that hold billions of dollars for public sector investment. We know that expanding the 1988 TIFIA loan program, to provide low interest loans to local governments, will leverage more investment. And we can create a federal infrastructure bank for additional investments.

What is most needed, however, is new leadership in Congress. Leadership occurs when congressmen/women get out of Washington and travel the nation to inform the American people of our infrastructure needs and financing solutions. Congress must work to build political support for these critical investments. This is precisely what we did in Denver when we asked citizens to support new infrastructure investments by increasing their property taxes. They voted "yes" in the midst of a brutal recession when their home values had diminished. We did not propose "smoke and mirror" solutions as Congress has when it borrowed from the Federal Reserve's surplus or sold oil from the Strategic Petroleum Reserve, which they did in funding the 2015 infrastructure bill. In educating Denver citizens about our infrastructure plans, we explained what the increase in property tax would be, exactly how the funds would be used, and why postponing these investments would cost taxpayers more down the road. I understood that people are smart and will make the right decisions when they are told the truth and given the facts.

The measures I list above, together with ideas from others, can transform America into a powerhouse once again and ensure her vitality for future generations. President Biden's bold infrastructure plan is urging Americans to think big. The longer we wait, the more it will cost. It's time to rebuild America. It is up to Congress to think boldly and to take action.

21. MiGs in the Air

Early on Saturday, March 4, 1996, I found myself in the secure communications room of the United States Coast Guard, an extraordinary organization that, at the time, was under my jurisdiction. Along with Nancy McFadden, my new General Counsel at the Department of Transportation, and some of the Guard's commanders, I was listening to radio traffic from off the coast of Florida. The crackling voices were coming from American Coast Guard and naval vessels that were prepositioned several miles southwest of Miami. The President's Chief of Staff, Leon Panetta, and Defense Secretary William Perry were at their desks also monitoring the situation. One week earlier, Fidel Castro's Cuban Air Force had shot down two U.S. civilian planes departing from Florida. Four Cuban Americans were killed in the strike. We were now monitoring a flotilla of boats piloted by Cuban Americans on their way to the site where the planes were downed. They intended to commemorate the deaths of their fellow Americans.

While I sympathized with them, I was worried. What if the flotilla provoked another confrontation with Cuba? What would happen if Coast Guard and naval vessels were caught in the middle? Would we counter-attack and start another international crisis? Could we lose lives in a military confrontation? I thought back to 1962, when Fidel Castro allowed the Soviets to plant missiles in Cuba, bringing the world to the brink of nuclear catastrophe. I wondered why my initial DOT briefings did not included a warning that I could be drawn into volatile international situations like this one. As I contemplated these questions while listening to the radio, I heard a guardsman yell, "MiGs in the air! Two MiGs in the air!" My heart rate soared. I had addressed disasters and threats of varying types before but never Cuban MiGs! I was thankful I was in a room of experienced military officers because I needed their guidance.

It seemed unreal. Only eight days before, Cuban Americans flying three civilian Cessnas had departed from Opa-Locka Airport in Miami to search for Cuban migrants on the seas who might be struggling in homemade rafts. The downed pilots were part of *Hermanos al Rescate.* "Brothers to the Rescue" was an organization of Cuban Americans who were all too familiar to Castro's spies in the United States. Some *Hermanos* had escaped the communist takeover of Cuba in 1959, and others were dedicated to the eventual overthrow of the regime.

A week earlier, the *Hermanos* had filed their required flight plan with the Federal Aviation Administration. They had planned to leave U.S. territorial waters and fly south of the 24th parallel into international airspace—still north of Cuba's twelve-mile zone. The area the *Hermanos* were targeting was legally accessible to commercial and civilian boats and aircraft.

While the three Cessnas were north of the 24th parallel, the Cuban Air Force scrambled a MiG-29 and a MiG-23. The Cubans trained their sights on the smaller planes and opened fire, shooting down two of the Cessnas and killing four Americans. *Hermanos* leader José Basulto, who was piloting the third plane, escaped and returned safely to Miami.

The attack caused uproar around the world. The Cuban

government—no doubt with Castro himself aware—had violated international aviation accords that specify how perceived threats from the air were to be handled.

When a government believes an aircraft is intruding its airspace, it is required to communicate with specific steps before attempting a forced landing. The Cuban MiGs did not take any of the required steps and methodically shot down the civilian aircraft without warning.

Circa 1996, Secretary Peña (Left) and Secretary of Defense William Perry
being briefed on the Coast Guard operations.
Photo courtesy of the Peña Family Archives.

President Clinton condemned the attacks and initiated unilateral, punitive actions against Cuba. He announced tighter restrictions on the movement of Cuban officials into the U.S. and suspended all commercial charter flights between Cuba and the United States. He called for the United Nations to sanction the communist dictatorship as well.

Within weeks, Congress passed legislation sponsored by Senator Jesse Helms of North Carolina and Representative Dan Burton of Indiana that allowed Americans to sue foreign investors who trafficked in American properties seized by the Castro government. Congress strengthened the U.S. embargo against Cuba. Secretary of State Warren Christopher asked for an emergency meeting of the U.N. Security Council, which condemned the attack the next day. The U.N. Security Council directed its International Civil Aviation Organization (ICAO) to investigate the downing of the planes. The European Union also condemned the attack.

Two weeks later, I represented the United States at the ICAO proceedings in Montreal, Canada. I met the families and relatives of the Americans who had been killed. On March 6, 1996, I became a lawyer again, formally presenting the U.S. complaint to the thirty-three members of the Executive Council of the ICAO. I did not hold back. I described the assault on the innocent Americans over international waters as "murder in the skies."

I presented radar and other data to demonstrate that the Americans' civilian aircraft had been in international airspace. I introduced recordings of the Cuban pilots who, immediately after firing on the planes, exclaimed in Spanish, using vulgarities, "We blew his balls off!" The transmissions made evident that they had done nothing to warn the civilian aircraft.

The Cuban government disputed our evidence with its own data. Rejecting their arguments, the ICAO adopted a preliminary resolution deploring the shoot-down and directing the Secretary General of ICAO to initiate a more comprehensive investigation of the incident and report on its final conclusions.

I did not feel that the ICAO's findings were strong enough. I left Montreal frustrated by the predilection of the ICAO to accommodate the various perspectives of non-democratic countries and to use softer language than the incident required.

Four months passed before the ICAO issued its final report denouncing Cuba and demanding that the Cuban government compensate the victim's families. In July, the U.N. Security Council condemned Cuba's actions. The U.S. Ambassador to the

U.N., Madeline Albright, presented the evidence I introduced to the ICAO. She helped secure the final condemnation of Cuba by most members of the international community, with Russia and China abstaining.

But on that Saturday morning when I was monitoring the Americans determined to lay wreaths at the crash site, nature intervened. The Americans encountered dangerously high seas and were forced to return to Miami. The Cuban MiGs retreated.

This painful episode highlights our ongoing need to update immigration laws. Each year, thousands are lost attempting to reach our shores and borders as they flee dangerous conditions in their homelands. We need to update our immigration laws so that future administrations, like President Trump's administration did, do not cage asylum seekers at the border, separating their children, while ignoring our well-established asylum laws.

During five short weeks between August and September in 1994, the Coast Guard rescued 29,000 migrants, mostly Haitians, in the Straits of Florida. It was called Operation Able Vigil and was the largest Coast Guard-led naval operation since WWI.

I flew over the Caribbean with the Coast Guard and saw for myself the unfolding tragedy. I traveled to our military base in Guantanamo, to review housing provided for the people rescued from the sea. It was painful to see the desperation on the faces of thousands awaiting repatriation to their homelands. The life-threatening risks they had taken had been in vain. The Commandant of the Coast Guard, sensing my frustration, later presented me a handmade wooden oar that had been found on one of the abandoned rafts. It hangs on a wall of my home today.

The oar is a reminder of our need to update and reform our immigration laws. I am outraged over the immoral separation of families at the U.S.-Mexico border, where children are placed in cages. The coronavirus has infected imprisoned immigrants who endured the postponement of naturalization services based on politics. Hundreds of thousands of young "Dreamers" face uncertain futures. These injustices were fueled by President Trump's labeling of Mexicans as "criminals and rapists" and calling Haitian and African nations "shit hole countries." These racist views drove his immoral curtailment of immigration, even while business and civic leaders demanded increased immigration. We have acted with more sensible and practical solutions before. Over thirty years ago, Senator Alan Simpson of Wyoming and Representative Romano Mazolli of Kentucky passed the Immigration Reform and Control Act of 1986. Known as Simpson-Mazolli and signed by President Reagan, the law criminalized the "pattern and practice" of employers who knowingly employed "unauthorized aliens." It provided amnesty for about three million undocumented immigrants on the condition that they pay a fine, back taxes, and remain free of any criminal activity.

Today the population of undocumented immigrants has grown to twelve million. Policy makers acknowledge the shortcomings of the 1986 Act. I believe that if the sanctions against employers had been vigorously enforced, we would have far fewer unlawful entries into the U.S. If employers knew that severe penalties would be imposed if they illegally hired undocumented immigrants, they would be more vigilant in their hiring practices and potential immigrants would learn that jobs are not easily available in the U.S.

In 2013, eight Senators led the passage of The Border Security, Economic Opportunity, and Immigration Modernization Act (S.744). Unfortunately, the bill died in the House of Representatives. Its enactment could have cured many of the deficiencies in the l986 Act. Today, we are left with the debacle that is President Trump's "Great Wall" on our southern border. We have spent over $2 billion to repair and construct 649 miles of fencing and barriers, leaving two-thirds of the border untouched. It is estimated that it will cost $6.5 billion to maintain these barriers over the next twenty years. Some have estimated that completing the "wall" will cost between $15 billion and $25 billion.

I see some of this fencing in my hometown of Brownsville, where it cuts through the local city park, college campus, nature preserves, farmers' fields, and residential properties. Many South Texas residents believe the fence has not worked; it has instead impacted the natural state of the Rio Grande and especially the native flora and fauna from El Paso to Brownsville.

All walls ultimately fail. The Great Wall of China, at one time six thousand miles long, did not keep out the Mongols under Genghis Khan. The Aurelian Walls built to protect Roman emperors were breached when the Bersaglieri of the Kingdom of Italy attacked. The Berlin Wall came crashing down as a result of worldwide pressures. Weak countries build walls, which ultimately fail. Strong countries need no walls.

Immigration must be assessed in unemotional and practical ways. Immigrants must be seen as a source of strength and growth for the future of our country. As in the past, today's immigrants will form the backbone of the America of tomorrow. They will serve our military, support an aging population, provide a workforce, and strengthen our economy. President Trump's inability to see immigration in this light showed his blind disregard for the important role immigration plays in building and strengthening America. An overwhelming majority of Americans support immigration reform. Nevertheless, we must challenge the misconceptions about immigrants that many Americans still harbor.

First, a country whose population does not grow in a sustainable way will weaken over time. It is simply a matter of mathematics. Immigration is a nation-building instrument. As the Wall Street Journal reminds us: "A tighter labor supply will sooner or later be a brake on growth if it isn't already as the workforce ages. Memo to the White House: The U.S. needs more legal immigrants" (WSJ, February 8–9, 2020).

Second, recent undocumented immigrants constitute *less than 4 percent* of our population and represent a net positive to our economy. Yet, they are portrayed as a threat and as a financial drain. What critics do not acknowledge is that tax-payer expenditures to support immigrants in public education, health care, and other social services *are outweighed by* the tax and economic contributions undocumented immigrants make to our nation. The non-partisan Congressional Budget Office came to this conclusion back in 2013. It found that if the House had adopted the immigration reform bill approved by a strong majority in the Senate, it would have reduced the federal budget deficit by $158 billion in the first decade after its passage, and by an additional $685 billion in the second decade.

Third, immigrants do not take jobs from Americans. Instead, they contribute to our nation's high level of productivity. Most Americans refuse the jobs that immigrants are willing to work. Just ask any meat packing plant supervisor, janitorial service owner, dairy farmer, or vegetable grower! And it was many of those frontline immigrant workers who lost their lives during the coronavirus to make our lives easier. Moreover, permitting twelve million undocumented immigrants to obtain legal status in 2013 would have increased our Gross Domestic Product over ten years by $832 billion. It would have increased earnings of all American workers by $470 billion according to The Center for American Progress.

Fourth, immigrants today, like immigrants of the past, over-whelmingly create small businesses that add to the economy by paying taxes and employing workers. A 2012 report by Fiscal-Policy.org found that 30 percent of the small businesses opened between 1990 and 2010 were created by immigrants. Geoscape found that Hispanic-owned businesses grew to 4.2 million in 2016, an impressive growth rate of 27.5% since 2012, double the growth rate for all U. S. firms.

Today, one out of every six small business owners was born in another country. Immigrant-owned businesses employ 4.7 million workers in the U.S. and generate more than $700 billion in revenue each year. As for Latinos specifically, we "had the highest entrepreneur rate of any ethnic group in the United

States...and accounted for nearly a quarter of new entrepreneurs in 2016, despite making up just 18 percent of the population," per Nera Economic Consulting.

Instead of reforming our immigration laws, President Trump considered using National Guardsmen to arrest and deport immigrants. This is impractical, wrong, and immoral. There is a more effective approach. The government should hire workplace agents to arrest, fine, and jail employers who continue to violate the 1986 law by hiring undocumented workers. This would discourage most people from even contemplating entering our country illegally, knowing that employers would not risk hiring them. This would compel Congress to enact new laws permitting needed temporary or seasonal workers with appropriate health, safety, and wage safeguards.

It is argued that allowing undocumented individuals to earn their citizenship would be unfair to those who are here legally. The same argument has been said about the many state and local amnesty benefits provided to tax evaders, child support deadbeats, and municipal law violators. These programs are criticized as unfair to citizens who comply with the law. Nevertheless, state and local amnesty laws will continue to be adopted because they satisfy more compelling public interests, such as collecting needed revenues, avoiding costly arrests and prosecutions, and allowing lawbreakers an opportunity to "come clean" and to start anew. These same public policy principles should apply to undocumented immigrants. "Amnesty" was a part of the 1986 immigration law signed by President Reagan, and it should be a part of immigration reform now.

We can—and must—forge effective reform of our immigration system, as it will renew our economy with an influx of both technical and essential workers. Otherwise, our nation will gradually weaken and decay as other nations grow and progress. By resolving this national controversy, we can avoid thousands of immigrant deaths and stop incarcerating children and separating families. Ultimately, the United States should lead a global effort to devise humane and safe immigration policies for all nations in order to provide critical workers to nations with worker shortages and ensure fair wages to individuals seeking new employment opportunities for their families back home. Equally important, resolving this divisive issue will free us to respond to more critical challenges facing our nation. President Biden has the opportunity with a Democratic Congress to finally pass comprehensive immigration reform. Let's not have more wooden oars hanging on our walls.

22. Communists and Kings

President Trump loved communists and kings. His relationships with Russian President Putin, North Korean Leader Kim Jung-un, and Saudi Royal Prince Bin Salman were disconcerting and frightening. President Trump's approach was dangerously at odds with the national security policies of past presidents. Malcolm Nance, in *The Plot to* Destroy *Democracy*", describes these misdeeds in great detail such as the destabilization of NATO and permitting Russian aggression.

President Bill Clinton approached similar leaders with "eyes wide open." Historically, the Secretary of State has led administrations on foreign policy and the Secretary of Commerce on global business matters. U.S. Presidents employ Cabinet Secretaries as surrogates around the globe both for geopolitical and commercial purposes. When I left the federal government in 1998, I had visited more than twenty-five countries to foster broad American security policies and to further support American economic interests abroad.

I was the first American Cabinet Secretary to visit Vietnam. I was both excited and uneasy about my visit to a country that, with Russian and Chinese aid, was responsible for the deaths of more than 50,000 American soldiers. I believed the Vietnam War was immoral and ill-conceived. I demonstrated against it and argued about it with my Father. I thought of my friends who fought there and the brother of a classmate who lost his life while flying a helicopter. I thought of the times I visited the Vietnam War Memorial in Washington, D.C. and the sobering sight of rows and rows of the names of dead Americans. I watched families and friends tearfully touch the wall. I had to bury my memories as I traveled to Hanoi. I was sent to represent my country, foster reconciliation, and promote capitalism. While the Vietnamese were still communist in theory, they had been adopting free market-based practices since the collapse of the Soviet Union in 1991. I arrived with mixed emotions.

My visit was in November 1995, a year after President Clinton lifted the long-standing American embargo against trade with the country. The American Embassy opened in Hanoi in July of that year. I was accompanied by an enormous interagency delegation for this historic mission. It included officials from the Department of the Treasury, the Export-Import Bank, the Overseas Private Investment Corporation, and representatives of the Departments of State, Labor, Commerce, and Agriculture—a full-court press. I added Patrick Murphy, an expert in aviation policy at DOT, because he was a wounded veteran of the war. He was appreciative and deeply moved.

American companies were able to do business in Vietnam. I was honored to witness Ellicott Dredges of Baltimore and the Vietnamese government sign a $12 million contract for port dredging equipment.

It was a time of hope and promise. They wanted us there. I was warmly welcomed when I became the first U.S. Cabinet Member to climb the steps of the Vietnam War Department. There was enormous symbolism in entering the place where anti-U.S. military strategies were devised. It signaled the embrace of a new relationship with the United States by Vietnam. This was also evident when I met with Transport Minister Bui Danh Luu to discuss rebuilding the roads, bridges, ports, and airports that had been destroyed.

November 1995, Secretary Peña and Vietnamese Transport Minister Luu descending Viet Nam War Building.
Photo courtesy of the Peña Family Archives.

Traveling throughout Hanoi, I saw thousands of Vietnamese people buying and selling goods and services in open markets. The city's residents moved about quickly, riding expertly through the streets on bicycles, weaving in and out of traffic with little effort. Their energy and vibrancy impressed me, and the vigor of the new Vietnam was met with equal enthusiasm from the dozens of American businesspeople who accompanied us. They were eager to do business.

The idea that a new Vietnam was rising was solidified during my meeting with Prime Minister Vo Van Kiet. Kiet had fought in the war against the French colonial government long before Americans arrived in South Vietnam. After joining the Communist Party in 1939, he rose through the ranks to become the most powerful official in post-war Saigon. When we met, he had already served four years as Prime Minister and was the leading proponent of *doi moi* (renovation). His Gorbachev-styled economic plan encouraged entrepreneurial initiatives and foreign investment—proof of which could be seen in the streets of Hanoi.

Kiet no longer wore the drab military garb of Ho Chi Minh and impressed us with his business suit. The communist leader personally welcomed us. Within minutes, Kiet, through a translator, announced that though our countries were enemies on the battlefield, the war was "water under the bridge." He wanted the war topic off the table quickly. He emphasized that he welcomed American businesspeople and investment, and he expressed delight that our delegation had come so quickly after the U.S. had normalized relations with its former foe. I was shocked at how the millions of deaths of Americans and Vietnamese and the billions of dollars wasted on the war were so easily dismissed.

I thanked the Prime Minister for his welcome, agreed that we needed to move both countries forward, and discussed matters important to the U.S. This meeting ended the trip on a high note. I could not have imagined a more successful initial trade and diplomatic mission.

While in Hanoi, we visited a small monument near Truc Bach Lake, where Vietnamese gunners shot down Senator John McCain's jet. The monument mistakenly portrays his jet as an Air Force plane, though McCain flew for our Navy. We took a picture nevertheless. I delivered the photo to the Senator, who appreciated the gesture and our efforts to set a new course in U.S.-Vietnamese relations.

Our presence in Vietnam sent a strong signal to China that it would be unwise to contemplate future military intervention. In an ironic twist of history, the country we had long fought now sought to become a close ally partly to shield itself from China's menace. To re-enforce our new relationship, the Vietnamese released two Vietnamese Americans who had been jailed for allegedly attempting a coup. Our government had been pressuring Vietnam to release the pair before any improvement in trade relations could be considered. The two Americans were soon flown out of Vietnam.

Since my visit, trade with Vietnam has increased to $82 billion in 2019, from $450 million in 1995. We have even provided military equipment for the country's defense. American tourists now frequent the country. Hopefully, the Vietnamese government will one day reform its domestic policies so that individual rights of citizens are protected.

I learned a key lesson from my trade mission to Vietnam. Once countries establish economic and other relations, they are less likely to engage in conflict. They can even become allies in combating other menacing powers. This is why President Trump's careless criticisms and attacks on Mexico and Canada are worrisome. If we ruin our trade relations with either country, China would be waiting in the wings to capitalize on our conflicts and jeopardize our economic and civic ties. Our relations have begun to deteriorate with Asian Pacific countries. President Obama secured the Trans-Pacific Partnership to strengthen U.S. relationships in Asia, an area growing in population and economic power. China is now making trade inroads in that region of the world because President Trump abandoned the "Comprehensive and Progressive Agreement for Trans Pacific Partnership." President Trump's reckless broadsides have weakened our trade relations around the world. Thankfully, President Biden has started to constructively re-engage in this significant part of the world.

The success of the Vietnam trip paved the way for missions to other volatile parts of the world, including Saudi Arabia. There we were tasked with rescuing our deteriorating aircraft manufacturing industry.

The recession of the 1990s caused Boeing and McDonnell

Douglas to hemorrhage money. Both companies were engaged in a highly-competitive global market with Airbus, their European counterpart, and they needed help.

If anyone could help, it was Ronald Brown, Secretary of Commerce. I met Ron when I was Mayor of Denver. It was Ron who helped secure $500 million from the Department of Transportation to finance our new airport. He was a prominent attorney with the powerful law firm Patton Boggs. He later became chairman of the Democratic National Committee.

Ron and I were seated next to one another in President Clinton's cabinet meetings. It was a unique experience that forged a special bond between us. My cabinet chair sits in my home today, with its legs scuffed by Ron's chair bumping mine. It reminds me of Ron, and I still have difficulty believing he is gone. He died tragically in a plane crash on a trade trip to Croatia as Secretary of Commerce.

It was Ron who encouraged me to visit King Fahid vin Abdulaziz in Saudi Arabia. While discussing the plight of American plane manufacturers, he told me about his efforts on a recent trip to Saudi Arabia to encourage the Saudis to purchase fifty aircraft for $6 billion from Boeing and McDonnell Douglas. He urged me to follow up with my own visit. I agreed.

Arriving in Riyadh in 1993, I was astonished by the country's wealth. Of course, I knew that oil produced extreme wealth, but the opulent private waiting rooms held for Saudi princes at the airport were overwhelming. And then there were the gold bathroom fixtures. I was provided a room at the royal family's hotel that occupied an entire floor. There were trays overflowing with nuts, fruits, and exotic foods to greet me. I was treated like a prince and felt a long way from my days of pulling sorghum husks out of my blistered skin in Brownsville.

I also experienced the ultra-religious and conservative culture of the country as my Chief of Staff, Ann Bormolini, had to wear full-length dresses, with long sleeves, in order to comply with the strict dress code imposed on women. Dress code restrictions were enforced by the Mutaween or "religious police."

1993, Secretary Peña with Saudi officials in Riyadh.
Photo courtesy of the Peña Family Archives.

After a number of meetings with government officials, I was finally to meet with King Fahd. Or so I thought. Fahd had come to power in 1982 upon the death of his Father. Ruling as the fifth King of Saudi Arabia, he had increasingly taken on a more Islamist role swapping the traditional title of "Majesty" for "Custodian of the Two Holy Mosques." However, King Fahd's religiosity did not prevent him from spending lavishly, owning extravagant yachts and planes, and traveling around the world in luxury.

The King—as a matter of royal prerogative, I suppose— arrived late to our meeting. Apparently, he had been fishing. Once seated, he proceeded to tell me through an interpreter about the long and friendly relationships he enjoyed with American presidents. He named each one, recalling his specific interactions with each president in fascinating detail. Then he discussed his bad knees and his desire to come to the U.S. to have surgery. I listened intently and respectfully to his lengthy monologue. Finally, with a few minutes remaining in our meeting, I was invited to speak.

I thanked King Fahd for his fascinating historical accounts, told him about my own knee surgeries, agreed that our countries enjoyed a long relationship, and then raised the subject of purchasing American aircraft. Without uttering a word, he nodded politely, and then rose to leave. Our meeting had ended as it had begun, with the King in complete control.

I flew home reminiscing about my life, hoping that the same polite attention and respectful tone my Father and Mother paid their foreign guests had served me well. It had. A few months later, Ron Brown and I joined President Clinton in an Oval Office celebration of the sale of American aircraft to Saudi Arabia.

Airbus and the European countries that supported it were in no mood to celebrate. They protested, arguing that it was inappropriate and unfair for a Transportation Secretary to lobby for U.S. aircraft manufacturers. They claimed we had violated the General Agreement on Tariffs and Trade (GATT). I responded that I was surprised by their concern that a lowly Transportation Secretary could compete against European heads of state who had been lobbying Saudi Arabia and other nations to promote Airbus long before my visit.

Much has changed since my experiences in Saudi Arabia in the 1990s. Our relationship has become more complex. We still engage in major arms sales, security training arrangements, and enhanced counterterrorism cooperation. Yet, it was the son of a prominent Saudi businessman, Osama Bin Laden, who masterminded the deadly 9-11 terrorist attack against the United States. Fifteen of the nineteen al-Qaeda terrorists responsible for the attack were Saudis. While we continue to urge the Kingdom to buy our planes and other American products, and to house American military bases, we condemn the funding of terrorist groups by certain Saudis and worry about our dependence on Saudi oil. Nevertheless, our countries share concerns about Iran's effort to develop nuclear capabilities, and we jointly oppose al-Qaeda and the rise of the Islamic State (ISIS).

Our oil relationship is most challenging. When the global price of oil dips below fifty dollars per barrel because of excess global oil supplies, U.S. energy companies either curtail production, shut down wells, or declare bankruptcy. This forces us to import more foreign oil. The Saudis are not pleased when U.S. production increases because it lessens our need to import their oil. This tenuous oil relationship presents vexing challenges for U.S.-Middle East policies.

In 2018, the barbaric killing of journalist Jamal Khashoggi by Saudi operatives alienated congressional support for Saudi Arabia, resulting in a Senate vote to end American military assistance for the Kingdom's war in Yemen.

Many believe that Mr. Khashoggi's murder was ordered by Saudi Crown Prince Mohammed bin Salman. President Trump's defense of the crown prince has muddied the U.S-Saudi relationship.

The Saudis are developing economic ties with countries in the Far East using oil as a carrot. As the U.S. imports less and less Saudi oil, they are attempting to diversify their economy. Did Trump have a strategy in dealing with Saudi Arabia? No one knows!

I vividly recall the Arab oil embargo of the 1970s that resulted from disagreements over our Middle East policies. Only time will tell if Trump's questionable conduct in the Middle East will ignite future repercussions. As I traveled the globe, I saw my role not simply as a cabinet member, but as an emissary for the President and the American people. I was treated with such respect and courtesy that I became uncomfortable with the attention that, at times, approached levels fit for the King Fahds of the world. It was gratifying to witness the global community's respect for our country, not only for our democratic ideals and institutions, but also for our unique cultural, economic, and political strength. I felt unabashedly proud to represent my country and most proud to witness how America represented hope, progress, and possibility to people all over the world.

President Trump's destabilizing criticism of our allies tarnished America's standing in the world. His instigation of the January 6 attack on our Capitol further demoralized emergent democracies around the world. How are U.S. officials viewed as they travel the globe representing the American people? I wonder if they are treated as well as I was.

After four years in the Department of Transportation, I was ready to return to Denver and resume a normal life. Several devastating airline crashes affected me deeply. I visited each crash site to meet with grieving families. It was always a difficult experience. To this day, when I learn of an airline crash somewhere in the world, those painful memories return.

And by 1997, I was the father of three small children. Nelia was seven years old; Cristina was five; and I now had a son, Ryan, who was not yet one. Cabinet jobs are difficult. I worked ten-hour days, then read a briefing book each night after the kids were asleep. I was "on call" seven days a week. My extensive travel, sometimes hastily arranged due to an emergency, meant I had little time with my family. With two girls in elementary school and a baby boy at home, this was a difficult occupation.

I campaigned for President Clinton's re-election. When he won a second term, I felt I had served my country well. I enjoyed a good relationship with President Clinton and Vice President Gore and had fulfilled my promise to serve a four-year term. Clinton's cabinet included talented and wonderful people, and it was an honor to work with each of them. The international experience was an unexpected bonus. My team managed the Transportation Department well, reducing the workforce by 10 percent, and introducing best practices to make the department more efficient. So, satisfied with my work, I notified the President of my decision to leave the administration.

At the end of Clinton's first term, I had completed sixteen

years in public office—four as a Colorado State Legislator, eight as Mayor of Denver, and another four as Secretary of Transportation. I believed that public service was a responsibility of every citizen, but I didn't think it should be a life-long career. Mine had been a long journey, from a small town in South Texas to Washington, D.C. I was honored to have been called upon, time and again, to serve my city, state, and nation. But it was time to move on to a new chapter in my life.

In December of 1996, I watched as our realtor drove a "For Sale" sign into the ground in our front lawn. We began packing, thinking about returning to Denver, and talking about new schools for the children.

Then the phone rang.

Part Five: Still in Washington, D.C. (1997–1998)

23. Energy Secretary

"Hello, Federico. It's Al Gore."

"Yes, sir," I responded, reverting to my South Texas upbringing.

"Federico, I am with the President in the Oval Office, and we have an issue. I know you are planning to return home, but we need you to run the Department of Energy."

What? The Vice President could not see me, but my jaw dropped literally almost to the floor.

I liked and respected Al Gore. I greatly admired and supported his push to "reinvent" government. We were allies in our effort to upgrade the nation's outdated air traffic control system. We traveled across the country together warning of the outdated vacuum tubes still used in air traffic instruments, and urged congressional legislation to allow the adoption of private sector practices.

In my dealings with the Vice President, I learned he could be uproariously funny, not at all the Al Gore normally seen in public. Once, on Air Force Two, he had a few of us nearly in tears laughing at his jokes. When he campaigned for the presidency in 2000, he remained coldly stoic in public. I thought his humor could have been an asset.

But on that December evening in 1996, he was not being funny. Gore explained that the President was going to finalize his second-term cabinet appointments the following day. President Clinton intended to nominate me as the new Secretary of Energy to succeed Hazel O'Leary. Hearing the Vice President say this was surreal. I seriously could not be having this kind of conversation...again!

I assumed that the new, second-term team had long been selected. I had already said farewell to my fellow cabinet members. I could not believe that my world was once again being placed upside down at Christmas. Surprisingly, the new cabinet had no Hispanic members, which would have set the President back in his promise to have an administration that reflected the country. Having been confirmed by a near-unanimous vote in the Senate four years earlier, I was again being asked to take on responsibilities that I was qualified to manage, albeit in a rather hurried and inopportune manner.

I thanked the Vice President profusely, but respectfully told him I already was packing, had listed my house for sale, and was heading home to Denver. I reminded him that I had notified the White House months before that I would leave after the President's re-election. He said he understood, wished me a good night, and hung up. A few minutes passed. I was still rattled when the phone rang a second time. It was President Clinton.

I repeated what I had said to Vice President Gore. He said he appreciated my feelings, but he emphasized that I was the last piece to the puzzle in filling out his second-term cabinet. He exuded great confidence that I would be an excellent Secretary of Energy, assured me he would support me, and that this was very important to him and the country.

"I really need you to do this, Federico," he said. I paused. I sensed he was being genuine. And it is extremely difficult to say no to the President of the United States.

I did not question my abilities, and I had some background and interest in energy policy. I understood the importance to the broader Hispanic community of my taking on the job. The President promised I would be able to select my own team. He was typical Bill Clinton—effective.

In between the two calls, I had fifteen minutes to talk to my then wife, Ellen. I was surprised when she wholeheartedly encouraged me to take the position. I thought she was anxious to get home. So, within minutes of hearing the President's plea, I relented. "I can't promise I'll serve the full four years," I added.

The President seemed relieved when he replied, "That's fine, just stay as long as possible."

I prepared to be announced as the next U.S. Secretary of Energy in the morning. It occurred to me that the appointment was rushed, and I worried that it would receive less than positive reactions. I was not known for my energy work, and I was concerned that there was insufficient time for a thoughtful announcement. Indeed, the hurried press release omitted key background information. In 1981, Secretary of Energy James Edwards had appointed me to a task force to investigate alternative uses for the plutonium plant at the Rocky Flats Nuclear Weapons facility located near Denver. Our committee back then produced "The Rocky Flats Long-Range Utilization Study" that laid the groundwork for effectively managing the site. As DOT Secretary, I worked with Secretary O'Leary on clean energy issues and understood many aspects of DOE.

My work to develop clean energy and alternative fuels when I was Mayor of Denver was not mentioned. Nor was my understanding of their impact on Colorado's mining industry. Notwithstanding these oversights, President Clinton introduced me as his new Secretary of Energy, along with the rest of his reshuffled cabinet. My cabinet friends were surprised to learn I was staying on and they appeared a bit nervous as they congratulated me. I was introduced as a seasoned cabinet member who had run DOT efficiently, could work with Congress as well as state and local governments, and understood the workings of Washington, D.C.

The list of Americans who have managed two departments at the cabinet level is not long. The list of Latinos who have managed two cabinet level departments is even shorter. I was the first Latino to serve in two cabinet positions in the history of the United States. It was not until I left Washington that I recognized the historical import.

The next day, I plunged into preparing for confirmation hearings for another department of government. Although I felt confident I could run the Department of Energy, I still had much to learn.

Over the shock of not returning to Denver, I quickly warmed to my new position. As I eagerly prepared for my Senate confirmation hearing, I was dismayed to learn it was being delayed. The Republicans had won control of the Senate in 1994, and Senator Frank Murkowski of Alaska now chaired the Senate Energy Committee, which would conduct my confirmation hearing. Murkowski was upset with the administration's position on Nevada's Yucca Mountain, designated by Congress years earlier as the long-term repository for our nuclear waste.

Senator Murkowski was a strong supporter of the Yucca Mountain site and wanted a guarantee from the President it would be opened. He used my confirmation as a bargaining chip. Weeks passed without my hearing. Ultimately, White House Chief of Staff Erskine Bowles sent a letter committing the administration to continuing the legal and engineering work on Yucca Mountain.

Bowles's letter mollified Murkowski. I finally received Senate confirmation on March 12, 1996, three months after my nomination and three days before my forty-ninth birthday, by a 99–1 vote. Republican Rod Grams of Minnesota voted against my nomination. I did not take it personally, understanding he wanted the Department of Energy abolished altogether.

My delayed confirmation is one example of the Senate

hijacking of the confirmation process by some Senators. Today, any member of the Senate can place a hold on a nomination while seeking to extract concessions from the White House. Although once used sparingly, this check on presidential power is now out of balance. It has been corrupted into a political tool that has warped our government.

Over the years, I have watched too many competent and qualified cabinet nominees abandon the nomination process for personal or family reasons. They cannot withstand the politically motivated delays, which have little to do with their qualifications, and ultimately withdraw their nominations in order to get on with their lives. The angst over many of President Trump's cabinet nominees was not new. I was subjected to similar treatment over twenty years ago. Thankfully, I had the stamina and perseverance to prevail. Most importantly, once confirmed, I could finally officially go to work for the benefit of the American people.

24. Tomorrow's Promises, Today's Challenges

I arrived at the Department of Energy sensing that its mission was more about the future than simply energy. Oil and gas had long been deregulated, and the independent Federal Energy Regulatory Commission and State Public Utility Commissions largely shaped electricity policy throughout the country. The building and oversight of nuclear energy plants were governed by the independent Nuclear Regulatory Commission. But in this dawning new age, technology was remaking the future, evidenced by breakthroughs in producing oil and gas, attention to climate change, and scientific advances in our national laboratories. And the incumbent responsibilities of the department grew to embrace new concerns, including protecting the nation's technological research from espionage and securing nuclear materials across the globe.

The dramatic collapse of the Soviet Union and the growing concern about Chinese nuclearization launched this new era, but it did not absolve us from the legacy of the Cold War. As Energy Secretary, I was responsible for certifying the safety and reliability of our nation's nuclear weapons to Congress. The cleanup of old atomic sites that were contaminating local communities would cost billions. And the United States had taken on the responsibility of ensuring that former Soviet nuclear stockpiles would not fall into the hands of terrorists.

Many started to believe that the world's oil supplies had already peaked and we were running out of oil. This movement, called "peak oil," made the development of alternative fuels increasingly important. The Department of Energy could accelerate the development of new energy, an exciting challenge for the future security of our nation.

The Department of Energy had already begun to support alternatives to oil and gas. Simultaneously, however, it continued to research new ways to explore for oil and gas. Horizontal drilling, hydraulic fracturing, and diamond-bit drilling were being tested at DOE laboratories in conjunction with the energy industry. Back then, when oil was trading at twelve dollars per barrel and many companies were going bankrupt, DOE's support became a national security imperative. Almost thirty years later, those efforts have put the country at the door of energy security—an astonishing achievement that carries tremendous implications for our nation's economy, foreign policy and, if handled correctly, the environment.

America's future was also taking shape in each of the Department of Energy's national research laboratories. Thousands of scientists and engineers were at work developing new resources, processes, and theories by which the U.S. was creating the modern age. Together, these laboratories comprised a preeminent federal research consortium that explored possibilities in strategic scientific and technological fields, including human genomics, robotics, hydrogen fusion, global warming, alternative fuels, intelligent transportation, and even the Higgs boson (or "God") particles—the very building blocks of the cosmos. I was inspired as I toured our national labs, seeing and feeling the promise of our future. The factories that produced our atomic weapons—with which the country ultimately faced down the Soviet Union—also produced tons of dangerous waste at sites throughout the country. Cleaning up the contamination of Hanford in Washington State, Rocky Flats in Colorado, and other locations was left to the Department of Energy. I was, of course, already familiar with Rocky Flats and the contamination it brought to Colorado. I strongly believed the federal government had a responsibility to protect the land and water near affected communities.

The Rocky Flats Nuclear Facility, located sixteen miles north west of Denver, produced 70,000 plutonium "triggers" (fission cores) for the country's nuclear arsenal. Although Rocky Flats provided high-paying jobs for thousands of Coloradans, it became a toxic nightmare for the surrounding community. Unfortunately, the Rockwell company operating Rocky Flats mismanaged the plant. In both 1957 and 1969, fires sent toxins into the air over the metropolitan area. Barrels of radioactive waste leaked and dangerous contaminants leached into the ground, ultimately tainting the water supply. Many Rocky Flats workers developed cancer and other illnesses for which the government had to provide compensation. Not surprisingly, Denver residents clamored for the site's closure.

As a State Legislator in the 1970s, I co-authored a study sponsored by DOE that developed options for the plant's future. I wrote a separate opinion calling for a major change in strategy to accelerate the Rocky Flats cleanup. Ironically, almost 20 years later, I would be the person responsible for the cleanup as the Energy Secretary. I now had the power, and I was not reluctant to use it. I immediately accelerated the closure and cleanup of Rocky Flats, which was finally shuttered in 2005. Where once highly unstable, dangerous weapons were made that could destroy humankind, now wild animals and native flora thrive in the 4,000-acre Rocky Flats National Wildlife Refuge.

As we dealt with the legacy of the nuclear age, it was clear that the nation still required nuclear arms for its defense. Working with our scientists and engineers, it was my job to ensure our nuclear weapons were not deteriorating and that they were safely secured and upgraded as necessary. Each year, I met with our nuclear scientists and engineers to review each individual nuclear weapon for safety and modernization. I certified to Congress that our nuclear arsenal was safe, secure, and reliable. It was a weighty responsibility, and I constantly worried about making a disastrous mistake. But fortunately, I had a great team of advisors. Additionally, the DOE scientists developed a way to accomplish this through the use of supercomputers. At the time, the Sandia National Laboratory supercomputer delivered 1.8 trillion calculations per second, or ten teraflops. In February 1998, I announced an $85 million contract with IBM to develop an even faster computer called Option White, which would conduct ten trillion calculations per second.

1998, Secretary Peña visiting Rocky Flats prior to its closure.
Photo courtesy of the Peña Family Archives.

These supercomputers would verify the safety of our arsenal. This development obviated the need to test weapons underground with expensive explosions that contaminated the earth. Since then, the Department of Energy continues to maintain one of the fastest supercomputers on the planet (Titan) at the Oak Ridge National Laboratory in Tennessee, which now sustains twenty-seven petaflops, or well over a quadrillion floating-point operations per second, much faster than the supercomputers that were in use when I was in office.

In the 1990s, the ability to safely design and test nuclear weapons while still enhancing their power supported President Clinton's goal to stop underground testing. With our advanced technology, he felt confident in signing the Comprehensive Test-Ban Treaty (CTBT) at the United Nations General Assembly in 1996.

I supported the CTBT, but unfortunately, many members of Congress felt otherwise. There were Senators who could not imagine the equivalent of a nuclear bomb being formulated in a series of computers. They were unhappy that other nations, like Iran, failed to sign the agreement. In 1999, the Senate defeated the treaty 51–48.

The arguments President Clinton and I made twenty years ago in support of the CTBT have since become more valid. Without the treaty, experts believe that about 2,000 nuclear tests have been carried out throughout the world, including recent tests in India, Pakistan, and North Korea. Absent American ratification of the treaty, it is almost certain that China, Iran, and Israel will never agree to it.

The lack of a united effort to eliminate underground nuclear testing adds to the instability of our world. Had the treaty been signed, and had the U.S. been able to convince other nations to sign it, nuclear tests could have been controlled. The use of nuclear power for electricity could have been more manageable in developing countries, with more protections and monitoring measures in place.

Today, we cannot know the nuclear intentions of Iran and North Korea. President Obama made a valiant effort, along with China, France, Russia, United Kingdom, and Germany, to negotiate a treaty with Iran to eliminate its stockpile of enriched uranium. Secretary of Energy Ernest Muniz, who served as my Undersecretary, negotiated the complicated Iran nuclear deal with Secretary John Kerry that was signed by all parties. President Trump recklessly renounced the treaty, and Iran can now develop a nuclear weapon. This is the result of a misguided, schizophrenic national security policy that undermines consistent, long-term efforts to make the world safer. Time will tell which other countries attempt to obtain nuclear weapons.

The Department of Energy and its scientific laboratories remain vital in addressing future nuclear challenges. The extraordinarily talented women and men in our national labs need enhanced support to work with the private sector to advance alternative energy, battery storage, artificial intelligence, climate change solutions, and other scientific advances. While China is making sizable investments in science, technology, and national security, our Trump-era leaders failed to adequately fund scientific research. The private sector alone cannot and will not advance our country's research. Remember that many advances critical to our economy, and beneficial to the private sector, came from governmental research. Nuclear energy, space exploration, the internet, global positioning satellites, and human genome discoveries are but a few. I am proud to have supported our national laboratories and our scientists, engineers, and technicians. I have urged President Biden to increase support for our national laboratories. After all, it's all about our future.

25. High-Stakes Strategies

A s I entered my second year in the Department of Energy in 1998, fears over peak oil prices had faded. Energy supplies were abundant and affordable. Oil was trading at twelve dollars per barrel, and natural gas was cheap. Although the low energy prices benefited consumers and industrial users, they caused massive shutdowns of wells that became unprofitable. This was not good news, especially in Texas. I was all too familiar with the boom-and-bust history of the oil and gas industry in light of Denver's experience in the 1980s, and I was resolved to do what I could to soften the economic impact.

We responded by supporting royalty relief and other benefits for the industry. Oil companies with leases on federal lands could reduce the rent payments when the price of gas fell below certain levels. Since traded prices were considerably below these thresholds in 1998, producers received financial relief. We supported the federal production tax credit, which provided an incentive to explore for natural gas through unconventional sources—a strategy that has provided us with ample natural gas today. The U.S. now exports natural gas to over thirty nations.

The abundance of oil and gas, and its attendant low prices, afforded us time to prepare for the next energy crisis and to find ways to transition to cleaner energy.

I also became concerned about our antiquated electricity grid needed to power our homes, offices, and factories. The power grid is a complex network of more than 200,000 miles of high-voltage transmission lines that span the country like a spider web. When congestion occurs either from physical or capacity constraints, it can cause power outages or force suppliers to buy electricity from less-constrained parts of the U.S. When suppliers are forced to pay higher prices, it means higher electricity prices for consumers. Our transmission system also remained vulnerable to the effects of bad weather and being "hacked" by foreign governments. Texas recently experienced the human and economic tragedy of a faulty system during record low temperatures that left 2.6 million without power for almost a month. In early 1998, Deputy Secretary Moler crafted legislation to address these issues, but it sadly received no support from Congress.

I was becoming increasingly aware of scientists' worries over climate change. I believed that our abundant energy supplies allowed us the luxury of time to develop an integrated plan for the future. With careful planning, we could anticipate our energy needs and propose ways to mitigate the impact of energy production on the environment.

The Department of Energy Organization Act, which created the department in 1977, gave me the perfect opportunity to address these issues. It required the Secretary of Energy to submit an energy policy to Congress every two years. I believed the nation deserved a thoughtful, organized approach to its energy needs and directed my staff to begin developing our "Comprehensive National Energy Strategy." The strategy was led by Robert "Bob" Gee, the Assistant Secretary for Policy and International Affairs. Bob hailed from the private sector and had been a member of the Texas Public Utility Commission.

With the support of a great team, I welcomed the opportunity to convert yet another government report into a sensible and constructive vision for the future.

Our new energy strategy included specific actions, timetables, and measurements. I pushed the team hard for specifics. I did not want platitudes, as they are too often of the lame language that Washington uses to sidestep action. Chief of Staff Elgie Holstein, with his solid energy and budget background, oversaw the effort. Kyle Simpson, an energy advisor with experience in both the government and private sector, focused on energy efficiency strategies and royalty relief for natural gas producers. Deputy Secretary Betsy Moler included provisions which introduced robust competition to the electricity sector to attract the capital needed to upgrade the nation's grid. It took a herculean, year-long effort to craft legislation to transform the enormously complex and stodgy electric utility sector.

Despite our efforts, the process of fashioning the energy strategy I had envisioned would prove cumbersome. We were required to circulate our draft among other federal departments, agencies, and, of course, the White House. The Office of Management and Budget worried about the impact the expenditures would have on the budget, and other agencies wanted their input. Everyone in Washington had an opinion on what should—and should not—be included.

The mind-numbing process took longer than it should have. This was "bureaucratic" Washington at its best. More than once, I called the White House to spur decisions and resolve disagreements among the many federal entities. We had to stave off lobbyists and special interests. In the age we are in today, when the influence of special interests has reached corrosive dimensions in Washington, I doubt we could produce such a plan.

The Comprehensive National Energy Strategy was a goal-oriented document with specific timelines. Senator Jeff Bingaman of New Mexico, then Chairman of the Senate Energy Committee, said it was one of best he had seen. This is a top-line summary of our five goals:

1. Improve the efficiency of our energy system. We proposed competition in the electricity sector to reduce electric prices and upgrade transmission lines. Our transportation, industrial, and building sectors could be more energy efficient by increasing fuel economy standards in vehicles and increasing solar and wind usage by 2010. Since the federal government was the largest user of electricity, we urged adoption of clean energy systems in federal buildings.

2. Minimize foreign-led energy disruptions by stabilizing domestic oil production, maintaining the readiness of our Strategic Petroleum Reserve, diversifying imports, and reducing fuel consumption.

3. Support energy production in ways that respect health and environmental values.

4. Expand energy choices with new scientific and technological advancements, including long-term investments in fusion, hydrogen-based, and methane hydrate systems.

5. Call for international cooperation on global issues by promoting competitive energy markets and facilitating the adoption of clean, safe, and efficient energy systems.

I also urged regional stability by reducing energy-related environmental risks to protect U.S. security interests.

I believe these five goals, with the 30 pages of specific energy strategies, helped move our nation toward greater energy security today. U.S. oil production is now 12.5 million barrels per day. We have become one of the largest producers in the world. New production, plus new energy efficiencies in the transportation and commercial sectors, has significantly reduced our oil imports. In 1998, we imported 10.4 million barrels per day of total crude oil products. In 2020 we reduced those imports to 7.86 million barrels per days, making the U.S. more energy secure. Thankfully, successive Bush and Obama administrations continued to make progress. They were supportive of wind and solar power, and continued private sector partnerships in developing advances in electric vehicles, battery storage, and other clean energy technologies.

Sadly, President Trump reverted back to coal production and rejected any effort to reduce global warming. Incredibly, he rolled back Obama-era improvements in vehicle fuel efficiencies, which were on track to double average fuel standards to 54.5 miles per gallon and cut carbon dioxide pollution by six billion tons. Even a number of car manufacturers rejected Trump's regulatory "rollbacks." Some are committing to the higher fuel-efficiency standards in California.

But back in July of 1997, while my team back home hammered out the details of our Comprehensive National Energy Strategy, I found myself jogging past Lenin's tomb in Red Square in Moscow. The White House had urged me and State Department officials to fly to Russia to address a number of emerging challenges.

26. Russian Revelations

"How was your jog in Red Square this morning?" my Russian counterpart asked. How did he know? I should not have been surprised that I was being followed. My security officers had previously warned me that we were entering a dicey environment. We could not discuss any sensitive matters in our hotel rooms, since they were presumed to be under electronic surveillance. Serious conversations would have to wait until we were within the more secure confines of the U.S. embassy.

The environment in Moscow in the late 1990s was eerie and disconcerting. Walking through a shopping mall, I noticed that Russians were quiet and reserved. They whispered to one another when out in public and their eyes darted about to see if they were being watched. I had expected that *glasnost*—the policy of openness and transparency instituted by Soviet leader Mikhail Gorbachev a decade earlier—had freed Russians to be more relaxed. But they had reason to be skeptical about whether their government's repressive practices had really landed in the dustbin of history. While the possibility that my hotel room might be videotaped or audiotaped perturbed me, it quickly became obvious that more sinister elements were at work when one of my staff members was threatened outside a restaurant by Russian mobsters. As he got out of his car, some thugs accused him of denting their car—which he had not—and demanded money. I understood this sort of harassment likely paled in comparison to what average Russians experienced on a daily basis, but it was nerve-wracking nonetheless.

My Russian interpreter told me he had been forced to abandon his restaurant business years earlier because he was tired of paying protection money to the Russian mob. I figured U.S. companies investing in Russia were experiencing these same problems.

I was disappointed to learn that President Boris Yeltsin, while bringing in more progressive cabinet ministers, had yet to improve the day-to-day lives of the Russian people.

My primary concern revolved around Russian export of nuclear expertise and technology to countries seeking their own nuclear capabilities. These countries included Iran, which wanted to finish building a nuclear reactor at Bushehr on the Persian Gulf coast. I was also worried about the vulnerability of their unguarded nuclear materials that could easily be stolen by other governments, or worse, by terrorists.

Two additional concerns involved Russia's mistreatment of American energy companies, and the country's questionable role in developing oil and gas in the Caspian Sea. I started negotiating with Energy Minister Sergey Kiriyenko, who became Prime Minister of Russia in 1998, regarding the inappropriate financial conditions or concessions being imposed on American energy companies. Although we secured some relief for our companies, over subsequent years they lost much of their investments in Russia. I met with Deputy Prime Minister Boris Nemtsov, a reformer with whom I would meet again in Baku, Azerbaijan several months later. Nemtsov was full of hope for his country, believing that more democratic and capitalistic policies were soon to come. He later became an outspoken critic of Vladamir Putin and was assassinated in 2016 not far from where we met in Moscow. His death was a devastating loss to Russians fighting for more freedom and openness.

One of the more fascinating Russians I met was Victor Mikhailov, Minister of Atomic Energy. A leading expert on nuclear power, Mikhailov was committed to using his country's expertise in the field to prop up the failing Russian economy and keep his scientists employed. Since the collapse of the Soviet Union, even once-favored professionals were struggling to survive. No prospective customer who had arrived in Moscow, however questionable, went unwelcome.

1997, Russia Minister of Atomic Energy Mikhailov (2nd From Left), Secretary Peña, and Minister Adamov (Right) on their way to dedicate the Russian Nuclear Safety Center. Photo courtesy of the Peña Family Archives

When I toured Russian laboratories during that visit, I found them in a state of shocking disrepair. Machines appeared rusted and antiquated, and buildings were empty of personnel. They were nothing close to our sophisticated scientific labs back home. The danger they posed to the Russians themselves was significant, and the danger they could pose to the rest of the world could be exponentially worse. We believed that some Russian scientists were selling nuclear goods and services to other nations. Minister Mikhailov, who titled his 1996 autobiography *I Am a Hawk*, was using his underpaid and unemployed nuclear scientists to export nuclear-related technology and services to China, Iran, Bangladesh, Belarus, Nigeria, and Vietnam. I was alarmed at his way of doing business. It was accelerating the proliferation of the global threats that the Comprehensive Nuclear-Test-Ban Treaty had sought to avoid.

Mikhailov's most controversial work involved the Bushehr nuclear facility in Iran. It was built in 1975 by Germany, at the direction of the Shah of Iran, to produce electricity. The project was abandoned after Islamic revolutionaries deposed the Shah. Eventually, the Russians stepped in and continued construction in the 1990s. With the radicalization of the Iranian government, the United States soon became concerned that Russian nuclear technology and fuel would be used for military purposes at Bushehr.

During my various meetings in Moscow, I was aided by Gary Samore, who was special assistant to President Clinton and the Senior Director for Nonproliferation and Export Controls. We pressured the Soviets to not proceed with Bushehr, but they contended that their nuclear reactor technology was for civilian use only.

I knew negotiations with Mikhailov would be difficult. I also knew that personal relationships are valuable in international arenas. So, before I left for Moscow, I purchased—at my own expense—cufflinks engraved with bear claws that closely resembled the Russian national symbol. The cufflinks were hand-crafted by Native American artisans in New Mexico. As any nuclear scientist in the world would be, Mikhailov was familiar with New Mexico. After all, the Atomic Age had begun there in 1945 with the testing of the first atomic bomb near Alamogordo. He seemed very appreciative of my gift, and he gave me a gift in kind. I was moved when he took down one of his personal paintings from his office wall to give me. And I knew that sharing a shot or two of vodka would help our negotiations, so I rendered my country a great service when the U.S. delegation, led by Vice President Gore, dined at a beautiful resort with Prime Minister Chernomyrdin and his team.

I was seated across from Mikhailov. Elgie Holstein sat next to his counterpart, who, being a jazz lover, kept toasting Louis Armstrong. As the night wore on, Mikhailov and I toasted each other and our countries many, many times. Russian toasts lasted so long it was a challenge to hold my arm up high for the duration. The first shot of remarkably smooth vodka easily gave way to a second, and then a third. Seven or eight shots later, having toasted our cultures, our leaders, and our dreams, we were barely functional, but very friendly. Elgie soon met me in the men's restroom, where we wondered at our ability to keep up, especially since we were not big vodka drinkers. I told him I was holding my own, and Elgie agreed he was doing the same.

As Vice President Gore prepared to leave the banquet that night, he walked past our table, and I introduced him to Mikhailov. His social propriety drowned, Mikhailov lunged at Gore with a hearty kiss. The Vice President, taken aback, quickly appraised the situation. "Just doing what's needed for my country, Mr. Vice President," I explained. Gore laughed and gave Mikhailov a bear hug. The next day, our negotiations went more smoothly.

The facility at Bushehr ultimately was completed, but not before the Russians agreed that they, and not the Iranians, would operate the reactor. Any spent nuclear fuel would be returned to Russia to minimize Iran's access.

During my second trip to Russia, our concern was that some of the country's nuclear materials might be missing. The vast majority of Americans back then did not know about our extensive efforts to secure nuclear materials left unprotected in the states of the former Soviet Union. To help prevent these materials from falling into the hands of terrorists or leaders of rogue states, Senators Sam Nunn, a Democrat from Georgia, and Richard Lugar, a Republican from Indiana, persuaded Congress in 1992 to pass the Cooperative Threat Reduction Program.

1997, Secretary Peña and Russia Minister of Atomic Energy
Mikilov signing agreement.
Photo courtesy of the Peña Family Archives.

Nunn-Lugar, as the law would be called, provided funding to secure and dismantle weapons of mass destruction and their associated infrastructure in Ukraine, Georgia, Azerbaijan, Belarus, Uzbekistan, and Kazakhstan—states that were spun off from the Soviet Union and were struggling to manage the nuclear stock left behind. Their limited resources were insufficient to allow them to protect their nuclear sites, and they needed help.

I saw up close the critical need for the projects that Nunn-Lugar was designed to fund. I was alarmed to learn about installations where piles of nuclear materials were inadequately stored. At one site, only a turnstile gate served as an entrance. No secure fencing, cameras, or security badge requirements—

none of the most rudimentary protections required by modern security systems. Almost anyone could enter and potentially remove what they wanted. In the middle of the night, a band of terrorists could easily swoop in and out, loaded with the very stuff nightmares are made of.

By the time Nunn-Lugar came up for reauthorization in 1998, it had helped deactivate hundreds of nuclear warheads, silos, and intercontinental weapons at sites around the world; secured enormous amounts of fissile material; and blended down tons of highly enriched uranium. There was no question that I would do whatever I could as Secretary of Energy to extend the program. I went to the Capitol to meet with Senator Lugar and others to urge continued funding for the program.

Much of the work to secure fifty-three different sites had been done secretly—especially the missions that removed dangerous materials to safe locations in the U.S. and elsewhere. At the end of one such mission, I was proud to welcome home the team that completed Operation Auburn Endeavor, which had airlifted especially vulnerable weapons-grade uranium out of the former Soviet republic of Georgia. It was satisfying to see a government program working as it was intended, and I found it immensely fulfilling to see the United States acting unselfishly to help protect untold millions from possible harm.

Although Nunn-Lugar had produced solid results over twenty-one years, Russia announced its intention to withdraw from the program in 2012. The Kremlin declared that it was more concerned about maintaining its military secrets than continuing to benefit from the financial assistance we were providing. The defeat of Senator Lugar in his 2012 bid for re-election, and the previous retirement of Senator Nunn, robbed the Senate of the expertise and passion needed to further this important work.

During Senator Lugar's re-election campaign, his opponent claimed that Indiana's Senior Senator was too cozy with his Democratic colleagues in the Senate. The sad truth is that few members of the Senate have done as much for national security as Richard Lugar. It is a tragic time indeed when patriotic stalwarts from opposing parties, like Senators Lugar and Nunn, cannot work together to solve the kinds of problems that otherwise could, literally, blow up the world. Today's partisan fighting in our nation's capital is disturbing evidence of a dysfunctional Congress that should be able to accomplish much more for the American people.

On November 20, 2013, President Obama awarded Richard Lugar the Presidential Medal of Freedom. I was proud to have played a role in Lugar's work, and I continue to hope the end of Nunn-Lugar never results in dangerous nuclear materials falling into terrorists' hands.

Though we made significant progress on nuclear matters, there was more to be had in dealing with the Russians.

It was all about oil.

27. Caspian Concerns

Although the Caspian Sea is known for producing more than 90 percent of the world's caviar, this enormous body of water has been the subject of great geo-strategic conflicts for centuries.

Even today, the Caspian Sea remains a cauldron of conflict. The strategic importance of the region stems from the oil and gas under its seabed. Where cultures and religions have clashed for centuries, now Russia, the West, and Iran collide over as many as 178 billion barrels of oil—thirty-three times the reserves in the North Slope of Alaska.

The Caspian Sea is ringed by covetous nations. To the north are Russia and Kazakhstan, and to the south sits Iran. On the west is Azerbaijan, and to the east is Turkmenistan. Each of these five nations are developing economies to increase their geopolitical weight. All the while, beyond the Caspian shorelines await the energy thirsty nations of China and Europe.

As the dominant power in the region, the Soviet Union explored for energy in the Caspian very early on. When the Soviet Union collapsed in 1991, dominion over the Caspian grew more complex and contentious. The geopolitical reality of a weakened Russia allowed smaller countries—abbreviated and referred to as the "Stans"—to believe they too could exploit the sea's enormous oil and gas deposits. President George H. Bush established diplomatic relations with the "Stans," and American energy companies quickly zeroed in on the region's resources. President Clinton, building on Bush's policy, received the President of Azerbaijan, Heydar Aliyev, at the White House in August 1997.

The Clinton administration protected western interests by supporting the construction of pipelines to transport oil and gas from the Caspian Sea to Western Europe. Russia already had a small pipeline exporting oil from the Caspian inland, and Iran was encouraging Turkmenistan to send its gas through Iranian pipelines. Iran's intention, of course, was to undermine sanctions that the United States and other nations imposed for Iran's support of terrorism. Russia wanted Europe dependent on its oil. It was in our national security interest to intercede. Consequently, as Energy Secretary, I became part of a multi-agency team tasked to implement U.S. policy in the region despite Iran's objections and Russia's worries. In this quagmire, Azerbaijan would prove to be the lynchpin. Thankfully, I had several experts assisting me: Robert Gee, Assistant Secretary for Policy and International Affairs; Elgie Holstein, Chief of Staff; and Kyle Simpson, Senior Advisor. We worked with the White House in developing America's Caspian strategy.

In November 1997, I led a five-day presidential mission to the Caspian region to begin negotiations with the leaders of Georgia, Turkmenistan, Azerbaijan, Armenia, and Turkey. It was my first visit to these countries. I was struck by their deep and rich history, their culture, and their people. The intense political conflicts among them made a very complex situation even more complicated.

The fundamental problem was that these Caspian countries could not agree on how to divide the landlocked sea. They bickered over the sites of their respective drilling operations. In the meantime, Iran intensified its campaign to draw the countries into its orbit by offering them shorter routes for their oil to reach market. We did not want Iran to have that leverage over Europe. Russia worried that it would be excluded from future pipeline opportunities, thereby diminishing the value of its oil and gas reserves. It did not want to cede ground to U.S. energy companies, even though billions of dollars were required to construct the pipelines. Russia's anxieties were exacerbated by low oil and gas prices in the 1990s that were devastating its economy. The political instability in the region was worrisome.

Compounding the challenge was the reality that strongmen ruled these lands. Nevertheless, many of the region's leaders looked to us to help them join the global energy economy. Of course, they were fully aware that entering into collaborative agreements with the U.S. would provide protection from future Russian aggression. The clout and respect the United States carried around the world was extraordinary.

In Turkmenistan, I met with the country's authoritarian President, Saparmurat Niyazov. Niyazov was in a territorial dispute with Azerbaijan over drilling in the Caspian. Riding through the capital city of Ashgabat, I saw Niyazov's image glorified on many buildings and in the newspapers. It was surreal. Ironically enough, Niyazov's top advisor was a young man who attended Texas A&M University. Not that it helped my cause any. It was clear that these were difficult people willing to keep their options open, especially with Iran. I nevertheless offered to help resolve their territorial dispute with Azerbaijan.

Following my conversations with Niyazov, I flew to Armenia to meet with President Levon Ter-Petrosyan to discuss the disputed lands of Nagorno-Karabakh. Armenia and Azerbaijan fought a six-year war from 1988 to 1994 over Nagorno-Karabakh, whose citizens had close kinship with Armenians. The Armenians won the war, taking 20 percent of the former landmass of Azerbaijan. To successfully work with Azerbaijan on a pipeline, I needed to help resolve its dispute with Armenia. This was a challenging proposition, especially since the strong Armenian American lobby in the U.S. convinced Congress to pass sanctions against Azerbaijan. I was trying to reconcile American law with the country's strategic interests. How I yearned for the days back at Transportation! Recently, the two countries again fell into conflict, with Azerbaijan regaining much of the disputed land. Russia supported Armenia while Turkey assisted Azerbaijan.

I met with President Suleyman Demirel and Prime Minister Mesut Yilmaz of Turkey to seek support for a pipeline from Baku, Azerbaijan through Georgia, and then to Ceyhan, Turkey. The Turks were receptive because every year hundreds of oil tankers treacherously traversed the Bosphorus Strait, which cuts through a segment of Turkey. They emphasized that so many tankers moving through such a small waterway increased the danger of collisions and potentially ruinous spills. The Turks did not want the development in the Caspian oilfields to add still more traffic to its dangerously congested area. A new pipeline could help prevent a potential disaster.

By far the most important part of my trip was meeting with President Heydar Aliyev in Baku, Azerbaijan. I arrived in Baku almost simultaneously with Russian Deputy Prime Minister Boris Nemtsov, whom I had seen in Moscow a few months earlier.

I developed a fondness for Nemtsov. He spoke English fluently and had traveled across the U.S. He was a happy warrior, an unabashed reformer in the administration of Boris Yeltsin, and was considered a likely future President of Russia. Nemtsov demonstrated heroic courage in opposing corruption and supporting personal freedom, free markets, and broad reforms in Russia.

Despite my warm feelings for Nemtsov, we were rivals that day in Baku. Russia is constantly at odds with Georgia. The Azerbaijani pipeline, crossing through Georgia, would move the former Soviet state farther away from the Russian sphere of influence and closer to the West.

President Aliyev invited Nemtsov and me to view by helicopter the collection of decrepit Cold War structures the Soviets had built in the Caspian in the 1940s, called "Oil Stones." Russia's need for energy prompted them to build these "Oil Stones" about twenty-five miles from shore. Once the Soviets realized that oil in northern Siberia was more plentiful, they abandoned the "Oil Stones." We could see from the air that the buildings had deteriorated and were polluting the sea. The old roads that connected the buildings and schools were still visible. Aliyev wanted Nemtzov to see what Russia had left behind.

Despite the demise of the "Oil Stones," Azerbaijan had preceded with its own explorations. Upon landing, President Aliyev invited us to participate in a "first oil" ceremony to celebrate the oil first piped to its shore. I watched as Aliyev and his advisors each dipped their hands into a bucket of oil and rubbed it on their cheeks. They laughed joyfully in front of the media. President Aliyev then turned to me, gesturing for me to do the same.

Aware of the importance of the invitation, I gamely followed, splashing oil on each cheek while it dripped on my suit and onto my shoes. Everyone thought it was funny. But the act of camaraderie was worth it, engendering a close rapport with Aliyev that paid off when we presented ourselves to the Azerbaijani Congress later that day.

The scene in the Congress reminded me of a Cold War movie. Deep-red curtains draped the stage, while several hundred parliamentary members were seated quietly and upright in their seats. Each seemed to wear the same dark-colored suit. It was clear who was in charge.

Standing before Congress, Aliyev, Nemtsov, and I quietly discussed the order of our presentations. President Aliyev suggested that I speak after him. Nemtsov objected strenuously, arguing that he was a higher-ranking official than me and that it would be an insult to Russia if I spoke before him. I was amused by the tussle and told Aliyev I was willing to speak third, a concession that surprised him. Sometimes being diplomatic pays off, as I would later discover.

With interpreters at the ready, Aliyev launched into a long speech about the glorious future of Azerbaijan, the importance of oil to the nation, and the need to have helpful partners in the process. It was a serious speech with subtle messages to the Russians about the importance of independence. Then Nemtsov took the stage and, in what seemed to be unprepared remarks, opened with Russian jokes that did not sit well with the audience. His speech was received with lukewarm interest. Then I rose, fully aware that my speech represented the culmination of years of hard work by the United States.

In prepared remarks, I thanked our hosts for the warm welcome, described U.S. interests in the area, mentioned our positive relations with Russia, and then delivered the intended message of the visit: the United States officially and firmly supported a new, east-west pipeline from Baku to Ceyhan, through Georgia. I made it clear that the United States opposed investments in Iran's energy sector, investments in an Iranian pipeline, and the transport of Caspian oil and gas through Iran. The audience rose and exploded with applause. I had to stop speaking. The standing ovation seemed to last forever. President Aliyev stood smiling and seemed to be clapping the loudest.

I felt a bit sheepish in not having alerted the Russians about my speech, which was seen as a frontal assault on the Russian position in the region. Greatly displeased, Nemtsov looked angry as he quickly rose and left the stage.

While my Baku speech signaled U.S. support for Azerbaijan's independence from Russia, I emphasized to my Russian counterparts that building and financing Caspian pipelines would require billions of dollars, and they were welcome to participate. Yet, no matter how much I emphasized that Russia was welcome to take part in the project, and that we would support other pipelines to her benefit, Russian officials remained suspicious. Clearly, they recognized the support the U.S. enjoyed among leaders of most Caspian Sea countries. Had they chosen a different path, perhaps the geopolitical problems that have become even more deeply entrenched in the region might have been lessened—if not completely avoided. Instead, Russia has continued its own production with minimal cooperation with the U.S.

Later, back in Washington, I met with President Nursultan Nazarbayev of Kazakhstan who was cognizant of the need to placate Russia. He had previously supported the Russian pipeline known as the Caspian Pipeline Consortium. It would run from the Tengiz oil and gas field in northwestern Kazakhstan to Russia's Novorossiysk terminal. But he agreed to the alternative routes we proposed. We now had agreements from all the countries ringing the Caspian Sea, with the exceptions, of course, of Russia and Iran.

Though tremendous tactical progress had been made with our Caspian mission, we faced a bigger challenge in persuading private companies of the pipeline's viability. To provide impetus, American governmental support would be required. And so, in June 1998, at a conference hosted by the United States Trade and Development Agency in Istanbul, I announced the creation of The Caspian Sea Initiative.

The Caspian Sea Initiative brought together, for the first time, three independent U.S. trade and investment agencies: the Export-Import Bank, the Office of Private Investment Cooperation, and the Trade Development Agency. They agreed to coordinate the development of Caspian energy resources and multiple export routes. Senator Chuck Hagel of Nebraska, later Secretary of Defense under President Obama, was present because of his strong support for the pipeline.

Seven years later, in 2005, after significant political and economic challenges, the pipeline was completed. Even as late as 2000, Russian, Iranian, and other analysts—including some in the West—were proclaiming the project would never be completed. At a cost of $4 billion from private sector investment, and following a decade of controversy, Energy Secretary Samuel Bodman joined the presidents of Georgia, Azerbaijan, and Turkey to ceremoniously open the pipeline.

President Ilham Aliyev of Azerbaijan, who had succeeded his Father, declared, "The realization of this project would not have been possible without the constant political support from the United States." Azerbaijan became a significant contributor to Europe's energy security and would help counter Russia's dominance in the European energy market.

Russia's 2014 invasion of Crimea and its threatening attitude toward its neighbors have shined a spotlight on its control of gas delivery throughout Europe. It makes clear the need for western nations to utilize new, market-based energy sources. But continued exploration of the Caspian Sea remains part of the solution to this problem.

Over the years, the United States has skillfully promoted its energy and security interests via free markets, technology, and transparency while spurring the diversification of energy production around the world. These efforts have contributed to a decrease in our energy dependence on the Middle East and were part of the Comprehensive National Energy Strategy I submitted to Congress in 1998.

Through its support of new energy development, the U.S. has, until recently, been able to counter Russia's incomprehensible and aggressive actions in the Caspian region. A marked change occurred on August 12, 2018, when, after twenty years of negotiations, the five littoral states of the Caspian Sea signed the "Convention on the Legal Status of the Caspian Sea." While not resolving all issues, this treaty defined the legal status of the five Caspian countries.

Unfortunately, there is now a "conspicuous absence" of the U.S. in the region, according to many analysts. The Trump administration withdrew from the Joint Comprehensive Plan of Action—the Iran nuclear deal. As a result, Iran's geo-economic priorities will re-emerge, threatening Europe's energy security needs and our own strategic priorities. And the cooling of relations with Turkey, Azerbaijan's close ally, could result in the Caspian Sea region being defined by Russia's geopolitical ambitions. Some European nations are mistakenly relying on Russian gas partly as a result of Trump's negative attitude toward them. Thus, all the work of the Bush, Clinton, Bush, and Obama administrations to protect our interests in the Caspian Sea may now have been undone. I worry that President Trump's questionable relationship with Russia undercut America's influence in this important part of the world. He undermined the consistent policies of previous administrations by permitting Russia to intervene in the Caspian Sea and elsewhere. This is another example of how America loses progress whenever a new administration whimsically changes course.

While most Americans do not have Caspian concerns on their minds, I pray that years from now we will not be compelled to expend precious human and material resources to once again stabilize an unstable part of the world. The ownership and control of oil and gas has for decades been a source of conflict. This will likely continue as China, India, and Southeast Asia develop further. Today, the United States has no constructive policy to address these challenges. I tried to continue and expand on the Caspian strategy started by President H.W. Bush, as did subsequent administrations. Sadly, under Trump, we abandoned any effective and sustainable energy policy either domestically or internationally. I believe President Biden will establish a robust energy strategy for our country

Traversing the Caspian Sea, negotiating with the Russians over the mistreatment of American energy companies, interacting with energy ministers from across the globe, addressing the needs of bankrupt energy companies, and dealing with the Saudis drove me to focus on making our country more energy secure. It was a matter of national security two decades ago and remains one today.

I believed that in the 1990s it made sense to collaborate with energy ministers in our hemisphere to coordinate energy policies—from trading electricity to constructing cross border oil and gas pipelines—to reduce energy dependence beyond our hemisphere. I came to appreciate the risks when a nation depends too heavily on oil and gas revenues while I attended an Energy Ministerial in Caracas hosted by the Venezuelan Energy Minister. He surprised us by excusing himself from our meeting to attend an emergency cabinet meeting. Declining oil prices had decimated his country's finances. The Venezuelan emergency reinforced my determination to protect our country from the uncertainties of oil and gas supplies and pricing—and the exogenous forces beyond our control.

Although my 1998 CNES policy focused on the national security implications of reduced energy production, I also supported Vice President Gore's efforts to address global warming. The challenge was to balance our need for energy independence with the imperative to reduce carbon emissions. Today, few leaders work to reconcile these seemingly conflicting priorities. Some focus exclusively on ending oil and gas production to address climate change while others, like President Trump, argued that climate change is a hoax and that we should "drill baby drill."

I believe these are false choices. We can reconcile oil and gas production with climate change. I was faced with an "either-or" challenge when I dealt with the recession in the 1980s as Denver's Mayor. As detailed in chapters above, I believed we could rebuild our economy and reduce air pollution at the same time. Similarly, I contend that we can gradually reduce our dependence on fossil fuels while transitioning to clean energy. In doing so, we can achieve energy security and build a strong economy.

Over the next two decades, a balanced and consistent policy of reducing consumption and maintaining some sustainable production can reduce oil imports to 10 percent. To achieve this, we must bring all affected parties together to embrace the national security imperative of energy security and to address climate change. Many constructive strategies can be implemented to reduce carbon emissions and create millions of new clean energy jobs. But we will not become more energy secure by persisting on our current track of pitting one party against another. We need a new approach.

Currently, petroleum represents 40 percent of all U.S. energy supply, providing over 70 percent of transportation fuel and 30 percent of industrial fuel. Americans consume about 20 million barrels of oil per day and we produce about 12 million barrels per day. We can reduce petroleum consumption by 40 percent down to 12 million barrels per day over the next two decades. During this period, we can maintain current oil and gas production, as we transition to cleaner fuels, and thereby reduce oil imports to 10 percent by 2040.

How do we accomplish this? By adopting higher fuel economy standards for cars and trucks, as President Obama proposed, to 54.5 MPG by 2025 and thereafter requiring 2 percent improvements each year. We must produce more sustainable ethanol and renewable diesel. Mass transit usage can be doubled by 2030. Consumption of aviation fuel can be dramatically improved. We should increase tax credits and other incentives to dramatically increase electric vehicles and charging stations. Electric vehicle sales have already increased to 8% of total sales in the second quarter of 2021. Thanks to Tesla's pioneering products, most major manufactures are now producing electric vehicles.

Our cars and trucks can be redesigned to reduce energy consumption by utilizing lighter-weight materials like aluminum and high-strength steel, and polymer composites like carbon fiber in manufacturing new vehicles.

The bottom line is obvious. Reducing consumption by 40 percent with these and other strategies will gradually lessen the need for additional oil production and accelerate a shift to non-carbon energy supplies. Shareholders, bond rating agencies, and changing consumer preferences are compelling alert energy company management teams and their boards to re-evaluate business strategies and explore new revenue sources. Major producers are investing in carbon capture technologies and alternative fuels, and adding battery charging centers for electric vehicles to service stations. BP and Royal Dutch Shell PKL, committed to net-zero carbon emissions, are investing their oil proceeds in renewable energy. We must offer the scientists, engineers and other resources of our national laboratories and provide additional incentives to energy companies to accelerate their transition to clean energy. It's a matter of national security.

While we improve our energy security by reducing consumption and maintaining production over the next twenty years, we can simultaneously reduce carbon emissions. We will get there. The technological progress we are making will allow us to change the world in the many ways we can—and should—imagine.

Some of our global competitors hope we fail to understand the opportunity before us. Our contemporary partisan conflicts blur our memories of the traumatic effects of the oil embargoes of the 1970s. We forget that manipulations of oil prices, often caused by the OPEC cartel and affiliated countries, have helped spark ten of the eleven major recessions of the past thirty-five years. The world of energy has become more complex, and the political instability of current and emerging energy-producing countries is cause for worry. I am hopeful President Biden will establish an effective and robust energy strategy for the future.

Our leaders can move America toward energy security while addressing climate change. We need a comprehensive vision and shared strategies to achieve these goals. We need a constant and persistent commitment over the next several decades by both Democratic and Republican administrations to succeed. I saw how long-term commitments by successive mayoral administrations, with the engagement and support of citizens, transformed Denver. We can do the same for America.

28. Secrets and Lies

On July 14, 1997, four months after becoming Secretary of Energy, I entered a secure facility buried deep in our building on Independence Avenue. I was taken along a well-lit but stark hall into an austere room known as the "vault" to be briefed on a security issue by counterintelligence officials. With me was Deputy Secretary Betsy Moler. The officers wasted no time jolting us with potentially devastating news: a serious breach of national security might have occurred years earlier at the Los Alamos National Laboratory, our premiere research center in northern New Mexico. I was astounded. Why had nothing been done before now?

Los Alamos scientists were responsible for the safety and reliability of our nation's nuclear deterrent. These were some of the very scientists who reviewed nuclear weapons to ensure they were maintained safely and securely. They had at their fingertips some of the nation's most important secrets. I learned that one of them was thought to have provided China with critical, highly-sensitive information about the W88 thermonuclear warhead.

The Chinese military had made extraordinary advances in its nuclear weapons program over a short period of time. It was understandable for people to suspect that China's progress was achieved through the illegal acquisition of information from Los Alamos. The FBI had several past and present Los Alamos personnel under surveillance. I was told the FBI wanted to keep certain individuals in their current positions and allow laboratory operations to proceed normally, to avoid alerting their suspects.

I was outraged by the idea that U.S. nuclear weapons data might have been provided to China by one of our own scientists. The implications were enormous. Any advances the Chinese made to accelerate their military might disrupt the order of power in the Pacific and the world. Not since the Rosenbergs—Americans accused of passing secrets to the Soviets in the early 1950s—had so serious a charge been leveled in our country. And it would not be the last. At the time of the Los Alamos investigation, known as Kindred Spirit, an FBI agent named Robert Hanssen had been selling secrets to the Russians for eighteen years. He continued for four more years until his arrest.

Since the suspicions about Los Alamos had to be shared with the broader intelligence community, my team, led by Deputy Secretary Moler and Chief of Staff Holstein, briefed the offices of Attorney General Janet Reno, Secretary of Defense William Cohen, FBI Director Louis Freeh, CIA Director George Tenet, and, of course, the President's National Security Advisor, Sandy Berger.

I soon learned that security deficiencies had been a concern at our national laboratories for years. To make matters worse, I became aware of long-standing, internal disagreements and personnel conflicts between and within the offices of Intelligence and Counterintelligence—in my own department. I immediately ordered a review of all security procedures at our nation's research facilities.

Having run large organizations, I was not surprised to find

institutional disagreements within an operation as large and complex as the Department of Energy. But I was furious about the tensions within DOE in matters involving the nation's security. I addressed the conflicts by creating new offices of Intelligence and Counterintelligence and required that each report directly to me. In early 1998, President Clinton issued a Presidential Decision Directive (PDD-61) ordering major reforms in national counterintelligence and in overall security at our nation's laboratories.

To emphasize the importance of the PDD, I brought the Directors of the national laboratories to Washington to personally impress upon them the urgency of the situation. I had them meet with the FBI and CIA. I refused to tolerate further security lapses. We continued to follow the investigative directives of the FBI on Kindred Spirit.

While all of this was going on, other DOE business continued, including my repeat trips to Russia and the Caspian region. Shortly after I returned from the June 1998 Istanbul conference, where I announced the creation of the Caspian Sea Initiative, I prepared to retire from DOE and return to Denver. I had informed the President of my plan to leave the DOE earlier in the year and was more than ready to return to private life.

Over the next two years, the Kindred Spirit investigation and subsequent Federal Court hearings became a debacle. As soon as word of the investigation was leaked to the press, Los Alamos scientist Dr. Wen Ho Lee, a Taiwanese immigrant who had come to the U.S. in 1964, was publicly announced as its prime suspect. At Los Alamos, Lee wrote computer code to design nuclear bombs and simulate their testing at the national laboratory. A tsunami of print, TV, and radio reports ensued as news coverage of the investigation turned frenetic and congressional investigations began.

On December 10, 1999, I watched from my home in Denver as a Federal Grand Jury indicted Lee on fifty-nine counts of mishandling classified information. The judge ordered him detained without bond and mandated to solitary confinement. Following several preliminary hearings, it became clear that the government had miscalculated, or worse, overreached. The case against Lee crumbled, and in the end a plea bargain was reached in which Lee pled guilty to only a single count.

At Dr. Lee's sentencing, U.S. District Judge James Parker harshly rebuked federal officials, stating they had "caused embarrassment by the way this case began and was handled." He further declared that they had "embarrassed our entire nation and each of us who is a citizen of it."

While I am not permitted to discuss confidential matters relative to this case, certain details, which became public after I left the department, have concerned me. The most egregious was that I was led to believe that the briefing I received in the vault in early 1997 was the first time the Kindred Spirit allegations had surfaced. In fact, suspicions about Lee had been shared several years earlier with the FBI and the White House.

Also, the behavior of the media was at best irresponsible and at worst dangerous to our democracy. To my dismay and consternation, a number of newspapers, without interviewing me, criticized the decisions I had made and the actions I had taken relative to Mr. Lee. The media did not know, or care to learn, that its characterizations of my actions as being too cautious were erroneous. Had they contacted me, they would have learned that my decisions were the direct result of FBI directives for the DOE to refrain from taking action against Los Alamos personnel while the investigation was underway.

I subsequently testified as a private citizen before the Senate Select Committee in late 1999 to describe my actions as Secretary of Energy. I urged that mandatory briefings be held on all security issues involving the DOE for each incoming Department of Energy Secretary, Deputy Secretary, and Undersecretary within thirty days following their swearing in. I testified that there needed to be a clearer understanding between the Executive Branch and Congress about which congressional committees should be briefed in cases of such high importance, how classified information should be treated by all parties, and what information should be provided to the public without jeopardizing ongoing investigations.

After the Lee case ended, some members of the media grudgingly admitted to their inaccurate reporting—a truly rare occurrence. Many Asian Americans and other citizens complained that the mistreatment of Dr. Lee had been due, in part, to his Asian heritage. Sadly, we see blame mistakenly ascribed because of ethnicity over and over. Following the Oklahoma City bombing in 1995, there was an immediate rush to suspect people of Middle Eastern heritage, when in fact it was the work of Americans Timothy McVeigh and Terry Nichols. An innocent Indian American was targeted unfairly for the Boston Marathon bombing before the correct suspects were identified. In an age when data circles the world in seconds, we must be certain the information we have is correct before we assert its truth. I am left to worry about civil liberties and basic civil rights in the U.S. in the years ahead. In his four years as President, Trump furthered the knee-jerk reaction to blame minorities with his outrageous statements. In doing so, he encouraged others to make unfounded statements about ethnic and racial groups here at home and across the globe. In doing so, he endangered all of us.

In early 1998, as I was planning my retirement from the DOE, the Monica Lewinsky story started to unfold. Like most Americans, I learned about the Lewinsky affair through press reports. I was present at the January 23 cabinet meeting when the President assured us there was nothing to the allegations and that the matter would resolve itself. Several cabinet members spoke to the media afterward, assuring the public of the President's innocence. Though saddened by the whole thing, I— like other Americans—had more important things on my mind. I was a father of three, with a newborn son, Ryan, and his six- and eight-year-old sisters. I did not want to raise them in D.C., especially if I remained a cabinet member. It was time to head home.

At my official farewell on July 1, 1998, several hundred employees came to say goodbye. Also present were reporters, most of whom asked reasonable questions about my reasons for leaving, what I had accomplished, and issues that awaited the new Secretary of Energy. One asked whether I was leaving due to a pending indictment against me. Some members of the audience gasped, but then quieted, awaiting my response. I was indignant.

"Please stand up and identify yourself and who you represent," I insisted.

The reporter did so, adding that his editors at UPI had instructed him to ask the question.

"Tell your superiors that they need to be much more respectful of people who are in government today," I told him. "It is ridiculous questions like that which often try to embarrass public officials and perhaps drive people away from government." I was clearly upset and exasperated with this type of media intimidation.

The audience erupted in applause. As the reporter sheepishly sat down, I could see other reporters shaking their heads, embarrassed by the antics of one of their own. A number of my fellow cabinet members called that afternoon to congratulate me for challenging the reporter, confiding that they wished they had confronted other reporters in a similar way. It had been a risky move, however. He could have returned to his office and written that the Secretary of Energy, in his last day in office, had "lost his composure" or "responded defensively" or, worse, was going on the offensive in an obvious attempt to hide something. At the moment, though, I didn't care. My personal integrity was at stake, and I was fed up with press reports that recklessly assailed the integrity or motivations of decent people.

My hesitancy in accepting a cabinet position six years earlier was because I held the impression that some political players in Washington become consumed by a sense of privilege and power. For some, these trappings corrode the ideal of public service.

I was committed to maintaining my integrity and values through the years of service to my country. I was pleased with the hard work and dedication of my teams at both the DOT and the DOE, believing we accomplished much in a short period of time. At a ceremony at the White House, I thanked the President and Vice President for the honor of serving, and they responded by thanking me for my service and wishing me well.

Finally, as the airplane door closed on my flight home, my fear of being called back began to subside.

Besides, it was hot outside and nowhere near Christmas.

Part Six: Denver (1999–2020)

29. You Can Come Home

The phone rang frequently with calls inquiring about my next professional step once I announced my resignation from the Department of Energy. I declined all offers emanating from Washington or cities where I had no personal connection. Staying in Washington was out of the question, and living anywhere other than Denver seemed illogical.

Some opportunities posed conflicts of interest with my government work. When I was invited to serve on the corporate board of a foreign airline, I declined because I had negotiated aviation rights for U.S. airlines against that airline's government. I also declined to provide advice to an Eastern European government involved in energy development.

The one inquiry that immediately caught my attention came from Jim Kelley, who headed the Denver office of Vestar Capital Partners, a private equity firm headquartered in New York. At the time, I did not know much about private equity, but the idea intrigued me. Discussions ensued with Dan O'Connell, the company's CEO, and by August I arrived at Vestar Capital in Denver as a Senior Advisor. I enjoyed the work, and in a few months became a Managing Director focusing on transportation, energy, media, and telecommunications companies. I found the challenge of investing significant amounts of capital in mid-sized companies fascinating and rewarding. I believed government was filled with talented, forward-thinking workers, but the private sector is just as remarkable, if not more so. On a day-to-day basis, Investment Managers evaluate economic trends, consumer behavior, and company strategies in excruciating detail, and I found the process of conducting due diligence enthralling.

I had a great job, the children were in good schools, and I was exhilarated to reconnect with Colorado friends. We bought a nice home near a wonderful park where the kids could play, and it was a relief to be back in a dry climate away from the humidity of D.C. Most importantly, it was a delight to be with people who were not fixated on my being a cabinet member. I enjoyed driving myself to work without a security detail and marveling again at the Rocky Mountains.

It soon became clear that my wife Ellen and I had grown apart. We sought counseling but could not find a way forward together. Telling our three children we were divorcing was the most painful experience in my life. We agreed on joint custody and faced the future as single parents. Coming from a tight-knit Catholic family I felt I had disappointed my children, my parents, and my family. I had never experienced anything as dreadful. I thought I had worked hard to avoid the pitfalls that come with public life and the all-consuming seduction of Washington power. Yet divorce was my reality at age fifty-four. Searching for understanding, it took years of counseling, prayer, and self-reflection for me to regain my footing.

My focus remained on my children as I tried to provide as normal a life as possible. It was difficult. One particular night, the exhaustion and stress overwhelmed me. The kids were in bed, and at one o'clock in the morning I was doing laundry with yet another anxious work day ahead. Dead tired, I broke down from physical exhaustion.

Fortunately, my children and I held it together. I still marvel at how resilient they were. Nelia graduated from Harvard University cum laude, earned two master's degrees, and is pursuing a PhD in Education. Cristina followed her creative writing passion to graduate from Hampshire College and received her Master of Education from Columbia. Ryan flourished in high school where he excelled in baseball. He graduated from Brown University and is now working in financial services.

Reflecting on the impact of divorce on children, I am reminded that I was blessed with parents who loved their children and kept our family intact. As children, and later as adults, we never worried about our parents separating. We grew up with the comfort of knowing we could visit them in Brownsville and envelop ourselves in the loving environment of home. I cannot imagine what my siblings and I would have done had our parents divorced, but I am thankful that my children have found the way to grow into mature and loving adults. I love them dearly and am very proud of them.

So, I did come home but with a changed family.

30. New Hope

Working late one evening in my Vestar office in July 2003, I received a phone call from Warren Toltz, a friend of many decades. He suggested that I call a woman he knew whom I might find intriguing. Her name was Cindy Velásquez, the General Manager of the local ABC television affiliate. I thanked him for thinking of me but gently told him I wasn't interested. He "threatened" to end our friendship if I did not make the call. Warren likely recognized that Cindy and I would enjoy becoming friends.

Warren had never spoken to me in this way, so I called Cindy and we met for dinner. I found her enchanting. We soon began dating. Though Cindy had a crowded schedule, we managed to fit time into our respective family and work routines to get to know each other.

By coordinating some of our business travel, we were able to meet in San Francisco, New York, and other cities. It all worked. Cindy was beautiful, intelligent, and driven. We were incredulous that our paths had never crossed. Since 1978, I had been in public life and Cindy had been in the television business working for the NBC and ABC stations in Denver. At KUSA, she began as a college intern and worked her way up through the ranks. When she became General Manager of KMGH-TV, she was one of the first Hispanics in the country to run a major market network affiliate and the first woman to run one in Denver.

We soon discovered we were committed to our faith and our families and that we shared similar philosophies of life. I marveled at Cindy's generosity to others, at how she cared about causes she believed in, and at the pain she felt at a stranger's tragedy. These were core values that we shared, and I loved her for them. She also embraced my children, who were much younger than her own daughter. I met Pilar on a trip to New York City where she lived following her college graduation. Pilar was beautiful, fun, and had boundless energy. She shared the same caring spirit of her Mother. Pilar returned to Denver, earned a master's from Regis Jesuit University in Denver, and became a teacher.

2019, The Peña family at Cristina and Scott's wedding.
Left to right are Pilar with Quinn, John with Jack, Ryan, Scott, Cristina, Federico, Cindy, Nelia, Danielle. Photo by The Shalom Imaginative.

I am thrilled that Cindy had the joy of meeting my parents in Brownsville while they were alive. They loved her dearly, and her easy and total embrace of the Peña family amazed me. That clinched it for me, and on September 2, 2006, we were married. Since then, we have flourished with our blended family. Pilar, Nelia, and Cristina have each married, and we are thrilled to have two grandsons, Jack and Quinn. Ryan enjoys his three new in-laws, Danielle, John, and Scott.

However successful Cindy was in her field, her real passion was caring for the underserved. For years, she served on the boards of nonprofit organizations that focused on women, education, and health care. But the passion we shared for health care issues became absolute in 2011 when my doctor told me I had tested positive for prostate cancer. Cindy had recently lost her Mother and brother to cancer at young ages. My Mother died of cancer in her nineties. Hearing the words "You have *prostrate cancer*" shocked me, since I had always tried to maintain a healthy lifestyle. I was scared, and I was confused. I had been assured the tests were just "routine." But suddenly my life had become anything but routine. I drove home dazed, unable to assimilate the news. When I arrived home, I could not remember how I got there. When I told Cindy my news, she broke down. The two recent losses in her immediate family had devastated her, and now cancer threatened her husband. She was reeling.

The day after my diagnosis, I dove headlong into hours of research. I read everything I could on the subject and began to understand the dimensions of the disease. Fortunately, I had friends who had survived prostate cancer who counseled me and lifted my spirits. I discovered an almost secret society of men who had the disease, and we shared experiences and advice. Unlike women who speak openly of breast cancer, men are generally silent about prostate cancer. So, I was doubly thankful to those men who reached out. I was blessed with excellent doctors who helped me understand the pros and cons of my options.

True to my nature, I would not make a hasty decision. I finally chose to have my prostate removed, an operation performed by the extraordinary physician, Edward Eigner.

Following the surgery, Cindy helped me walk around the floor of the hospital the same afternoon. Soon she helped me walk around our neighborhood, and finally I began running and biking again. I thank God continually for my many blessings—especially for my wife, our children, and that I remain cancer free.

I was determined to share my experience with as many people as possible. I tell every male friend to get an annual PSA test, and I have supported those who have been diagnosed—just as others aided me. I believe that I can provide other men a sense of confidence that they, too, can be survivors.

I gradually recovered and our lives went back to some semblance of normality, until another shock hit us. This time, doctors found a cancerous spot in one of Cindy's lungs. She had not smoked a day in her life. We endured another round of terror. Again, we were fortunate to have good health insurance and access to great medical care. Within a week of her diagnosis, Cindy had a lobectomy of her right lung. Recovery was tough and it was my time to walk with her, and see her through her challenge. She was courageous through it all, and eventually she, too, was declared cancer free.

Our family's health care challenges motivated us to support the local city hospital, Denver Health, where Nelia and Cristina were born. Aware that we had the resources to secure the finest medical care for ourselves, we knew that many others did not. So, Cindy joined the Denver Health Foundation Board, and we served as co-chairs of the capital campaign to build a neighborhood health clinic in an often-ignored neighborhood in southwest Denver. It is a beautiful clinic that quickly reached capacity. In addition to Denver Health, Cindy had for years supported Clinica Tepayec, a medical clinic providing services to the underserved, including undocumented families. I remained dedicated to promoting and improving education, and I served as chairman of A+ Denver, an organization that promotes academic achievement of low-income and minority school children. I am motivated by the fact that under current conditions, it will take forty years for Hispanic and Black students to catch up to non-minority students in Denver Public Schools. This is a startling reality. America's demography is rapidly changing, and without commensurate progress in educating the country's vast pockets of underserved people, we are headed for a national disaster.

2021, The new Federico F. Peña Family Health Center in West Denver
supported by Cindy and Federico.
Photo courtesy of the Peña Family Archives

Together with Denver oilman Tim Marquez and his wife Bernadette, Cindy and I created the Latino Leadership Institute at the University of Denver. It trains young professionals, through a nine-month program, to become leaders in the broader community. I mentor a number of these individuals who are rising to positions of influence to become the next generation of leaders in Colorado. As I enjoyed my new business and civic ventures, I assumed I was done with active political engagement. I should have known that I could not abstain from matters important to our nation.

31. Obama

Amid the challenges in our personal lives and our commitments to business and community affairs, Cindy and I kept our passion for caring about the country. I still followed local, state and national events, and I anguished over the thousands of lives lost and billions of dollars wasted in Iraq and Afghanistan under the Bush-Cheney Administration. I cringed over the national deficits that George W. Bush's mismanagement of government engineered, exposing our nation to an upcoming national recession. It was a setback from the elimination of the deficit and reduction of our national debt that we had engineered under the Clinton Administration. As a businessman, I found the weakened economy especially disconcerting. And those economic challenges would pale in comparison to the subsequent COVID-19 disruptions.

In just eight years, after inheriting a budget surplus and growing economy in 2000, the Bush administration drove the nation into horrendous debt—and into war. The United States faced a crisis that was taking us dangerously close to a second Depression. Just like Franklin Delano Roosevelt and Bill Clinton, it would take another Democrat to revive our economy and rescue the country. The words of Yogi Berra could not have been more apt: "It was *deja vu* all over again." The looming 2008 presidential election afforded our country's voters an opportunity to choose a President capable of seeing the nation through its latest crisis. I watched men and women, who in early 2007 envisioned themselves to be the Democratic Party's standard-bearers, begin to gear up for the campaign. I knew Hillary Clinton, of course, and John Edwards, John Kerry's running mate in 2004. I knew Senators Joe Biden and Chris Dodd. I knew Bill Richardson, who succeeded me as Secretary of Energy and was elected Governor of bordering New Mexico. I knew Dennis Kucinich. The only potential candidate I had never met was Barack Obama, the Junior Senator from Illinois.

I thought any number of the prospective candidates would do a good job in the White House. Though I cared deeply about who would be nominated, I had not been engaged much on the national level for almost a decade and did not expect to become involved in the Democratic primary. Except that the kids and Cindy had fallen for Obama.

In the early months of 2007, Pilar, our oldest daughter, had moved into the Obama camp and started talking to her Mother and then to Nelia about him. Ryan and Cristina followed soon thereafter. I watched with interest as my family got swept up in what became more of a movement than a campaign. They were not timid about pushing for my support.

I told them I would study the candidates' platforms before making a decision, handling the matter the way I handle everything: by analyzing and assessing. I reflected on my friendships with Bill and Hillary Clinton and considered my loyalty to them. President Clinton had appointed me to two cabinet positions, and I respected Hillary's intelligence and commitment to many causes that I supported. Many of my friends were supporting Hillary. I considered my relationship with Bill Richardson, the only Hispanic in the race, and my past dealings with Biden,

Dodd, and Kucinich.

The more my family became involved in Obama's campaign in Colorado, however, the more he caught my attention. I read his books and listened to his speeches. I grew impressed with his vision of a new America. His campaign theme, "Hope and Change," seemed to echo my own: "Imagine a Great City." Like me, he was the underdog candidate. Then one afternoon in late May, my executive assistant, Renee Hamilton, walked into my office with a look of excitement on her face.

Renee has been with me as a trusted and loyal colleague for many years. One of the most competent individuals I have ever met, she was accustomed to fielding calls from high-profile individuals. But this was *Barack Obama*. The eagerness in her voice reminded me of the time President Clinton first called.

Senator Obama was the only candidate to call me personally. I took the call and after a few pleasantries, Senator Obama said he would like to meet when he came to Denver. "I know we don't know one another yet, but I would still like your support. It would mean a lot," he said.

A few weeks later, our first meeting was arranged at a campaign stop north of Denver. Cindy, Pilar, and Nelia were already planning to attend, so I joined them. We met Barack and Michelle and their daughters at the regional airport in Jefferson County. It was Sasha's birthday and the girls talked about the party waiting for them back in Chicago. After a few pleasantries, Obama and I peeled off to a private conference room in the hangar.

Senator Obama was serious and respectful. He was thoughtful as he shared his vision for the country. He sounded me out, aware and respectful of my relationships with the other candidates. His candor impressed me. He made it clear that my support would be very important to him, acknowledging that Hispanics, like women, represented a cornerstone of Hillary's base. He did not assume that this first meeting was going to convince me—and he was right. I thanked him for the meeting, told him

I would give serious consideration to our conversation, and that I would be in touch.

In the days that followed, I called a friend in Chicago, attorney Manny Sánchez, who knew Obama well. I asked Manny if there was anything about Obama I needed to know. He assured me that Obama was a devoted family man, that he was honest, and that I would not make a mistake by endorsing him. I continued to study Obama's positions as I watched him grow as a candidate.

In the days ahead, I reflected on my life and all I had experienced. I considered the challenges facing our nation and worried about our world in tumult. I watched the Senator connect with the electorate in a way that could rally the country. He was as qualified as his rivals to be President. It became clear to me that helping Barack Obama win the nomination and then the presidential election was the right thing to do. I decided to endorse him.

Under normal circumstances, an endorsement from me would not mean much. But these were not normal circumstances. I would not be endorsing the only Latino running, Bill Richardson. I would not be supporting Hillary Clinton, whom I respected and knew from my six years in Washington, six years that would not have been possible without the faith and confidence of her husband, President Clinton.

Out of courtesy, I notified my friends in the Clinton and Richardson camps that I would be endorsing Senator Obama. On September 7, 2007, on a national teleconference, I announced my support and accepted Senator Obama's offer to become a national campaign co-chair. In turn, the campaign touted me as a former Clinton cabinet member and Hispanic leader from a key battleground state. I immediately began receiving calls from friends and associates. Some were congratulatory. Others were not. Some sought insights about my decision. I found myself at odds with people I had known for years. Some conversations were not pleasant, especially with those who were supporting other presidential candidates.

The Latino vote was especially critical in a number of key states as the fight for the nomination unfolded—as it would be later in the election. My wife and I flew to Miami for the first presidential debate in American history broadcast on a Spanish-language television network. With simultaneous coverage from English-language networks and international press, the debate received great attention in the Latino community. As we entered the United Bank Center for the debate, it was clear that we were vastly outnumbered by Latinos supporting Hillary.

Minutes before the debate, Cindy and I greeted Obama backstage so he would know he had some supporters in the audience. We talked briefly about possible debate topics. Making our way to our seats, Cindy and I passed by the other six candidates, lined up to be introduced to the live audience of about 300 and a television audience of millions. The tension was palpable, as the candidates had the demeanor of gladiators preparing for battle. I was surprised. I had expected to see more comity among them. At the mid-point of the debate, Senator Obama's performance concerned me. He had taken a late flight from California and it showed. He was exhausted, even lethargic. During the break, I walked up to the stage to tell him, "You have to show more energy and more emotion. These are Latino voters!"

He looked at me and replied, "Got it." And he, in fact, did get it...and rallied in the second hour. By the time the debate ended, I was confident he had made an important breakthrough with Latinos.

Following the debate, several friends asked me to support their candidate following the primaries because they believed that Obama would fall by the wayside. I respectfully declined and told them that I thought Obama was going to win. They looked absolutely mystified. Others, whom I had considered friends, purposely avoided me altogether.

The campaign was tough. We were being outspent, most high-profile Democrats supported Hillary and the Clinton machine was in full gear. As a co-chair, I traveled throughout the western states, and Iowa and Pennsylvania, eight states in all, and I could see we were gaining traction. When Obama won in Iowa, African Americans swung to him and away from Hillary, as did a fair share of Latinos.

2008, Candidate Obama and Peña in Pueblo campaign event.
Photo courtesy Obama Presidential Library.

As our support grew, one of Hillary's pollsters went public with his "findings" that Latinos would not vote for Obama because of his race. I knew the pollster and called him to personally voice my disgust. I reminded him that African Americans had supported my mayoral race and African American mayoral candidates in Denver were supported by Latinos. The same had been the case with Harold Washington in Chicago in 1983, Tom Bradley of Los Angeles in 1973, and many others. I told him his results were inaccurate, and I intended to challenge him publicly. I was right. He misjudged the intelligence of Latinos— who continued to move into the Obama camp in large numbers.

A critical moment in the campaign arose over the controversial statements of Reverend Jeremiah Wright, who was a pastor of Obama's church. I met with Obama and a few of his advisors and discussed how he should respond. While some suggested Obama avoid the race issue, I asked him what was in his heart. He responded that he wanted to address race issues head on and I replied, "Then do it." I could not have been prouder of him when he delivered his historic speech on race in March 2008 in the Philadelphia Constitution Center.

After Obama secured the nomination, I attended a delicate meeting in Washington where Hillary and Barack jointly hosted Latino leaders in an attempt to unify the party. Feelings were still raw, however, and emotions were on full display. Some of Clinton's supporters were still upset by my Obama endorsement. After the meeting, I joined Hillary's supporters for dinner, and after some uncomfortable moments, we acknowledged that we would not let this contest ruin our relationship. I emphasized that Obama would welcome their ideas and input in a new administration. Eventually, most came to support Obama, which was crucial in the campaign against Senator John McCain.

2008, Federico Peña speaking on behalf of Candidate Obama at the National
Democratic Convention in Denver.
Photo courtesy of the Peña Family Archives.

To her credit, Senator Clinton was essential to uniting the party behind Obama. She knew how important the election was to the country. I was impressed—and very grateful. By the time of the national convention in Denver that showcased many Latino leaders and activists, the party was united wholly behind Obama-Biden.

In the general election, Barack Obama won with an overwhelming 67 percent share of the Hispanic vote. His victory drove a stake through the heart of the Republican southern strategy that was dependent on white voter misgivings about African Americans and minorities. The Democratic nominee for president broke through the Republican line to carry the western states of Colorado, New Mexico, and Nevada for the first time since 1964. After months of campaigning throughout the country where I represented Obama in debates, media interviews, and community forums, I celebrated his victory on election night with Cindy in Grant Park in Chicago. Latino voters had flexed their political muscle, with all signs pointing to their new geo-strategic importance. And our influence was bound to grow in the future. We made the West the new battlefield, and Latinos were now the group to pursue for the foreseeable future. More recently, as a supporter of Joe Biden, we built on the "Southwestern Strategy" by winning in New Mexico, Colorado, Arizona, and Nevada with strong Latino support.

Today, it is imperative that Latinos vote in the same proportion to the general electorate to fully flex our political power. I can't help but feel that in this tectonic political shift, my mayoral election way back in 1983 in Denver might have played a small but historic part.

Soon after Obama's election, I was back in Washington as a member of the transition team. We began identifying candidates for cabinet and sub-cabinet positions. I reminded everyone who asked that I was not interested in a federal appointment, although my name was bandied about continually. Many thought I wanted an appointment as a justice or ambassador. I wanted nothing. I wanted only for Obama to be the best President possible. This time my wishes were respected, although many friends and associates remained puzzled by my stance.

Months later, when President Obama did in fact have the opportunity to fill the seat vacated by Justice David Souter, I picked up the phone and encouraged him to choose Sonia Sotomayor. I could not have been happier when he announced her nomination.

I was proud of the role I played in electing Obama. Hope and Change had prevailed. And my own hope in America's future once again had been reinforced.

Returning to Denver from Washington had brought great and unexpected change in my life: a fulfilling career in business, a painful divorce, a wonderful remarriage, frightening bouts with cancer, and a rededication to causes I cared about. Through it all, I developed a new rhythm in life, honored the work my parents and ancestors did before me, and discovered a newfound confidence in the hope and promise that is America.

2012, Federico Peña having lunch with President Obama in the White House.
Photo Courtesy of Obama Presidential Library.

Afterword

During the years while writing this book, much has changed. Joe Biden was elected President, and Donald Trump grudgingly left office while attacking our fundamental principles of democracy. Under President Trump, we did not have a shared a vision for the future of our nation. He did not provide us a unifying direction other than a vague notion of "America First." While other industrialized nations have had some sense of where they want to belong in the world, even during the COVID-19 crisis, we were unsure under Trump of where we were headed. And we were certainly not united. Uncertainty bred needless discontent, and millions of Americans were indeed discontented.

We as a people, as a nation, can be so much more with visionary leadership. I came from a generation that had some level of certainty about our own vision. We wanted to stop a war, end poverty, safeguard our environment, protect consumers, and guarantee equal rights for all. From these youthful efforts sprang my commitment years later to not only "Imagine a Great City" but to help build one as well.

To those who have abandoned hope, particularly with the dysfunction in Washington and the damaging conspiracy theories about the legitimacy of Biden's presidential election, remember the Denver experience, and my personal journey, as a source of inspiration and encouragement.

It is not too late for Americans to develop a shared vision of where we want to go. President Joe Biden, whom I supported, is fighting for the "soul of America." This will require us to agree on what our nation's soul looks like. The soul of America, when it was formed by white, Anglo-Saxon immigrants, may appear to have been different from our soul today. Or was it? Are the fundamental principles of our founders—rejecting tyranny, embracing religious and individual freedoms, believing in democratic principles of equality and independence—still applicable today? I believe they are, albeit with an American society that is more religiously, racially, and ethnically diverse. I maintain that we still can believe in the fundamental ideas of our founders even if we look different than they did.

Our diversity requires us to better understand one another. We must be willing to genuinely listen to each other, appreciate our backgrounds and personal histories, and forgo—or at least suspend—our biases and preconceptions. I did this as a Mayor with a strong civil rights background and a deep Latino history. As a Mayor of a predominantly Anglo constituency, I learned to listen to those with different political and genealogical backgrounds in order to form new relationships and forge compromises. By appreciating the attributes of one another and reaching balanced compromises, Americans can visualize what America's soul should look like, just as Denverites imagined what a "Great City" should look like. Most importantly, the soul of America will not be found in the halls of Washington but in the neighborhoods, rural communities, and metroplexes across the land. Our soul will be discovered through honest and direct dialogue, which may at times emit anger, resentment, and tears. But these conversations and interactions can bring a new level of mutual respect and even love for one another. We will recognize that the perceived threats to us lie not within our nation but beyond our boundaries, from powers seeking to trounce on our discord. For example, these foreign enemies are doing this with damaging cyber attacks and divisive social media messages, while we remain divided. It is time for Americans to unite and rally together just as we did during the Depression, WWII, and following 9-11.

By discovering the soul of America, we can then look forward and imagine a greater country. Maintaining hope will be challenging given the bitterness of our disappointing politics, and an economy that has neglected the middle class and the working poor. We must also address the schisms that remain from the divisive rhetoric of President Trump. This is not an easy task. Nor was the struggle to re-unite our nation after the Civil War. I believe our country is enduring what it must before it can breathe itself back to life. As in life, a blow that knocks us down moves us to rise again with a renewed vigor and determination to succeed.

I believe the basic strengths of our country—our people, values, institutions, and system of governance—will sustain us going forward. I relied on the principles and virtues I learned from my parents and ancestors to see me through periods of personal crisis. So, too, must America depend again on the values that made her great while she sets her sights on the future.

The period we are traversing is unique. Our country is undergoing a historic metamorphosis in every aspect, especially demographically. In the simplest terms, a new America is being born...literally. The America of today is not the America of even twenty or thirty years ago. The complexion of America is changing, for the better. When we saw Americans from every race, religion, and ethnicity rise to fight the coronavirus, we witnessed the strength of our diversity. Just visualize the front-line doctors, nurses, scientists, epidemiologists, and vaccine researchers who battled the virus for months. Sick patients were not worried about the ethnic or racial backgrounds of the talented and dedicated doctors and nurses tending to them. Nor were their relatives and or loved ones. Rather, we were thankful for their dedication and compassion for the sick and dying. Many perished in the battle to save us. Other Americans from all backgrounds, many of them immigrants, were the critical workers picking our fruits and vegetables, working in meat-processing plants, staffing our grocery stores and restaurants, and running our schools, fire, and police stations. Their courage in the face of the threat of illness and death helped to restore and define the "soul of America." All we need to do is open our eyes to a demographically changed America—the soul of America— and realize that it's making us greater. We did this decades ago when we accepted the poor and uneducated immigrants from Ireland, Italy, England, and eastern European countries. We need to do it now.

Complicating our challenge of imagining a greater America is the impact of social media and its abuse by foreign governments. Traditional media, both liberal and conservative, encourages us to look upon our country through its particular political lens in a mad effort to maintain ratings. As a result, the right and the left have hardened their beliefs. Each side sees and hears only what it wants, causing a disparateness in our social fabric that borders on disunion.

Like me years ago, many Americans have reached a crossroads with a level of disillusionment generated from the fiery politics of both the left and the right. However disconcerting, firebrand politics do have a place in America's social discourse. But in the middle of the firestorm lies the frustrated center— disappointed by extremes as it watches an incomprehensibly public and vicious battle with so much at stake.

It was the frustrated center that rallied Denverites together to overcome a devastating recession. The people of Denver saw a brighter future in the face of adversity and moved vigorously in its direction. They welcomed immigrants and transplants from every state—like me—and appreciated their involvement in re-shaping their city. As a result, Denver today has a new mindset—and the human resources, spirit, and passion to keep imagining what it can still become.

We can bring great change in our own communities, neighborhoods, and cities. At the local level, it is easier to have rational discourse, share similar dreams for our families, and find common ground. The great majority of citizens in our locales want strong, local economies with decent jobs. They want safe and fun neighborhoods, great schools, and wonderful communities to raise our families. These are dreams we can fulfill in our cities both large and small.

I hope my reflections have conveyed how civility, respect for others, determination, and inspirational and hopeful visions can help to bridge the divide in our country. I have learned the art of compromising, of listening to others, and of imagining a walk in another's shoes. I came to appreciate the constructive ideas and contributions of neighborhood leaders, developers, unionists, environmentalists, energy producers, and ethnic and racial and religious groups

Some argue that leaders should not compromise. I have found that in politics, business, and personal relationships, accepting reasonable and balanced compromise always trumps dead-end divisiveness and failure. It is not the "art of the deal" that matters but the "art of being willing to deal."

Counter-arguments can be made for any one of my ideas. Life itself is not an orderly unfolding of logic and rhyme, and seldom does anything reveal itself step by step. But progress on any of the challenges I have addressed will beget progress on other fronts. For example, once we resolve our broken immigration system, and the divisive emotions it breeds, we can move forward on other imperatives. We can rebuild our country's infrastructure and move toward energy security. We can address climate change in a deliberate and meaningful way. We can reduce income inequality and heal a battered country torn by racism. And when these and other issues are addressed with a unified strategy, we will all benefit. I believe that all Americans, when given a comprehensive vision for their future, supported with coherent, honest, and clear-headed solutions based on facts, will rally and imagine—and then pursue—our new potential.

The overarching lesson of my professional and personal life is that we can *imagine a greater country*, not by yearning for our past achievements, but by embracing our future opportunities. This requires a bold vision that invites Americans from all backgrounds to join the effort. It requires determination that does not bend to criticism or obstacles. It requires the courage to take risks.

"There are," John F. Kennedy brilliantly stated, "risks and costs to a program of action, but they are far less than the long-range risks and costs of comfortable inaction." I subscribe to those words and believe they contain lessons for our nation today. And by holding to a dream, we must dare to imagine that it one day will come true.

The history of America is a story of a nation on a path to self-realization. Ours has been a journey of fits and starts, of progress and regression, and of hopes and dreams often delayed. Yet the American model has made us an exceptional country—one that leads the world rather than conquering it. Our model uses freedom to unlock the potential of each human being rather than to suppress its citizens. But we must find the courage to improve this framework.

When I came of age, I enrolled in the struggle to make America what it presumes to be and tells the world it is: a nation of equality that offers opportunity and redress for its citizens. As Americans, we contribute on a daily basis to advance our country to become what the founders imagined. When my forebear, Tomás Sánchez, forded the Rio Grande to found the city of Laredo, Texas 260 years ago, he must have imagined the town that would come to be. When my ancestor, Santos Benavides, fought to defend Laredo, he must have imagined his beloved community finally safe from authoritarian rule.

When my Grandfather, Eduardo Peña, served for almost a quarter of a century on the Laredo City Council, he must have imagined the many ways his public service could improve the lives of the people in his hometown.

And when this descendant of theirs, a Latino kid who grew up to fight for the poor and the powerless, turned a city around and served in the highest councils of our nation's government, he imagined a greater America.

He still does.

Acknowledgments

For several years after I left Washington, D. C. and returned to Denver, a number of friends suggested I write a book about my experiences in government and business. I struggled to begin what I knew would be a great commitment of time and energy and simply postponed the effort.

My extraordinary wife Cindy encouraged me to just start writing. I completed this work after her numerous and priceless reviews over the years. I thank her for her encouragement and patience as I worked late evenings and weekends.

I was unable to acknowledge all the individuals who supported me throughout my life and career. I apologize to so many in Denver and Washington, D.C. who helped me accomplish so much, but I hope they understand that I could not reference each of them. I do, however, want to humbly thank them for all their contributions and sacrifices.

I thank Jesse Treviño, a friend and former speechwriter at the Department of Energy, who sat with me for hours, extracting more personal impressions and re-drafting many passages. I could not have described the works of my ancestors without the guidance of my second cousin, George Farias, who captured this rich history in his book *The Farias Chronicles*. I borrowed heavily from his work, and over the years he forwarded me additional information and source materials. Two books written by my Tío Willie Peña, *As Far as Schleiden* and *Merriweather + Peña Family History*, were each valuable source materials. Karen Carter also provided valuable editing early on.

A number of former associates lent their insight and helped me recollect the past. Mort Downey, my former Deputy Secretary at DOT; Gary Samore, former member of the National Security Council; Betsy Moler; Bob Gee; and Kyle Simpson each provided thoughts on my work at the Department of Transportation or the Department of Energy. Tom Gougeon assisted in reconstructing events and activities from my Denver mayoral days, and Steven Katich helped me chronicle our efforts in securing Major League Baseball for Denver. Tom Nussbaum, dear friend and mayoral Campaign Manager and my first Chief of Staff, and his wife Sherri Seiber, long-time friend and counselor for much of my political career, reviewed early drafts for accuracy. Renee Hamilton, my executive assistant, devoted hours to editing my drafts.

References

Albuquerque Journal. https://www.abqjournal.com/

Burrough, Bryan; Tomlinson, Chris; Standford, Jason. *Forget The Alamo.* New York: Penguin Press, 2021

Comprehensive National Energy Strategy, report, April 1, 1998, Washington, D.C. https://prop1.org/thomas/peacefulenergy/cnesM.pdf.

Farías, George. *The Farías Chronicles: A History and Genealogy of a Portuguese/Spanish Family.* Edinburg, TX: New Santander Press, 1995.

Garcia, Ann. "The Facts on Immigration Today." Center for American Progress, August 14, 2013. https://www.americanprogress.org/.

Greenberg, Amy. *A Wicked War: Polk, Clay, Lincoln, and the 1846 U.S. Invasion of Mexico.* New York: Vintage, 2013.

Hinojosa, Gilberto. *A Borderlands Town in Transition, Laredo, 1755-1870.* Austin, TX: Texas A&M Press, 1983.

"Hispanic Businesses and Entrepreneurs Drive Growth in The New Economy." Geoscape, 4th Annual Report, 2016. https://ushcc.com/.

Inslee, Jay. "100% Clean Energy for America Plan." Jay Inslee for Governor, 2019. https://www.jayinslee.com/issues/100clean.

Merrell, Melissa, and Jonathan Schwabish. "How Changes in Immigration Policy Might Affect the Federal Budget." Congressional Budget Office, 2015. https://www.cbo.gov/publication/49868.

Muñoz Martinez, Monica. *The Injustice Never Leaves You: Anti-Mexican Violence in Texas.* Cambridge, MA: Harvard University Press, 2020.

NERA Economic Consulting. https://www.nera.com/

Natural Resources Defense Council. https://www.nrdc.org/

Peña, William M. *Merriweather + Peña, Family History.* Self-published, 2003.

Peña, William M. *As Far as Schleiden, A Memoir of World War II.* Self-published, 1991.

Biography

Federico Peña has enjoyed success in law, politics and business. Born and raised in a South Texas border town, he has made Denver his home for nearly fifty years. Elected Mayor in 1983 preceding a disastrous recession, he managed to revitalize Denver with his vision of "Imagine a Great City". He is credited with Denver International Airport, bringing Major League Baseball's Colorado Rockies to Denver and spurring the redevelopment of 600 acres of abandoned land next to downtown. He converted 32 city blocks into the historic LoDo district, the thriving urban mecca of housing and business that it is today.

Federico led two cabinet positions under President William Clinton, in Transportation and Energy, and later served as a Co-Chair of the Obama for President Campaign in 2008. Returning to Denver from Washington, D.C., he has worked in private equity and social impact investing and has served on numerous corporate and non-profit boards.

With roots as a civil rights attorney, Federico continues to work for systemic change in education and good government. He is a loving husband, father, and grandfather and is grateful to be an adopted son of the great state of Colorado.

CPSIA information can be obtained
at www.ICGtesting.com
Printed in the USA
BVHW071142260522
638205BV00007B/206

9 780578 925820